Learning Chinese in Diasporic Communities

AILA Applied Linguistics Series (AALS)

The AILA Applied Linguistics Series (AALS) provides a forum for established scholars in any area of Applied Linguistics. The series aims at representing the field in its diversity. It covers different topics in applied linguistics from a multidisciplinary approach and it aims at including different theoretical and methodological perspectives. As an official publication of AILA the series will include contributors from different geographical and linguistic backgrounds. The volumes in the series should be of high quality; they should break new ground and stimulate further research in Applied Linguistics.

For an overview of all books published in this series, please see
http://benjamins.com/catalog/aals

Editor

Rosa M. Manchón
University of Murcia

Editorial Board

Volume 12

Learning Chinese in Diasporic Communities. Many pathways to being Chinese
Edited by Xiao Lan Curdt-Christiansen and Andy Hancock

Learning Chinese in Diasporic Communities

Many pathways to being Chinese

Edited by

Xiao Lan Curdt-Christiansen
University of Reading

Andy Hancock
University of Edinburgh

John Benjamins Publishing Company

Amsterdam / Philadelphia

The paper used in this publication meets the minimum requirements of
the American National Standard for Information Sciences – Permanence
of Paper for Printed Library Materials, ANSI z39.48-1984.

Library of Congress Cataloging-in-Publication Data

Learning Chinese in Diasporic Communities : Many pathways to being Chinese / Edited
     by Xiao Lan Curdt-Christiansen and Andy Hancock.
    p. cm. (AILA Applied Linguistics Series, ISSN 1875-1113 ; v. 12)
    Includes bibliographical references and index.
    1. Chinese language--Study and teaching--Foreign speakers. 2. Chinese diaspora.
        I. Curdt-Christiansen, Xiao Lan, editor of compilation. II. Hancock, Andy,
        editor of compilation.
PL1065.L385   2014
495.182'4--dc23   2014008331
ISBN 978 90 272 0529 2 (Hb ; alk. paper)
ISBN 978 90 272 0530 8 (Pb ; alk. paper)
ISBN 978 90 272 7024 5 (Eb)

John Benjamins Publishing Co. · P.O. Box 36224 · 1020 ME Amsterdam · The Netherlands
John Benjamins North America · P.O. Box 27519 · Philadelphia PA 19118-0519 · USA

Table of contents

Preface

As a consequence of historical migration patterns and current globalization, Chinese communities can be found scattered throughout the world. These both sizeable and small diasporic communities, composed of settled and newly arrived citizens, are characterized by diversity and a dynamic interplay of variables. They include multiple places of origin, varied relationships with the host society and allegiances to several different spoken varieties of Chinese. Communities are also distinguished by an element of social cohesion through ties to a common writing system and shared cultural inheritance. The primary aim of this book is to explore these similarities and differences, the many pathways of learning 'Chinese' and being 'Chinese', in and across diasporic communities, within the influential and ever-changing socio-linguistic, educational and political landscape of dominant societies.

China's emerging position as one of the world's largest economies and leader of global trading has fuelled demands by politicians and business sectors in many countries for Chinese to be taught in state schools to support economic activity with China. This growing popularity towards mainstreaming the learning of Chinese frequently ignores how Chinese learners in diasporic communities frame their identities in relation to thoughts about cultural norms and practices and attitudes towards heritage language, including the privileging of different spoken varieties of Chinese and the opportunities and tensions when Chinese language learning is mainstreamed. This volume therefore also sets out to examine the complex nature of language acquisition; language attitudes and ideologies as well as cultural and linguistic practices and identity formation in Chinese diasporic communities.

The volume is organized around four themes: family socialization patterns in Chinese homes; community-initiated complementary/heritage Chinese schools; diverse models of bilingual Chinese education and the interwoven relationship of Chinese language; and identity construction and culture. In this way, the book attempts to provide a comprehensive account using several layers of analysis from the macro level of educational language policies in society to the micro level of parents' socialisation and language practices in the home. Each section includes chapters written by prominent scholars and researchers in the field located in a variety of countries, including Singapore, Australia, Canada, the United Kingdom (England and Scotland), Malaysia, the United States, and the Netherlands. Most chapters describe different sociopolitical and cultural contexts in order to provide insights into the significance of sociocultural, educational and linguistic environments that create, enhance or limit the ways in which diasporic children and young people acquire their heritage language.

It is hoped that the book will have international appeal for researchers, educators and teacher-educators, students and practitioners in the fields of Chinese language education and bilingual education. It is also hoped that the information gained from the range of chapters will contribute to a better understanding of individual countries and their own history of Chinese diaspora as well as acting as a stimulus for readers to debate and reflect on the bilingual models, methodological approaches and theoretical perspectives. This, in turn, is intended to support further analysis, both within the countries represented in this book and also within other educational contexts.

Acknowledgments

This book is a team effort, thus, the editors wish to gratefully acknowledge the authors who have contributed to this volume. We are particularly in debt to Claus Curdt-Christiansen for his thorough reading of the entire manuscript, Jonathan Hancock for his help with the indexes and Baoqi Sun for her careful reference checking. We would also like to thank Kees Vaes, senior acquisition editor at John Benjamins, for his support in bringing this volume to publication. Finally, we would like to dedicate this book to these special individuals in our lives, Baijie, Amanda, Juliet, Jonathan and Daniel.

Contributors

Louise ARCHER is Professor of Sociology of Education at King's College, London. Her research focuses on educational identities and inequalities, particularly in relation to race, class and gender. She has conducted research on British Muslim students, access to higher education, and urban youth and schooling. She is currently leading large studies on children's science and career aspirations, and on how to improve disadvantaged students' engagement with science and museums.

Shen CHEN is Associate Professor at the School of Education, University of Newcastle, Australia. He is responsible for an undergraduate language teacher education program and a postgraduate TESOL program for domestic and international students. His research interests cover culture in language education, computer-assisted language learning, intercultural studies and international education. He is recognised as one of language education leaders in Australia, as demonstrated by his numerous invited presentations at Australian and international universities and his publications in a wide area of language education and teacher training.

Xiao Lan CURDT-CHRISTIANSEN is Associate Professor at Institute of Education, University of Reading, UK. Educated at McGill University, Montreal, Canada, she has been actively involved in research projects on children's literacy practices and language development in family domains, heritage language schools, and mainstream classrooms. She is the guest editor of a special issue on Family Language Policy for *Language Policy* and an associate editor of *International Journal of Learning*. Currently, she is working on a book, *The Politics of Textbook in Language Education,* with Csilla Weninger (Routledge). Her publications have appeared in *Language Policy; Canadian Modern Language Review; Cambridge Journal of Education; Language and Education; English Quarterly; Language, Culture and Curriculum; Sociolinguistic Studies and Heritage Language Journal,* among others.

Patricia (Patsy) DUFF is Professor of Language and Literacy Education and coordinator of the graduate programs in TESL and Modern Language Education at the University of British Columbia, Vancouver, Canada. She is also co-director of the UBC Centre for Research in Chinese Language and Literacy Education. Patsy has a longstanding interest in the teaching and learning of English, Chinese, and other languages. The primary focus of her research, grants, and graduate student supervision is in the area of language socialization theory and research in multilingual contexts internationally. Her books include *Inference and Generalizability in Applied Linguistics, Case Study Research in Applied Linguistics, Language Socialization* and, most recently, *Learning Chinese: Linguistic, Sociocultural, and Narrative Perspectives* (De Gruyter 2013).

Becky FRANCIS is Professor of Education and Social Justice at King's College, London. She has followed a research career focusing on education and social in/equalities. Her academic expertise and publications centre on social identities (gender, race and social class) in educational contexts, social im/mobility, social identity and educational achievement, and feminist theory. She has written many books on these topics, including the most recent Identities and Practices of High Achieving Pupils (2012, Continuum, with Christine Skelton and Barbara Read).

Andy HANCOCK teaches at the Institute of Education, Teaching and Leadership at the University of Edinburgh. He is Director of the MEd programme Additional Support for Learning (Bilingual Learners) and Co-Director of the Centre for Education for Racial Equality in Scotland (CERES). He is Course Organizer of the Postgraduate Diploma in Education (Upper Primary Stage) and contributes to the Language and Literacy strands of the Initial Teacher Education (ITE) programmes. His Ph.D. focused on the biliteracy development of Chinese children in Scotland. He has published several articles and contributed chapters to a number of recent publications on literacy practices in Chinese communities and student teachers' perceptions of multilingual classrooms.

Kasper JUFFERMANS earned his Ph.D. from Tilburg University in 2010 with a dissertation on literacies and multilingualism in The Gambia, West Africa. He was subsequently involved, also at Tilburg University, in the IDII4MES project investigating discourses of Chinese-Dutch identity and heritage. A sociolinguist and Africanist, he is interested in language and literacy ideologies, education and mobilities, in Africa, Asia and Europe and the spaces in between. He has guest edited (with Jef van der Aa) the special issue *Analyzing voice in educational discourses* (Anthropology and Education Quarterly 44/2). Kasper is now attached to the Language, Culture, Media and Identities research unit at the University of Luxembourg.

Duanduan LI is Associate Professor of Chinese Applied Linguistics in the Department of Asian Studies at the University of British Columbia and Co-Director of the UBC Centre for Research in Chinese Language and Literacy Education. She has served as Director of the Chinese language programs at Columbia University (New York) and UBC for over ten years. Much of her research, teaching, graduate student supervision, and textbook and curriculum development in recent years has been devoted to understanding and advocating Chinese heritage language (CHL) learning and better understanding the distinct backgrounds, needs, motivations, identities, experiences, and learning trajectories of both CHL and non-CHL learners. Her other areas of specialization are intercultural pragmatics, second language socialization, and pedagogical grammar.

Jinling Li is a Ph.D. candidate in the School of Humanities and a member of the Babylon Center for Studies of the Multicultural Society, Tilburg University. Her research investigates Chinese-Dutch youth identity discourses in and beyond complementary schooling as part of a European project funded by HERA. Being a first generation Chinese migrant in the Netherlands and a former Chinese language educator and interpreter, Jinling is interested in multilingualism, multilingual education, language ideology, identity discourses, acculturation and globalization.

LI Wei is Professor of Applied Linguistics at Birkbeck College, University of London, where he is also Pro-Vice-Master and Director of the Birkbeck Graduate Research School. His research interests are in the broad areas of bilingualism and multilingualism. Amongst his publications are the award-winning *Blackwell Guide to Research Methods in Bilingualism and Multilingualism* (with Melissa Moyer 2008; Wiley-Blackwell), a two volume set of *Contemporary Applied Linguistics* (with Vivian Cook 2010, Continuum), and *Translanguaging: Language, Bilingualism and Education* (with Ofelia Garcia 2014, Palgrave). He is the Principal Editor of *International Journal of Bilingualism* (Sage).

Chan LÜ got her Ph.D. from Carnegie Mellon University, Pittsburgh (US). She is Assistant Professor of Applied Linguistics and Chinese Language Program Coordinator at the Department of Modern Languages and Literatures, Loyola Marymount University, Los Angeles (US). Her research focuses on English-Chinese biliteracy acquisition among school-aged learners in different instructional settings.

Ada MAU, Ph.D. is a social researcher in London, UK. Her research focuses on educational and social equity, identities, and heritage language learning. Her research interests also include migration, multilingualism, social justice, social and cultural policy, informal learning, and youth cultures. She is a member of the British Chinese Research Network. She is also part of the Early Years and Families team at the Learning Department at Tate Britain and Tate Modern.

Xiaomei WANG (Ph.D, City University of Hong Kong) is a senior lecturer at the Faculty of Languages and Linguistics and Malaysian Chinese Research Centre, University of Malaya. Her research focuses on language spread, language maintenance and language shift, multilingualism, linguistic landscape, ethnolinguistics and teaching

Chinese as a second language. She has published dozens of papers in *International Journal of Multilingual and Multicultural Development, Oceanic Linguistics, GEMA, Journal of Chinese Sociolinguistics* and other refereed journals. Her book *Mandarin Spread in Malaysia* was published by University of Malaya Press in 2012.

Dongbo ZHANG (Ph.D., Carnegie Mellon University) is an Assistant Professor in the Department of Teacher Education at Michigan State University. Prior to the current appointment, he worked as a Research Scientist at the Center for Research in Pedagogy and Practice, National Institute of Education. His research interests include second language acquisition and pedagogy, bilingual children's literacy acquisition, and reading and vocabulary knowledge.

Yuzhe ZHANG gained her Bachelor of Arts (Chinese) degree from Henan University, Kaifeng, China in 2007, and a Master of Applied Linguistics from Huangzhong Normal University, Wuhan, China in 2010. She is currently studying for a Ph.D. degree in Education at the University of Newcastle, Australia. Her research interests include Chinese linguistics and literature, language education, teacher education and comparative education.

Shouhui ZHAO is Associate Professor at the Department of Foreign Languages, University of Bergen, Norway. He obtained his Ph.D. in linguistics from the University of Sydney, Australia. His work has appeared in *Language Policy, Current issues in Language Planning, Asia-Pacific Education Researcher, International Journal of Bilingual Education and Bilingualism* and numerous other journals. His recent work was published by Springer (2008, with R.B. Baldauf, Jr.) and Cengage Learning Asia (2010, with Dongbo Zhang). Professionally trained as a language teacher, Dr Zhao has taught and researched Chinese language and culture at seven universities in five countries before he joined the University of Bergen.

ZHU Hua is Professor of Language and Communication at Birkbeck College, University of London. Her research expertise is in language and intercultural communication, multilingual socialisation and practices among diasporic and transnational communities, and phonological development of monolingual and bilingual children. She is author of *Exploring Intercultural Communication: Language in Action* (Routledge 2014) and editor of *The Language and Intercultural Communication Reader* (Routledge 2011). She is currently working on a research method book *Research Methods in Intercultural Communication: A Practical Guide,* Wiley-Blackwell and a book that looks into the link between globalisation and workplace interactions *Crossing Boundaries: Weaving life, work and scholarship* with Adam Komisar. She is the series editor of Routledge book series of *Language and Intercultural Communication* with Claire Kramsch.

List of figures

List of tables

Introduction

Xiao Lan Curdt-Christiansen & Andy Hancock

University of Reading / University of Edinburgh

其实，所有的故乡原本不都是异乡吗？所谓故乡不过是我们祖先漂泊旅程中落脚的最后一站。

(杨明: 我以为我有爱)

In fact, aren't all homelands originally strange lands? The so-called homelands are nothing but the last stop of our ancestors' journey, the land they chose to stay.[1]

(Yang Ming: I think I possess love)

In almost all countries of the world, Chinese people have a visible presence. Chinese people live not only in China, Taiwan and Hong Kong, but are dispersed all over the world, crossing borders as migrants, international students, business people, or simply to further their career. This is a book about becoming 'Chinese' in the many and various last stops of Chinese ancestors' migration journey, in the diasporic communities across the globe. It explores the many pathways of learning 'Chinese', being 'Chinese' and becoming 'Chinese'. In this context 'Chinese' encompasses different varieties of Chinese language in both spoken and written form, a wealth of shared cultural knowledge, and linguistic expressions as well as symbolic manifestations.

Although the book is primarily about learning and teaching Chinese, the chapters within it go beyond the confines of formal education to include the educational input of parents, communities, and community-based organizations, taking place in homes, schools, and community schools. The focus of the book is on Chinese heritage language learners, rather than a somewhat narrow concept of learning linguistic forms and 'traditional Chinese culture' passed on to them through homes and communities. It recognizes the duality of individuals living *in* and *with* multiple languages and a variety of sociocultural practices. This duality not only determines unique and creative language use (code switching, styling, or translanguaging), it also enables the use of languages and sociocultural practices as resources to create new meanings, adapt to changing situations, and

---

1.   Translation is provided by X.L. Curdt-Christiansen

face challenges. The scope and discussions of the chapters are therefore not limited simply to the construct of 'heritage language' (HL) as inheritance matters that need to be maintained and passed on. Rather, heritage language is viewed as a language in motion, a language that meshes constantly with local languages and cultures, that evolves with global sociopolitical changes and is a part of a larger sociocultural system.

Aims of the Book

In multilingual societies all over the world, linguistic practices entail an ecological approach to language development and language use. The purpose of this book is to examine how and to what extent sociocultural and linguistic environments and conditions, including family, community, and government sponsored educational institutions in different sociopolitical contexts, create, enhance or limit the ways in which diasporic children and young people acquire the 'Chinese language'. Its central argument is that learning the 'Chinese language' is an ideological struggle, filled with sociocultural values, political power issues, economic opportunities and identity formation.

The book is primarily addressed to those who teach and research in the area of Chinese language and, in particular, bilingual education and, more broadly, within the field of situated language learning and language development. As a collected volume, the book examines the complex nature of language development, involving language attitudes and ideologies as well as linguistic and literacy practices in formal and informal educational contexts. It is therefore accessible to non-specialists in Chinese teaching, including, for example, students and scholars from the social sciences, such as anthropology, political science, psychology and sociology, as well as to those involved in language policy and sociolinguistic research. The book can be used as a primary text for teachers seeking education in Chinese language acquisition and as a supplementary text in teacher education courses dealing with language policy, sociolinguistic studies and bilingual education.

New perspectives on learning Chinese

Although Chinese is considered to be one of the most widely used languages in the world, a re-evaluation of how Chinese people (Sinophones) learn to speak, read and write is needed in the light of new theoretical perspectives, research methodologies and analytical frameworks. In particular, the ways in which Chinese heritage language learners maintain and develop their HL and acquire "the symbiotic social and cultural processes that accompany HL learning" (He 2011: 588) deserve continued investigation. There are a variety of factors that warrant a book that thoroughly examines the implications of teaching and learning in a transnational, intergenerational, and intercultural context.

Firstly, the recent growth of China's economic and political power in the world combined with globalization on an unprecedented scale has increased the demand for learning Chinese, both as a heritage language and as an international language. Related to this are new perspectives which require us to understand different approaches to Chinese language education in diasporic communities.

Secondly, the increasing demand for learning standard Chinese (Mandarin) suggests that there is a need to redefine what is meant by the term 'Chinese language', as diasporic communities in their daily communications use a variety of Chinese languages in addition to their host country's language. As a result, the process of becoming linguistically competent and literate in Chinese language entails learning different varieties of Chinese language and writing systems (classic or simplified characters), depending on the individual's home country and region. Families, based on their natural linguistic resources (Fishman 1991; Spolsky 2009) and literacy facilities, socialize their children into different sociolinguistic norms and literacy practices. While differing in their migration experiences, educational backgrounds and resettlement patterns in different parts of the world, these parents still adhere to certain traditions and cultural values from their Chinese heritage, most importantly high aspirations for their children's education and academic success. There are, however, a number of significant questions to be asked. How are these values communicated to their children? What role does Chinese language play in this process? Why do members of some migrant groups maintain their language, while members of other groups lose their language? Why do some children become bilinguals while other children become monolinguals, although they grow up in the same linguistic environment? To what extent do parents impede and prevent or support and promote Chinese language acquisition or bilingual development? Seeking answers to these questions has the potential to shed light on the roles and functions of Chinese in relation to politics, economics and social systems.

Thirdly, although Chinese learners share cultural traditions and learn one unified written language, they come from different countries (regions) and therefore have different socioeconomic backgrounds and educational experiences. The heritage language schools also differ with regard to language of instruction (standard vs. regional variety), pedagogical approaches, and the instructional tools for supporting the teaching of the Chinese script (pinyin or zhuyinfuhao). There are different philosophies underlying each school's mission and goal in teaching Chinese language. There is, therefore, an urgent need to identify the similarities and differences between these schools, located within complex webs

of political, ideological and historical contexts and socio-cultural-linguistic practices worldwide, and to establish how Chinese is taught, what teaching approaches
are employed, what teaching materials are used in heritage language schools and
what socio-linguistic and political environments are likely to enhance or constrain
multilingual development.

Fourthly, learning a language is closely related to the culture reflected in that
language. Hence the relationship between language and culture needs to be re-
examined as there are visible tensions between newly arrived and earlier generations of migrants. This re-examination affects three areas of language learning and
teaching – the teaching of intercultural pragmatic competence, the use of cultural
resources in the classroom, and the cultural assumptions that underpin pedagogical approaches to teaching and learning.

To the extent that appropriateness of language use is based on sociocultural
norms, it is necessary to re-examine the culture in diasporic contexts as younger
generations of migrants are submerged in substantially different social and cultural values. Both families and educational institutions need to address this aspect
of language teaching.

The link between language and culture also has important ramifications for
the choice of materials. Currently, Chinese language materials often focus on cultural topics related to heritage countries, which presupposes knowledge of traditional cultures. Is such an approach justified in the teaching of Chinese language
in diasporic contexts where children are exposed to a different culture outside the
hours at the heritage school?

Finally, the degrees to which language maintenance and language shift have
occurred vary greatly from one community to another. The comparison of different educational contexts, sociolinguistic situations and political environments
can shed light on language attitudes and linguistic practices and the ideologies
that reflect and refract broader societal beliefs and values. How to strike a balance
between linguistic allegiance and new language adaptation? How to negotiate language ideology and identity? How to counteract economic pressures and balance
institutional impositions with language maintenance? These are some of the major
issues that arise in the teaching and learning of Chinese in diasporic communities,
and they are examined in depth in this book.

Structure of the book

The book is divided into four parts in order to help the reader navigate the various chapters. Each of the four parts forms a discreet and coherent unit within the
book by developing a field of study either through offering descriptions of research

literature reviews or through descriptions of specific research studies across the globe. These parts also interconnect and overlap as each makes an important contribution to the multi-dimensional theme of learning and teaching Chinese in diasporic communities. Most of the chapters draw on a specific country with their own history of Chinese diaspora, unique educational systems and diverse sociolinguistic and political features in which Chinese heritage language learners are located. When viewed as a whole, it is hoped that general themes and patterns will also emerge. In this way the reader can not only gain knowledge and understanding of distinct contextual factors but also consider some of the similarities and differences within and across Chinese diasporic communities.

Part I, *Family socialization patterns in Chinese language learning and literacy practices* consists of two chapters examining the factors that might impede or enhance bilingual development and the acquisition of the Chinese language. The chapter by Duff provides a synthesis of research on how children in diasporic Chinese families are socialized by and through the languages (Chinese and the mainstream language) into the practices of their different communities. Comparing and contrasting Chinese families situated in different geographical locations of the world, the review examines both theoretical and methodological underpinnings of research in Chinese language socialization. Closer attention is paid to studies on Chinese heritage-language socialization, with a focus on the functions and forms of code-switching, shaming, narrativity and literacy texts in traditional Chinese diaspora homes as well as in mixed heritage ones. Duff calls for future research to concentrate on discontinuities, syncretism, and innovations in Chinese language learning and use across home, school, and community settings and across multiple timescales in order to better understand the relationship between being and knowing/using Chinese in contemporary societies.

The chapter by Curdt-Christiansen takes a novel approach to studying language socialization using the lens of the newly emerged framework of Family Language Policy (FLP). The author argues that FLP is an important field of investigation as it sheds light on the role of parents and family members in determining how languages are transmitted across generations and under what conditions languages are maintained and lost. Using interviews with and participant observations in bilingual English-Chinese families, the chapter investigates multilingualism in Singapore by focusing on how FLP is explicitly and implicitly planned for children's language and literacy education. Curdt-Christiansen takes a broader view of FLP and shows how it is connected to political, educational and economic forces external to the families as well as to micro factors within families that mutually influence and shape the participants' ideologies about languages and influence parental decisions about their language use patterns and their interventions to manage and modify home literacy practices. The research sheds light on current language policy in Singapore and shows how parents value bilingual proficiency and also how English carries greater educational, social and economic status compared to Chinese with its affiliation with cultural heritage and ethnic identity.

Part II, *Complementary/heritage Chinese schools in diasporas* consists of four chapters exploring the pedagogical and research implications of the growing number of children and young people of Chinese heritage who are learning Chinese part-time in classrooms that operate outside of mainstream schools. This community-initiated provision includes a range of schools catering for the diverse needs of Chinese communities in terms of spoken varieties, countries of origin and occasionally faith affiliations. The title of this section acknowledges the different terminology used to describe these schools around the globe. The authors in this section examine Chinese schools in a variety of countries and provide insights into instructional practices and resources and how teachers and learners navigate and respond to learning and teaching approaches, curriculum content and language use in the classroom.

The chapter by Hancock employs Hornberger's Continua of Biliteracy as a framework for a critical analysis of the Chinese complementary school phenomena in Scotland. In particular, attention is paid to how prevailing language policies shape children's biliteracy experiences, including a shift towards learning Mandarin (Context); how texts are frequently used by teachers to guide children to an appreciation of Chinese cultural values (Content); how teachers sometimes deviate from 'mundane' practices in order to generate an interest in learning Chinese literacy (Media); and how children draw on their biliterate resources to support their Chinese learning (Development). Each element of the continua is supported by data gathered from classroom observations, interviews with teachers and conversations with children.

Lü's chapter also examines biliteracy learning based on classroom observations but from the perspective of a Chinese Heritage language school in the United States. It describes traditional practices around texts, such as learners reading aloud either individually or together, teacher-dominated questioning, and teachers providing corrective feedback on learners' pronunciation or intonation. However, observations also show that there are times when teachers incorporate language games into lessons to make learning more enjoyable for children learning Chinese at the weekend. The author examines some of the challenges for this type of grassroots provision such as teacher retention and recruitment and concludes with some suggestions for enhancing pedagogy in Chinese heritage language schools through developing partnerships with mainstream educators and parents.

The chapter by Li and Juffermans is concerned with the metapragmatics of Chinese where the effects and conditions of language use themselves become objects of discourse. Using transcripts from a complementary school classroom in the Netherlands, the chapter examines the subtle ways of speaking about and referring to Chinese and explores the implicit and more explicit meanings attached to the particular use of different language varieties of Chinese. The authors also suggest that consideration is given to Chinese as a polycentric language, i.e. as a language that operates on various scales and has multiple centers, and that these centers are continually shifting as a result of historical, demographic, economic, and political changes. It describes how teachers, parents and young people have adjusted or are adjusting to or catching up with this changing situation, as to what counts as Chinese. The authors believe a clearer understanding of the metapragmatics of Chinese is useful, because it provides a window into dynamic socio-cultural identities and the changing hierarchies of language varieties within Chinese diasporic communities.

The final chapter in this section, by Li Wei and Zhu Hua, also takes a socialization orientation and focuses on classroom interactions in Chinese complementary schools in England. It shows how teachers use the opportunity of language and literacy teaching to pass on cultural values to the pupils, and how the pupils react to this kind of socializational teaching. Like Li and Juffermans, the authors make the crucial point that the ideologies embedded in teaching are not static but changing across the generations as a consequence of the on-going process of migration and globalization. A study of classroom discourses reveals the tensions between the teachers' and pupils' language repertoires and preferences and cultural understandings, and how the pupils negotiate a new set of identities through the process of language and literacy learning. In common with all the chapters in this section, Li Wei and Zhu Hua recognize the key function of community-inspired Chinese schools in supporting and maintaining the heritage language and literacy skills of different generations and also their role in providing spaces where competing language ideologies, beliefs and practices are played out. The authors conclude by acknowledging complementary/heritage schools as important research sites for opening up further debates over interculturality and analyzing the varied dimensions of multilingualism in contemporary Chinese diasporic communities.

Part III, *Bilingual Chinese education models* consists of three chapters describing state or privately funded bilingual programs in different parts of the world. The chapters grapple with the complex issue of what bilingual programs are employed and promoted in the teaching of Chinese as a heritage language or additional language; and how political decisions can expedite or slow down language loss and language shift.

The chapter by Wang situates Chinese language education in Malaysia, where the Chinese are the second largest ethnic group. It takes a historical look, and for each phase of development of Chinese teaching, the medium of instruction, syllabus, curriculum allocation, and learning outcomes are critically discussed against the sociopolitical background during that period. Special attention is also paid to the characteristics of current models of Chinese language education in different types of schools in Malaysia where the government provides schooling in Chinese at primary level while more options are available to Chinese parents at the secondary stage. The medium of instruction is discussed in relation to the social, economic and political opportunities and access to the national language (Malay), global language (English) and heritage language (Chinese). The achievements of Malaysian Chinese education are highlighted as well as some of the challenges and issues in relation to the present syllabus and curriculum of Chinese teaching in Malaysia.

The context for Zhao and Zhang's chapter is the unique bilingual educational model in Singapore which requires all students to study two compulsory languages: English as the main medium of instruction in all schools at all levels and one of the state-assigned mother tongues, specific to an individual's heritage background, including Mandarin Chinese. The chapter begins with an inter-textual analysis and a critical evaluation of the inconsistencies in curriculum reform documents in terms of objectives and pedagogies and the downgrading of the importance of teaching and learning Chinese characters (*hanzi*) in Singapore's primary schools. This is followed by a quantitative analysis of Chinese language teachers' and primary school students' perceptions of *hanzi* and their place in Chinese language education. In particular, the survey suggests a more optimistic picture of children's interests in and their awareness of the functions of *hanzi*, whilst the teachers were concerned about the reduction in writing *hanzi* in the new curriculum. The authors argue that there is, therefore, evidence of discrepancies between the views of stakeholders (teachers and students) and what is depicted in the curriculum policy documents, and the teaching and learning of *hanzi* needs to be given greater prominence in the next round of educational reform in Singapore.

The chapter by Chen and Zhang locates models of teaching and learning Chinese in the context of the progressive national language planning policy in Australia. A chronological investigation of Australian governments' language policies is presented to reveal how provisions for learning Chinese have changed over time from local Chinese community schools with a separate curriculum to mainstreaming Chinese language teaching based on a developing national curriculum to meet the needs of an ever increasing number of learners of Chinese in schools all over the nation. Some of the challenges are noted, such as providing a differentiated syllabus to cater for the various needs of learners, including ethnic

Chinese students and students from a non- or mixed Chinese heritage. A critical examination is provided of a new heritage language syllabus for Chinese learning in New South Wales, drawing on interviews with teacher educators, student teachers and graduates of the Chinese teacher education programmes in several universities. The authors argue that the research reveals a number of concerns, such as a mismatch between curriculum design and curriculum implementation, and they provide some suggestions to enhance Chinese language teaching and learning to support the social, economic and political demands of Australia.

Part IV, *Chinese language, culture and identity*, consists of two chapters that address individuals' perceptions of and views on the complex and important issues of identity, language attitudes and ideology in the process of learning (or not learning) Chinese. The chapter by Francis, Mau and Archer takes a post-structuralist approach and analyses young British-Chinese people's constructions of the relationship between language and ethnic identity, drawing on data from two studies: Chinese complementary school attendees, and young people of Chinese/mixed heritage that constructed themselves as not being able to speak Chinese. Findings indicate that those young people attending Chinese complementary school strongly viewed fluency in their heritage language as fundamental to Chinese identity. Interestingly some of these young people used moral and nationalistic discourses to challenge the possibility of identification as 'Chinese' without fluency in 'mother tongue'. For those young people not able to speak the language, it was discovered that this did not preclude their identification as Chinese: these young people drew on a range of signifiers of Chinese culture, connection, and engagement to position themselves as wholly or partly 'Chinese'. The authors argue that, despite discourses that produce idealized notions of 'essential' features of Chinese culture, in practice young people demonstrate agency in their diverse productions and understandings of 'Chineseness'.

Finally, the chapter by Li and Duff also looks at agency and motivations toward learning Chinese and its relationship with ethnicity and identity construction. It critiques previous research in this field as categorical or essentialist and takes a theoretical stance that envisages Chinese heritage language learning motivation as dynamic, multilingual, nonlinear, and a contingent process. The participants involved in the study are young adults recruited from a Chinese language program in a university in Canada and their accounts generate a sense of their diverse lived experiences including transnational migration histories, achievements/motivations and negotiation of identity. Furthermore, features of the participants' individual learning trajectories include different L1s from different regions/geographies, affiliations, expertise, and investments in and even misgivings vis-à-vis learning and using Chinese at certain stages. The authors believe that this type of storytelling has implications for improving curriculum, pedagogy, learning materials, and policies.

Looking into the reality of learning Chinese in diasporic communities, the volume draws attention to patterns of variance and invariance in conditions of family language socialization, informal and formal language input, and instructional environment and materials used in becoming 'Chinese'. The authors in the book not only raise questions and concerns about learning Chinese as a heritage and second language from both macro and micro language policy perspectives, but also make suggestions and new directions for future research.

References

He, A.W. 2011. Heritage language socialization. In *The Handbook of Language Socialization*, A. Duranti, B. Ochs & B. Schieffelin (eds), 587–609. Oxford: Blackwell.

Fishman, J.A. 1991. *Reversing Language Shift: Theoretical and Empirical Foundations of Assistance to Threatened Languages*. Clevedon: Multilingual Matters.

Spolsky, B. 2009. *Language Management*. Cambridge: CUP.

PART I

Family socialization patterns in language learning and literacy practices

Language socialization into Chinese language and "Chineseness" in diaspora communities

Patricia A. Duff
University of British Columbia

Language socialization research provides a rich, socioculturally-oriented theoretical framework and set of analytic tools for examining the experiences of newcomers and other novices learning language in a range of educational settings, both formal and informal. This chapter first presents an overview of language socialization principles and then highlights several personal narratives of language socialization within Chinese diaspora communities in different geographical settings. Next, studies on Chinese heritage-language socialization are examined with a focus on the functions and forms of codeswitching, shaming, narrativity, the socialization of taste during meals, and literacy texts in traditional Chinese diaspora homes as well as in ethnically mixed or blended ones. The chapter recommends, in closing, that future research should examine to a greater extent continuities, discontinuities, syncretism, and innovations in Chinese language learning and use across home, school, and community settings and across multiple timescales in order to better understand the relationship between being and knowing/using Chinese in contemporary societies.

Introduction

Language socialization (LS) provides a rich theoretical and methodological orientation to language learning. Using ethnographic approaches for the most part, it aims to account for the processes by which novices are apprenticed or mentored into the linguistic and nonlinguistic ideologies, values, practices, and stances (affective, epistemic, and other) of particular sociocultural groups across a range of contexts (Bayley & Schecter 2003; Duff 2008; Duff & Hornberger 2008; Duranti, Ochs & Schieffelin 2011; Schieffelin & Ochs 1986; Watson-Gegeo 2004). These aspects of linguistic and cultural life, behaviours, and dispositions constitute what Bourdieu (1977) refers to as *habitus*, a construct that a number of language socialization (LS) researchers (e.g. Duff 2007; Garrett & Baquedano-Lopez 2002; Ochs & Schieffelin 2011) and Chinese as a Heritage Language (CHL) scholars (e.g. Dai & Zhang 2008) have also found helpful in understanding enculturation and social life.

For many heritage language (HL) learners, like first language (L1) learners and young bilinguals worldwide, language socialization begins at home through everyday interactions with parents, relatives, and others in their social worlds, through a variety of oral interactions and genres (songs, rhymes, stories, and other verbal routines), and through the literacy practices they observe and in some cases learn to participate in themselves (Duff 2010, 2011; Duff & Talmy 2011; He 2008a, 2008b, 2012). Their language socialization is therefore (potentially) mediated by other people and by various semiotic resources, including visual, embodied, and aural modes as well as by mass media, and virtual or online engagements. Prevailing language policies and ideologies also mediate their dispositions toward acquiring and using the HL. Their learning of and about language and culture may take place inside and outside the home by means of their participation in activities in community HL programs and with tutors (e.g. Jia 2006; Lei 2007), through formal public or private schooling, and by means of home language and literacy practice with siblings, parents, grandparents, and guests. It may occur monolingually, bilingually or multilingually, depending on the linguistic ecology and history of the family and community (Wang 2008).

For some HL learners, however, their engagements with their familial HLs are much more receptive than active, and their knowledge is latent or tacit, often marked by language shift to the dominant language of the wider community and attrition in their mother tongue (if that is the heritage language). Other HL learners may have no meaningful engagements with their HL or another closely related language until they are much older, when they may choose to study a standard variety of the language, such as Mandarin, through secondary, postsecondary or other programs. The home language may be Cantonese, Hokkien, or another dialect, but only Mandarin may be available through formal education later.

Many scenarios in fact exist, just as many definitions of HL learners do (e.g. Li & Duff 2008). Irrespective of whether the learner becomes proficient in the HL or not, discourses of ethnic legitimacy, authenticity, and identity ("Chineseness") are often conflated with cultural and linguistic competence and this essentialist association between proficiency and ethnic authenticity can be very contentious, as I illustrate below. The title of this volume itself connects "learning Chinese" with "becoming Chinese," much as McDonald's (2011) book does, with its title *Learning Chinese, Turning Chinese*. Furthermore, this juxtaposition of learning Chinese and turning or becoming or being Chinese begs the question as to whether socialization into Chinese identities ("Chineseness") and non-linguistic cultural dispositions cannot also take place in and through other languages, such as Indonesian or English.

To date, there have been relatively few studies of children's *language socialization* – explicitly framed as such – in Chinese diaspora households where one or more variety of Chinese is spoken. There has been more research within three other sociolinguistic domains: (1) socialization within Korean or Hispanic diaspora families, especially in the U.S., (2) studies on Chinese children's socialization in HL educational programs *outside* the home, and (3) studies of young children's LS in English-speaking homes.

In this chapter, I outline some of the basic theoretical principles of LS and describe how and why it is a very compelling lens through which to examine bilingual or multilingual socialization in home and community settings. I then present examples of Chinese HL socialization specifically and some of the issues that emerge in sinophone contexts. The review of LS and existing research in CHL reveals that family language socialization needs to be examined within its broader social, political, and ethnolinguistic context and in relation to some of the circulating discourses surrounding cultural authenticity (i.e. Chineseness) associated with HL retention and use.

Language socialization: Negotiating languages and identities in diaspora settings and discourses

LS represents an academic approach to human development and cultural practice originating in linguistic anthropology and cultural psychology that examines how novices learn "the ways" of the communities they are in or that they seek membership in so they can become successfully integrated and engaged within them. Naturally, language is a critical element, since it mediates the socialization process and also constitutes one of the intended outcomes of LS – namely, communicative competence or linguistic/literate proficiency. Reviews of LS in bilingual and multilingual contexts relevant to Chinese children's experiences (e.g. Bayley & Langman 2011; Duff 2007, 2010, 2011; Duff & Hornberger 2008; Duranti, Ochs & Schieffelin 2011; Garrett & Baquedano-Lopez 2002; Zuengler & Cole 2005; Watson-Gegeo & Bronson 2013) and other sources underscore the contingencies among a number of influences in learners' socialization and language development. These may include novices' interactions with more experienced members of the communities (parents, other caregivers, siblings, and teachers, among others), media influences, the perceived and actual status of the languages and cultures, particularly in linguistically diverse diaspora communities, and the choices, agency, and social positioning of the learners by themselves and by others (Duff 2012; He 2003).

LS in Chinese diaspora and other minority contexts may also take place against the backdrop of an earlier history of discrimination and language shift resulting from pressures to assimilate to the dominant language of the community at the expense of the HL, a legacy which may have continuing consequences for attitudes and possibilities. In some contexts, however, earlier sociopolitical pressures that resulted in language loss by one or more older generations may actually inspire efforts to revitalize the language within the younger generations.

Despite such pressures to assimilate or to adopt a socially dominant language such as English, many ethnic Chinese families are very successful at keeping their ancestral language or one closely related to it alive within their homes and communities for generations. However, families and individuals who have *not* been able to maintain their HL often – but not always – lament this outcome, sometimes with considerable regret and shame (Duff & Li 2008; Li & Duff this volume). Others who have "lost" Chinese, for whatever reason, may also find themselves positioned in disadvantageous ways as a result, even if that loss or shift toward other languages was a matter of deliberate choice and agency on their part or that of their families (i.e. letting go of Chinese while strategically embracing other languages in order to integrate into dominant cultures). Examples of this phenomenon follow.

The first example comes from a narrative of such transnational and crosslinguistic identity politics where the younger generation, for reasons to be explained, is not socialized into Chinese and therefore does not retain Chinese and feels quite conflicted about this situation. Ien Ang (2001), a professor of cultural studies in Australia, described the many contradictory ways in which non-Chinese-speaking yet ethnically Chinese people like her are viewed. These perceptions or positionings and the ideologies they betray about equating nation, ethnicity, and language are important to examine when considering Chinese LS because they are part of the broader context for diaspora members with respect to Chinese language(s), often from an early age but also across their lifespan.

An ethnically Chinese *peranakan* (a southeast-Asian born and bred person) from Indonesia, Ang emigrated to the Netherlands with her family as a child, where she became a fluent Dutch speaker and received her secondary and post-secondary education. Ang's book, *On Not Speaking Chinese: Living between Asia and the West*, was inspired by an invitation to give a lecture in Taiwan in the early 1990s. As she noted in the preface, "… I felt I couldn't open my mouth in front of [the anticipated audience] without explaining why I, a person with stereotypically Chinese physical characteristics, could not speak to them in Chinese" (p. vii). In the book she interrogated the meaning of "Chineseness" and "Asianness" in "the West," including Australia, a country that in the 1990s reinvented itself as politically and economically part of greater Asia. She also observed how language ability and race factored into that alignment with Asia. Yet, to her consternation, in the

Netherlands, Australia, and other countries, she found herself frequently asked whether she could speak Chinese, questions which indexed local identity politics and her perceived "difference" and yet betrayed assumptions about the durability of Chinese proficiency in the wake of transnational migration and multilingualism in other languages. Indeed, she described her own (hybrid) experience of being in the "Chinese diaspora" as ambivalent at best, not only because of not speaking Chinese but also in light of other discourses surrounding the emerging "global political and economic power" of "China" and "Chineseness" (p. 12).

Historical marginalization and potential privilege and many other social factors and situations thus create multiple kinds of Chinese identities and alignments, she argues, which cannot and must not be essentialized or fetishized. Ang goes on to write, in her critique and deconstruction of the notion of the Chinese diaspora, that "[d]iasporas are transnational, spatially and temporally sprawling sociocultural formations of people, creating imagined communities whose blurred and fluctuating boundaries are sustained by real and/or symbolic ties to some original 'homeland'" (p. 25). With respect to her own lack of Chinese language knowledge, she noted that her mother, owing to travel to China in her youth, "speaks and writes Chinese fluently, [but] carefully avoided passing this knowledge on to me. So I was cut off from this immense source of cultural capital; instead, I learned to express myself in *bahasa Indonesia*." (p. 28) Thus her earlier socialization, unlike her mother's and in fact as a result of her mother's choices and actions, ensured that she would not become proficient in her HL – or be able to add "this immense source of cultural capital" to her personal repertoire. Rather, she was socialized into Indonesian, Dutch, and English – a trilingual who was nevertheless perceived to have a major linguistic deficiency. Later in the Netherlands, for example, as on the streets of Taiwan on the visit when she gave her lecture, she was called (or perceived as) a "fake Chinese", precisely because she admitted to not speaking Chinese. This labeling by others signaled not just the intergenerational loss of (Chinese) language ability potential, but also the assumed loss of perceived authenticity as a Chinese person.

Duff and Li (2008) presented a similar account by a younger Chinese Indonesian person, "Tony," in a study that took place in western Canada. For Tony, growing up a generation later than Ang in Suharto-era Indonesia near the end of the twentieth century, learning Chinese was actually illegal, as was the display of written Chinese characters in public. Yet the effect on his interlocutors of his disclosures about not speaking Chinese, was the same: he was not considered a culturally authentic Chinese person without being able to speak the language once people learned that his ethnicity was Chinese. He then internalized that view and the shame resulting from his lack of proficiency, which became the impetus for his university-level study of Chinese. Unfortunately, Ang's and Tony's experiences are all too common in the Chinese diaspora, particularly among Generations 1.5 and 2.0, and later waves of immigrants despite differences in the political, cultural, and familial contexts that gave rise to language shift and language loss.

Louie (2004), too, writes about this phenomenon as an American-born Chinese ethnographer who conducted research initially on her first visit (which she described as her "return") to her family's ancestral village in Guangdong and then documented her own and others' experiences of Chineseness across borders and their negotiation and production of identities in the process – as overseas Chinese, as hybrid Americans, and as non-proficient Chinese speakers, for example. An excerpt from the narrative of another Asian American who participated in the university-based "In Search of Roots Program" she researched as a participant-observer (during which participants travelled to China to document their personal histories as well as considering their own diaspora stories), also conveys this ambivalence about their Chinese language and cultural knowledge:

> I don't speak their language, I don't know their customs, I don't dress like them, I DON'T LOOK LIKE THEM, I said. But it was only fear speaking. Fear of feeling lost, fear of feeling stupid, fear of feeling alone…   (J.O. 1991)

Thus, fear was "speaking" in part because of the fear and shame of *not being able to speak or act Chinese* according to local norms, which is generally the driving force of LS. Given that *huaqiao* (overseas Chinese) have resided for centuries, if not millennia, all over the world, the desire among so many to maintain their ancestral language(s) (one or more of the many dozens of dialects considered "Chinese") attests to its significance in their lives and their individual and collective histories. Perhaps the sense of loss is all the more keenly felt in comparison with other languages/cultures because the Chinese languages, cultures, fine arts and literatures, and philosophies have such a long and storied place in the "imagined community" of Chinese (speakers) (Anderson 2006).

As McKay and Wong (1996) observed, even Chinese youth in their diaspora research context – recently arrived Taiwanese or Mainland Chinese immigrants in northern California – took up the discourses of Chineseness and the languages of their homes or wider society in quite distinct ways as a result of their socialization, social roles, and other aspects of identity and peer groups. In their study, the sinophone immigrant students needed to negotiate competing, interacting discourses in their midst, which the authors described as: (1) model-minority discourses (idealized representations of parents and students, particularly with respect to children's expected academic achievement); (2) colonialist/racialized discourses on immigration (society's positioning of immigrants in negative ways); (3) Chinese cultural nationalist discourses (issues of "being Chinese" or "Taiwanese"); (4) social and academic school discourses (e.g. doing and being

"ESL"); and (5) gender discourses (e.g. athleticism and masculinity for boys; model behavior on the part of girls). Those discourses and the people in students' social networks with whom they experience(d) language socialization – in addition to other ideologies referred to earlier regarding the status of particular languages and speakers who can or cannot speak their home languages – constitute the push and pull of bilingual and multilingual LS. Even within the same household these ideologies and discourses affect Chinese HL socialization processes and outcomes differently, according to such factors as birth order (the first child, or eldest sibling, being more likely to retain the HL than younger ones), gender, peers, and English language proficiency.

In summary, the affordances of successful LS within the family go well beyond opportunities to hear, speak, read and write a language regularly at home and are moderated by prevailing ideologies and discourses connected with proficiency in the HL in relation to other languages, cultures, and identities in the diaspora environment. LS research must therefore carefully examine these macrosocial and microlinguistic contexts and dialectics in which Chinese HL development and use are embedded.

Research on LS in Chinese families

From the preceding discussion and narratives regarding the contexts and ideologies in which LS takes place, we now turn to a review of important research in CHL socialization by scholars drawing explicitly on LS theory. The findings are typically based on sustained and fine-tuned micro-analysis of discourse and interaction between and among children, teachers, parents, and sometimes grandparents leading to broader insights.

Agnes He is the scholar most closely identified with Chinese HL socialization research in American Chinese diaspora settings (e.g. He 2006, 2008a, 2008b, 2010, 2011, 2013). The primary observational data in her studies come from Chinese HL classrooms, supplemented by interviews with participants about aspects of their earlier Chinese socialization at home and at school and about their identities. In addition to examining interaction among co-participants in particular sociocultural events, LS researchers such as He examine the various "indexical" meanings of parts of the linguistic code that are being used and acquired (e.g. word order, intonation, lexis, syntax, morphology, turn-taking mechanisms). These elements and their meanings and social significance (relationships to social identities, events, status, beliefs, and broader cultures) are then explicated. She has examined linguistic devices and the identities and stances (e.g. moral evaluation) that are inculcated as these forms are used and internalized by learners. She has also analyzed the artful and strategic use of codeswitching in home interactions in relation to indexicality (He 2013).

In addition to her micro-analysis of discourse, He has been able to construct typical trajectories related to CHL retention and use, with explanations for them, by linking ethnolinguistic observations at different stages in a number of children's and adolescents' lives. Resulting from this work, He (2008b; 2011) proposed a number of "hypotheses" – namely, that socialization and thus development will be most successful when (1) learners feel "rooted" in their heritage culture, or strongly affiliated and identified with it; (2) learners anticipate social and economic "benefits and rewards" as a result of their learning of the HL; (3) learners desire to communicate in the HL (rather than another language) in the here-and-now, in interactions with their older relatives at home, for example; (4) the English community surrounding the HL community has a positive attitude toward the Chinese language; (5) the use of Chinese "by choice" rather than by necessity (in the latter case, possibly when not all family members are proficient in English) enhances children's attitudes to the language and they see bilingualism (and Chinese as part of that) as an enrichment not a liability; (6) "rich and diverse input" in the HL, in both oral and literate modes, at home and elsewhere, contributes to success in HL literacy development in particular; (7) the greater alignment between or sensitivity to English discourse norms in Chinese HL contexts creates a more positive environment for HL learning for children; (8) learners' successful acquisition of the language of the dominant community (e.g. English) and integration within that community enhances their attitudes toward development and the use of HL; (9) "[t]he degree of success in CHL development correlates positively with the ease with which the learner is able to manage differences and discontinuities presented by multiple speech roles in multiple, intersecting communities" (p. 597); and finally, (10):

> As the CHL learner copes with the multiple linguistic codes in the contexts of family, peer groups, and school institutions, s/he is engaged in a double process of socialization into given speech communities and of acquisition of literacy as a means of asserting personal meanings that have the potential to transform the speech community. In other words, CHL can be used both to inherit heritage practices and to transform the very practices that motivated CHL learning in the first place.   (He 2008b, p. 118)

The principle conveyed in this final hypothesis is important yet often overlooked. HL "maintenance" is sometimes construed as being very reproductive and conservative, in intention, implementation, and outcome. However, as contemporary LS research demonstrates well, a perhaps more common outcome of bilingualism and other forms of language contact is *syncretic* forms and practices, reflecting not just cultural and linguistic preservation and transmission but also *transformation* (e.g. Curdt-Christiansen 2013; Garrett & Baquedano-Lopez 2002; Kulick 1992). Therefore it is important to observe how languages are mixed, how registers and genres may be introduced, changed, and lost, and how customs evolve, and particularly so within Chinese homes where multiple varieties of Chinese and other languages co-exist in the family's and community's collective communicative repertoire. Below, I illustrate this principle and highlight a few areas that other researchers have investigated in CHL in terms of LS by means of codeswitching, shaming, narrating, discussing taste, or using material semiotic resources. (Readers are referred to Duranti et al. (2011) for many other thematic foci in recent LS research.)

Code-switching and forms of address

Like He, Zhu Hua (2010) has examined LS within CHL diaspora communities, but in the United Kingdom. One area of focus in her research is interactions within the family and especially the use of address forms (e.g. pronouns, kinship terms such as *gege* 'older brother', and given names), either in Chinese or English, to fulfill particular social functions. In excerpts of bilingual family discourse she analyzed, she noted how the older of two young brothers (age 10) referred to himself as *gege* – in violation of Chinese sociolinguistic norms – when trying to convince his brother to let him play with a toy. The younger brother (age 5), in contrast, referred to himself in greater accordance with English norms, by first person pronoun – and in English – and referred to his older brother by his English name, not his Chinese name or by the kinship term "older brother". The mother also used address forms and languages strategically and differentially to try to mediate a small dispute between the brothers about who could play with a model car, addressing the eldest son by his Chinese name but the younger son by his English name.

Zhu Hua concluded that "[t]he strategic use of address terms by the parents and children … is part of a language socialization process in which the younger generations of diasporic communities not only internalize the social, cultural, and linguistic traditions of the parents, but also play an active role in constructing and creating their own social and cultural identities. In addition to this, the use of address terms brings about changes to the community and to family norms" (p. 200). As in He's analysis, Zhu Hua sees LS as multidirectional and dynamic, as both an enactment of traditions, ideologies, and practices, but also a site for contestation, innovation, and transformation in intercultural contexts.

Shaming

One of the earliest and most enduring topics of LS studied across languages, cultures, and communities has been that of shaming, a socially very powerful and potentially stigmatizing form of socialization into normative practices and ideologies (Lo & Fung 2011; Schieffelin & Ochs 1986; Ochs & Schieffelin 2008). A single word, phrase, or (other) negative assessment can have a huge and lasting effect and the cumulative effect of multiple such occurrences is clear. For example, scornfully calling a crying child – and especially a boy – a "crybaby" or a "sissy" or a "loser" or "wimp" is a form of shaming in English that conveys the stance that children shouldn't cry in particular situations, and that it is a form of weakness and embarrassment for the child and parents. The purported function of shaming, teasing, threatening, or humiliating novices in other ways, from a LS point of view, is to pressure them to comply with established practices, moral sensibilities and thus cultural competence in the group or risk being ostracized or sanctioned in other possibly more severe and enduring ways.

Although the role of shaming in LS has been examined in many other languages, less research has examined how it functions in Chinese diaspora families. Fung (1999) describes shaming as the "quintessential sociomoral emotion" (p. 181) and one that is pervasive in Chinese cultures. Shaming is also closely connected with notions of personal and collective "face" and honour. In Fung's study of nine Taiwanese families, she studied the socialization taking place through shaming from a very early age. Examining a large corpus of recorded data, she looked for explicit means of socialization, such as the phrases "'shame on you,' 'shameful,' 'ashamed,' and 'losing face' (e.g. *xiuxiu Han, xiu si ren, hao xiu, cankui, diu, Han, diu si ren*), gestures for shame (e.g. striking index finger on cheek), idiomatic expressions for shame (e.g. 'I want to bury my head into the ground,' 'You made your mother lose face,' 'Aren't you embarrassed for yourself?')" (p. 192). She also examined implicit forms of shaming such as turning away from the child, reminding him or her that others were observing the interaction, or spanking the child in public or in view of the camera; and then other contextual markers of shaming such as warnings, deep sighs, and frowns. The shaming was typically enacted by a parent or caregiver but could be meted out by peers or siblings as well, often taking a parental cue.

Fung also reported that the shaming behavior continued, sometimes long after the child had complied with local norms and ceased the earlier shameful behavior, for instance when a previous transgression was recalled or reinvoked by a parent, again to socialize the child about past wrongs. Sometimes the shamer sought an explicit confession or admission of wrongdoing and not just a stop to the offending behavior. In other cases a child challenged the shaming as unfounded or unfair. Shaming is thus a very potent and ubiquitous form of early socialization in the home and likely in other settings such as schools and should therefore be studied further in multimodal (e.g. visual, embodied, oral/aural, written) discursive ways, particularly in intercultural and bilingual diaspora contexts.

However, as Lo and Fung (2011) point out, shaming is not always charged with negative affect; sometimes, it can be done in a manner that appropriates a practice or label that might be construed as stigmatizing and then uses it for more lighthearted purposes, constituting a kind of mock shaming or teasing. This observation serves as a reminder that in research looking at pragmatic behaviours, such as speech acts, with a particular sociomoral function, it is important to examine the practice and the forms over time to see their evolution and also the different social meanings that are indexed in different contexts and interlocutors' uptake of feedback.

Narrativity

Socialization into and through narrative practices has been another longstanding focus of LS research since the seminal research by Heath (1983) and others (cf. Ochs & Taylor's 1995) 'father-knows-best' dinnertime narrative research; Ochs & Capps 2001). Not only is the manner of narrating important in LS (e.g. narrative structure, participant frameworks, and roles, voicing, and footing), but so too is the content – what is tellable to whom, in what contexts, by whom, and for what social, emotional, didactic or other purposes.

Miller, Koven and Lin (2011) observed differences between Taipei and Chicago families in terms of their narration of events involving their children (Chinese and English speaking, respectively), emphasizing the morally didactic (and often shaming) tone in the Taiwanese retellings much more so than in the American ones. One area that Miller et al. suggest for future LS research is socialization and narrative inequality (i.e. "privileging of some ways of narrating experience over others" (p. 194)) in family and other settings. Younger children, for example, or elders may not be considered legitimate, accurate, or competent storytellers, and gender inequalities may also surface, as Ochs and Taylor (1995) also reported. Other areas for future research on narrative include aspects of code choice, narrative roles, and notions of appropriate content in multigenerational, bilingual Chinese diaspora settings. Although not suggested by Miller et al. *transnational* narratives mediated by the internet (by Skype, email, or other messaging or social networking tools) offer other promising and increasingly routine forms of intergenerational narration and socialization in physically separated Chinese families. Therefore, these forms of narrative engagement and mediation merit further attention as well.

Dinnertime discourse: Speaking in (and about) good taste

A great deal of LS work within families takes place around the family dinner table, perhaps the prototypical setting for LS and for research on it (e.g. Blum-Kulka 1997, 2008). Even in the popular press, writers commonly extol the benefits of families eating together and recount the negative sociological effects of busy urban families no longer regularly sharing meals together around the same table precisely because it plays such an important role in the discursive construction of families and in family members' socialization and wellbeing.

By examining dinnertime discourse (narratives, explanations, arguments, jokes), scholars have learned how children are socialized into knowledge and ideologies connected to such aspects of life as work by hearing about it from their parents (e.g. Paugh 2008); into morality and spirituality (e.g. Ochs & Capps 2001; Ochs & Taylor 1995); manners, politeness, and gossip; bilingualism or multilingualism; various speech acts (such as ritual openings and closings of meals, blessings and prayers, requests for food or condiments to be passed around the table); humor and irony; and into explicit discussion about the taste of the food being consumed itself (e.g. Ochs, Pontecorvo & Fasulo 1996; see Blum-Kulka 1997, 2008, for a review of related work).

Considering the last point, socialization into "taste", the ways in which children and others (e.g. visitors from another culture) learn to orient to and comment on particular aspects of food in meals (e.g. whether a particular dish is too salty, spicy, bland, or rather, very tasty, fresh, and tender) and also its status as source of pleasure, ethnic identity, or reward (DuFon 2006) is highly relevant in Chinese culture(s). The importance of gathering over multicourse family meals together within the home, in restaurants, and other venues cannot be overstated as a site of LS. Cross-cultural comparative work has been done with other cultures, but the linguistic socialization of taste within Chinese diaspora homes and other aspects of family dinnertime discourse has received little attention in LS research. One recent exception is research conducted not in a diaspora context but in a homestay situation in China with American summer school students, where the researcher found that nearly a quarter of turns at talk at the dinner table were in some way related to taste or ideologies and beliefs about (Chinese vs. American) food – what kinds of food are healthy, tasty, seasonal, complicated to cook, and so forth (Kinginger 2013). This topic therefore represents another fertile area for future research on learning, becoming, or, as conversational analysts might say, "doing being" Chinese in diaspora contexts.

Socialization through other semiotic resources, networks, and activities

Although most LS research to date, across languages, has focused much more on speech than on literacy practices, textbooks and other aspects of literacy constitute another crucial mode and means of socialization, particularly in CHL settings. Here I consider several recent studies that have explored socialization into and through Chinese literacy, first by analyzing the textbooks that are used, and second, by focusing on the interactions among co-participants in literacy events, such as children, their siblings, and grandparents.

Jiang (2010) and Chiu (2011) examined Chinese textbooks and other materials used by children in Canadian diaspora homes, in family-based language and culture programs (*sishu*), and in HL schools over the past century. Both noted how the textbooks have depicted the 'ideal Chinese child' – one who is obedient, a devoted student of Chinese, one demonstrating filial duty and perseverance, and one who, in the case of the materials originating in China as opposed to Taiwan, makes efforts to visit China and its grand, iconic historical, cultural, and geographical landmarks, and is well acquainted with great Chinese writers and thinkers, such as Confucius. In the past, the materials carried strong and explicit political messages as well, especially those oriented to (Mainland) China and the various ruling regimes and ideologies through the 20th century (Jiang 2010).

The textbooks examined by Jiang and Chiu were intended for use in HL programs or Chinese schools for Chinese settlers and their descendents in Canada in the early to mid-twentieth century as well as in contemporary settings in Western Canada and other parts of North America. They convey clear socializing messages, through different periods of history, past and present about how children should act, speak, think, write (e.g. to write letters back to China, which was taught through Letter Writing courses, *chidu,* in the mid-20th Century), dress, and represent themselves, their families, and their homeland. The role of the Chinese language and literacy practices, the choice of canonical or classical literary texts, the choice of dialects (major Chinese varieties such as Cantonese vs. Mandarin, rather than Hakka or Taishan, which were spoken by many early settlers) and script systems, and (other) forms of moral education were all instrumental in constructing the ideal patriotic and filial Chinese child and the diaspora more generally.

Curdt-Christiansen's (2003) study of triliteracy development in families with children from Chinese backgrounds in the Canadian province of Quebec, also explores the language and literacy resources and instructional activities used to socialize young children at home and in community HL schools into the ideologies, cultural practices, "cultural capital" and identities connected with Chinese literacy. Interestingly, in the ten families in her larger sample, many of the parents were, like her, of the generation where early literacy in China was very restricted to particular political works and slogans, and especially those of Chairman Mao. Yet the same individuals, as parents, were now in the position of socializing their children into early literacy behaviors, activities, print environments, genres, and resources in Chinese (*and* English and French, to the extent possible) that they themselves had not had the opportunity to experience firsthand during the Chinese Cultural Revolution (1966–76). In addition, they were socializing the children into a work ethic associated with a broad and deep education (including fine arts and music) and Chinese language/literacy education, which emphasizes endurance and effort in learning. As one parent in her study remarked in an interview regarding the importance of Chinese language maintenance in the next generation in Canada, "You may give up anything else, but not Chinese [language]. Why? Simply because you are Chinese!" (p. 205; translated from the original Chinese). Echoing examples cited above from Indonesian Chinese immigrants, this conflation of language and identity was frequent among parents and children in the study and is shared by many first-generation Chinese immigrant parents. The large number of Chinese HL schools in Canada, the U.S., Australia, and Great Britain demonstrates this as well. In this sense, Curdt-Christiansen reported that the parents saw it as their role to apprentice their children into membership in the Chinese language, culture, and community, and into Chinese identities, as well as to foster "connection" and "communication" with an "ancient civilization" (p. 207), a recurring theme in the textbooks reviewed by Chiu (2011) as well.

The Chinese language itself helps mediate those functions and affords people who speak it opportunities for social and professional advancement, empowerment, and "participation in community life" (p. 208), according to the parents in Curdt-Christiansen's study. Furthermore, grandparents were often instrumental, within the home, together with parents, in working with children on their Chinese homework, reading to them and speaking Chinese to them, and encouraging them to persist with their studies, and providing a Chinese-literacy-rich home environment with engaging age-appropriate Chinese language materials. Parents also emphasized the importance of English in the children's lives and futures and assisted them with that language too – more so than with French, although that is the dominant language in Quebec and a language they also acknowledged to be important for their children's current education and cultural edification. Yet, one of the girls in the study who had come to Canada at age 4 and had already been in the country for six years, wrote in an essay (translated from Chinese): "I will continue learning Chinese so that I can serve my motherland when I grow up." (p. 232). Presumably, that 'motherland' referred to China, not Canada. Again, that sentiment likely was a reproduction of textbook discourse, which Chiu (2011) reported on as well.

In a later article, Curdt-Christiansen (2013) highlighted the *syncretic* literacy practices found in Chinese families in Montreal and Singapore, involving interactions between young children and the grandparents who traditionally have played such a prominent (albeit often 'imperceptible' or implicit) role in Chinese children's caregiving, socialization, and education. For instance, by observing their elders' interactions with literacy (i.e. implicit socialization), the children gain an appreciation of the importance of different forms of literacy texts and practices in their own lives and those of adults. Furthermore, by engaging actively in language play, playing riddle games connected to literacy (e.g. Chinese characters) and literary texts, the focal child in the Montreal CHL context (Lingling) learned to solve language problems as well as have fun through interactions with her Grandmother Ling. Rather than present literacy as a serious and rote process of character memorization and reproduction, as was the case in the Singapore home, the orientation to CHL literacy in the Montreal home was relaxed and engaging, much less structured than typical literacy activities in CHL schools (or in the Singaporean focal family). Lingling took an (inter)active role in the literacy games and in the production of various other syncretic texts. She and her (seemingly progressive) grandmother reportedly blended "traditional Chinese values and Western educational philosophy to create their own patterns of literacy practice" (p. 367).

This research demonstrates distinct possibilities for conducting research on Chinese heritage language and literacy socialization that examines the creative, syncretic aspects of language play (when that is allowed to occur) and the blending of home and school languages, literacies, traditions, and genres. To date, very little such LS research has been conducted in CHL contexts.

LS in international adoptive families

A relatively recent development in Chinese diaspora-related research has been an examination of linguistic and cultural socialization within families into which Chinese children have been adopted internationally either by ethnically Chinese or non-Chinese (typically White, Anglo) parents. There is much potential for research on LS in this type of setting. Fogle's (2012) pioneering study on L2 socialization within adoptive American homes with Russian or Ukrainian children is very instructive in that regard and especially when children resist parents' attempts to learn and speak the children's L1 or resist other ways in which parents attempt to socialize them. In Fogle's study, for example, children resisted a father's narrative strategies soliciting reports by the children about their day at school. The agency of emerging bilinguals such as adopted youth in LS processes and outcomes was underscored in that study.

With respect to Chinese adoptees specifically, for nearly a decade Louie (2009), a Chinese American anthropologist, has examined cultural socialization in international adoptive homes in the U.S. with young Chinese children. With ethnographic research sites in the Midwest and on the west coast, and using participant observations and dozens of interviews, she has been especially interested in White parents' construction of "Chineseness" through various kinds of symbols (Chinese clothing – their "native costumes", panda bear toys, dragons, calligraphy). She has also examined family activities or events such as Chinese New Year celebrations and patronage of local Chinese restaurants ostensibly to facilitate the children's socialization into Chinese culture and identification with their ethnic roots – or what they assume is authentic Chinese culture – as well as into "American" ones. This process becomes particularly interesting for LS research when the (White) middle-class parents themselves and the Chinese-adopted children's non-Chinese siblings (including adoptees of other ethnic/racial origins in some cases) are themselves being socialized into the same traditions alongside their children, without any real prior personal experience with or expertise in them. Although Louie's main focus is not language learning but, rather, the construction and production of Chinese identities, including racialized identities, she observed the role of Chinese language learning as one of the areas of symbolic competence that parents often invest heavily in and therefore attempt to socialize their children into, if not at home, then through community resources. She writes:

> The importance of attending Chinese-language school encapsulated many of the discussions and debates that parents have about the place of Chinese culture in their family's lives. When asked why they wanted their child to learn some Chinese, the majority of St. Louis parents told me that they would like their children to be able to say a few words in reply if spoken to in Chinese. Attending Chinese-language school also provided an opportunity for children to socialize with other adopted and nonadopted Chinese Americans from the local community. But at the same time, because Chinese-language school represented a substantial time commitment (every Sunday afternoon, plus homework), parents had to decide how, when, or whether they wanted to take it on. Some families made arrangements with private tutors who could adapt to their schedules and curricular needs.   (p. 311–312)

Louie also noted that beyond being a means of socializing their children, the "practice of Chinese culture" both inside and outside the families' homes served as "an involuntary performance to help establish their legitimacy not only as adoptive parents but also as adoptive parents of children of color" (p. 304). In other words, parents' socialization patterns and efforts had a crucial performative dimension – of demonstrating to others that they were attending to their children's past lives and reconstructed ethnic identities – and thus were sensitive, worthy, adoptive parents. When a Taiwanese American advisor reported that he had not felt it was important for his own children to retain Chinese when they were growing up, the adoptive parents in her study felt that "they did not have the luxury to make this choice on behalf of their children" (p. 312), that it was their responsibility to provide cultural continuity and pride in their children's lives.

Therefore, with greater transnationalism among Chinese people than ever before, and families that are not only mobile or migratory but also increasingly diverse or blended ethnolinguistically, LS offers many productive avenues for examining the processes, ideologies, and outcomes of language choice, code-switching, narrativity, pragmatics, and the use of semiotic tools such as textbooks and the Internet for the socialization of both children and their interlocutors into syncretic communicative practices, identities, and ideologies.

Conclusion

Socialization into Chinese diaspora languages, cultures, and communities offers many possible pathways to an appropriation of habitus, not all of which lead to the development of high levels of proficiency in varieties of Chinese language. Although members of the far-flung diaspora community as well as those in the non-Chinese mainstream may place a premium on Chinese linguistic competence as evidence of one's Chineseness and ethnolinguistic authenticity, young Generation 1.5, 2.0 or 3.0 Chinese may feel much less affiliated with the language and with its traditional cultures, dispositions and values, given the others in their immediate environment which may have more prestige and power and with which they find greater resonance, acceptance, and affiliation.

However, as He (2011) and other scholars (Li & Duff this volume) point out, for those who *do* identify with the Chinese language and desire to learn and use it, LS into Chinese often follows a very complicated nonlinear pathway that may involve multiple additional languages and Chinese varieties as well, and periods of lesser vs. greater connection with the HL and with activities and networks that are likely to build proficiency. Early home-based and HL-school socialization into Chinese may alienate children from the language, especially if their parents are not highly proficient in the locally dominant and more prestigious community language and if the methods and materials for teaching Chinese are viewed as too regimented, rote, uninteresting, and pedantic, especially in comparison with other forms of learning that children experience through mainstream schooling, for instance. Thus, the interplay of linguistic and cultural socialization, identity construction, and innovation in terms of sociolinguistic roles, code choice, norms, and interactional strategies, among other aspects of discourse, deserve much closer examination. Such pursuits are especially relevant and timely, given the very large and diverse Chinese diaspora worldwide, the increasingly dominant status of Mandarin globally, and the growing access of diaspora members to oral and written Chinese online as well as more traditional and formal language education.

In conclusion, future research in Chinese HL socialization should examine to a greater extent four sets of issues: (1) continuities, discontinuities, syncretism, and innovations in (Chinese and other) language learning and use across home, school, and community settings (Duff 2008); (2) CHL socialization across multiple timescales, looking at trajectories of socialization across the lifespan, both within and across generations, ideally through both cross-sectional (cross-generational) and longitudinal research designs (e.g. Wortham 2005); (3) the relationship between proficiency in Chinese and Chineseness, considering that many people of Chinese ethnic descent no longer speak any variety of Chinese, and a growing number of non-Chinese people who are learning Chinese to high levels of proficiency are also questioning their own sense of Chineseness and their sinophone identities; and (4) the changing status of certain nonstandard varieties of Chinese – including nonstandard dialects of Mandarin – spoken in many diaspora homes and the ways in which speakers of those languages are both positioned and socialized within home and Chinese school settings in relation to more standard current prestige varieties. These topics should be addressed in a forward-looking international research agenda on Chinese (heritage) language socialization.

References

Anderson, B. 2006. *Imagined Communities,* 2nd edn. London: Verso.

Ang, I. 2001. *On not Speaking Chinese: Living between Asia and the West.* London: Routledge.

Bayley, R. & Langman, J. 2011. Language socialization in multilingual and second language contexts. In *Handbook of Research on Second Language Teaching and Learning,* Vol. 2, E. Hinkel (ed.), 291–302. New York NY: Routledge.

Bayley, R. & Schecter, S. 2003. *Language Socialization in Bilingual and Multilingual Societies,* 128–147. Clevedon: Multilingual Matters.

Blum-Kulka, S. 1997. *Dinner Talk: Cultural Patterns of Sociability and Socialization in Family Discourse.* Mahwah, NJ: Lawrence Erlbaum Associates.

Blum-Kulka, S. 2008. Language socialization and family dinnertime discourse. In *Encyclopedia of Language and Education,* Vol. 8: *Language Socialization,* P. Duff & N.H. Hornberger (eds), 87–99. Dordrecht: Springer.

Bourdieu, P. 1977. *Outline of a Theory of Practice.* Cambridge: CUP.

Chiu, L. 2011. The Construction of the "Ideal Chinese Child": A Critical Analysis of Textbooks for Chinese Heritage Language Learners. MA thesis, University of British Columbia, Canada.

Curdt-Christiansen, X.L. 2003. Growing up in Three Languages: Triliteracy Practices of Immigrant Chinese Children in Quebec. Ph.D. dissertation, McGill University, Canada.

Curdt-Christiansen, X.L. 2013. Implicit learning and imperceptible influence: Syncretic literacy of multilingual Chinese children. *Journal of Early Childhood Literacy* 13(3): 345–367.

Dai, J.E. & Zhang, L. 2008. What are the CHL learners inheriting? Habitus of the CHL learners. In *Chinese as a Heritage Language: Fostering Rooted World Citizenry,* A.W. He & Y. Xiao (eds), 37–51. Honolulu HI: National Foreign Language Resource Center, University of Hawai'i .

Duff, P. 2007. Language socialization as sociocultural theory: Issues and possibilities. *Language Teaching* 40: 309–319.

Duff, P. 2008. Language socialization, participation and identity: Ethnographic approaches. In *Encyclopedia of Language and Education,* Vol. 3: *Discourse and Education,* M. Martin-Jones, M. de Mejia & N. Hornberger (eds), 107–119. Dordrecht: Springer.

Duff, P. 2010. Language socialization. In *Sociolinguistics and Language Education*, S. McKay & N.H. Hornberger (eds), 427–455. Bristol: Multilingual Matters.

Duff, P. 2011. Second language socialization. In *Handbook of Language Socialization*, A. Duranti, E. Ochs & B. Schieffelin (eds), 564–586. Malden MA: Wiley-Blackwell.

Duff, P. 2012. Identity, agency, and SLA. In *Handbook of Second Language Acquisition*, A. Mackey & S. Gass (eds), 410–426. London: Routledge.

Duff, P.A. & Hornberger, N.H. (eds). 2008. *Language Socialization. Encyclopedia of Language and Education*, Vol. 8. Dordrecht: Springer.

Duff, P. & Li, D. 2008. Negotiating language, literacy and identity: Chinese heritage learners' language socialization. World Congress of Applied Linguistics, Essen, Germany, August.

Duff, P. & Talmy, S. 2011. Second language socialization: Beyond language acquisition in SLA. In *Alternative Approaches to SLA*, D. Atkinson (ed.), 95–116. London: Routledge.

DuFon, M. 2006. The socialization of taste during study abroad in Indonesia. In *Language Learners in Study abroad Contexts*, M. DuFon & E. Churchill, E. (eds), 91–119. Clevedon: Multilingual Matters.

Duranti, A., Ochs, E. & Schieffelin, B. (eds). 2011. *The Handbook of Language Socialization*. Malden MA: Wiley-Blackwell.

Fogle, L. 2012. *Second Language Socialization and Learner Agency: Adoptive Family Talk*. Bristol: Multilingual Matters.

Fung, H. 1999. Becoming a moral child: The socialization of shame among young Chinese children. *Ethos* 27(2): 189–209.

Garrett, P.B. & Baquedano-Lopez, P. 2002. Language socialization: Reproduction and continuity, transformation and change. *Annual Review of Anthropology* 31: 339–361.

He, A.W. 2003. Novices and their speech roles in Chinese heritage language classes. In *Language Socialization in Bilingual and Multilingual Societies*, R. Bayley & S. Schecter (eds), 128–146. Clevedon: Multilingual Matters.

He, A.W. 2006. Toward an identity-based model for the development of Chinese as a heritage language. *The Heritage Language Journal* 4(1): 1–28.

He, A.W. 2008a. Heritage language learning and socialization. In *Encyclopedia of Language and Education*, Vol. 8: *Language Socialization*, P. Duff & N. Hornberger (eds), 201–213. Dordrecht: Springer.

He, A.W. 2008b. An identity-based model for the development of Chinese as a heritage language. In *Chinese as a Heritage Language: Fostering Rooted World Citizenry*, A. He & Y. Xiao (eds), 109–124. Honolulu HI: National Foreign Language Resource Center, University of Hawaii.

He, A.W. 2009. Sequences, scripts, and subject Pronouns in the construction of Chinese heritage identity. In *Beyond Yellow English: Toward a Linguistic Anthropology of Asian Pacific America*, A. Reyes & A. Lo (eds), 366–384. Oxford: OUP.

He, A.W. 2010. The heart of heritage: Sociocultural dimensions of heritage language acquisition. *Annual Review of Applied Linguistics* 30: 66–82.

He, A.W. 2011. Heritage language socialization. In *The Handbook of Language Socialization*, A. Duranti, E. Ochs & B. Schieffelin (eds), 587–609. Oxford: Blackwell.

He, A.W. 2013. The wor(l)d is a collage: Multi-performance by Chinese heritage language speakers. *The Modern Language Journal* 97(2): 304–317.

Heath, S.B. 1983. *Ways with Words: Language, Life, and Work in Communities and Classrooms*. Cambridge: CUP.

Jia, L. 2006. The Invisible and the Visible: Language Socialization at the Chinese Heritage Language School. Ph.D. Dissertation, University of Texas at San Antonio.

Jiang, H. 2010. A Socio-Historical Analysis of Chinese Heritage Language Education in British Columbia. MA Thesis, University of British Columbia, Canada.

Kinginger, C. 2013, July. Language and taste socialization in study abroad. Paper presented at the Research Symposium on Sociocultural, Discursive, and Transnational Perspectives on the Learning of Chinese (and Other Languages). Centre for Research in Chinese Language and Literacy Education. The University of British Columbia, Canada.

Kulick, D. 1992. *Language Shift and Cultural Reproduction: Socialization, Self, and Syncretism in a Papua New Guinean Village*. Cambridge: CUP.

Lei, J. 2007. A Language Socialization Approach to the Interplay of Ethnic Revitalization and Heritage Language Learning. Case Studies of Chinese American Adolescents. Ph.D. dissertation, State University of New York (SUNY), Albany.

Li, D., & Duff, P. 2008. Issues in Chinese heritage language education and research at the post-secondary level. In *Chinese as a Heritage Language: Fostering Rooted World Citizenry*, A.W. He & Y. Xiao (eds), 13–36. Honolulu HI: National Foreign Language Resource Center.

Lo, A., & Fung, H. 2011. Language socialization and shaming. In *The Handbook of Language Socialization*, A. Duranti, E. Ochs, & B. Schieffelin (eds), 169–189. Malden MA: Wiley-Blackwell.

Louie, A. 2004. *Chineseness Across Borders: Renegotiating Chinese Identities in China and the United States*. Durham NC: Duke University Press.

Louie, A. 2009. Pandas, lions, and dragons, oh my!: How White adoptive parents construct Chineseness. *Journal of Asian American Studies* 12(3): 285–320.

McKay, S.L., & Wong, S-L.C. 1996. Multiple discourses, multiple identities: Investment and agency in second-language learning among Chinese adolescent immigrant students. *Harvard Educational Review* 66(3): 577–608.

McDonald, E. 2011. *Learning Chinese, Turning Chinese: Challenges to Becoming Sinophone in a Globalized World*. London: Routledge.

Miller, P.J., Koven, M., & Lin, S. 2011. Language socialization and narrative. In *The handbook of language socialization*, A. Duranti, E. Ochs, & B. Schieffelin (eds), 190–208. Malden MA: Wiley-Blackwell.

Ochs, E. & Capps, L. 2001. *Living Narrative*. Cambridge MA: Harvard University Press.

Ochs, E., Pontecorvo, C. & Fasulo, A. 1996. Socializing taste. *Ethnos* 1(2): 7–46.

Ochs, E. & Schieffelin, B.B. 2008. Language socialization: An historical overview. In *Encyclopedia of Language and Education*, Vol. 8: *Language Socialization*, P.A. Duff & N.H. Hornberger (eds), 3–15. Dordrecht: Springer.

Ochs, E. & Schieffelin, B.B. 2011. The theory of language socialization. In *The Handbook of Language Socialization*, A. Duranti, E. Ochs & B. Schieffelin (eds), 1–21. Malden MA: Wiley-Blackwell.

Ochs, E. & Taylor, C. 1995. The 'father knows best' dynamic in dinnertime conversation. In *Gender Articulated*, K. Kall & M. Bucholtz (eds), 97–120. New York NY: Routledge.

Paugh, A. 2008. Language socialization in working families. *Encyclopedia of Language and Education*, Vol. 8: *Language Socialization*, P.A. Duff & N.H. Hornberger (eds), 101–113. Dordrecht: Springer.

Schieffelin, B.B., & Ochs, E. 1986. *Language Socialization across Cultures*. Cambridge: CUP.

Wang, S. 2008. The ecology of the Chinese language in the United States. In *Encyclopedia of Language and Education*, 2nd edn, Vol. 9: *Ecology of Language*, A. Creese, P. Martin & N.H. Hornberger (eds), 169–180. Dordrecht: Springer.

Watson-Gegeo, K. 2004. Mind, language, and epistemology: Toward a language socialization paradigm for SLA. *Modern Language Journal* 88: 331–350.

Watson-Gegeo, K. & Bronson, M. 2013. The intersections of language socialization and socio-linguistics. In *The Oxford Handbook of Sociolinguistics,* R. Bayley, R. Cameron & C. Lucas (eds), 111–131. Oxford: OUP.

Wortham, S. 2005. Socialization beyond the speech event. *Journal of Linguistic Anthropology* 15: 95–112.

Zuengler, J. & Cole, K. 2005. Language socialization and L2 learning. In *Handbook of Research in Second Language Teaching and Learning,* E. Hinkel (ed.), 301–316. Mahwah NJ: Lawrence Erlbaum Associates.

Zhu Hua 2010. Language socialization and interculturality: Address terms in intergenerational talk in Chinese diasporic families. *Language and Intercultural Communication* 10(3): 189–205.

CHAPTER 2

Family language policy

Is learning Chinese at odds with learning English?

Xiao Lan Curdt-Christiansen
University of Reading

This inquiry examines how family languages policies (FLP) are planned and developed in twenty bilingual families in Singapore with regard to their children's Chinese language and literacy development. The study focuses on how parents perceive Chinese and how their beliefs are transformed into active language practices. Data sources include *de facto* language practices in home domains, parents' language ideologies, and literacy activities and private tuition used as their language management. The findings reveal that all parents hold an unambiguous belief in the benefits of developing Chinese language, both in terms of cultural identity and in terms of providing overt socioeconomic opportunities. The study shows that FLPs are constantly interacting with and shaped by nonlinguistic forces – the national language policy and the educational system. When facing the sociopolitical and educational realities in Singapore, these parents are coerced to place Chinese and English into a dichotomous position resulting in lower expectations for their children's Chinese proficiency and less sufficient provision of Chinese literacy resources.

Introduction

Along with being recognized as an efficient, English-speaking and well-organized city-state in South-East Asia, Singapore is also known for its bilingual policy. In this chapter, I explore through the lens of Family Language Policy (FLP) how Chinese language, as one of the country's official mother tongues, is practiced and planned explicitly and implicitly in twenty English-Chinese bilingual Singaporean families. FLP is an important field of investigation as it determines how languages are transmitted across generations and under what conditions a language is maintained or lost (Fishman 2004). Few studies, however, have examined the broader socio-political and economic forces that shape parental decisions on what languages to practice and how to practice them. This study examines how language policies on different levels (national and educational institutions) influence and interact with the FLPs of the participating families, and how these interacting variables influence patterns of language and literacy practices. It focuses on the role of parents as this is shaped by the socio-cultural, political, ideological and economic forces at the macro level and by their own educational experiences, their understanding of the significance of languages for their children's future, and their language management and practices at the micro level. Inevitably, this exploration involves the broader issues of the impact of English as the language of modernity and political economy on the status and role of the heritage languages in a multilingual society. Thus the study has significant implications with regard to the politico-economic accessibility which linguistic abilities/disabilities afford or constrain; the dichotomous relationship between English and Chinese; the critical role that language plays in perpetuating social inequality; and the sociopolitical influence of the language policy, especially the Medium of Instruction (MoI), on parents' intervention in their children's biliteracy development.

Theorizing family language policy

Family language policy has been defined as explicit and overt planning in relation to language use and literacy practice within home domains and among family members (Curdt-Christiansen 2013a; King, Fogle & Logan-Terry 2008). While often explicit and observable, it can also be informal and unintended, as a default consequence of ideological beliefs (Fishman 2004; Lo Bianco 2010; Spolsky 2009). It is "shaped by what the family believes will strengthen the family's social standing and best serve and support the family members' goals in life" (Curdt-Christiansen 2009: 326).

In this chapter, I elaborate on Spolsky's theoretical framework of *language policy* to explicate how FLP is connected with broader political, educational and economic forces external to families as well as micro factors within families to mutually influence and shape family members' perceived values about languages, their language use patterns, and the observable measures that parents use to control and manage the 'desired' linguistic behaviors (e.g. Canagarajah 2008; Curdt-Christiansen 2012; King et al. 2008; Lane 2010). Figure 2.1 provides a graphic representation to illustrate the dynamic relationship between FLP and its sociolinguistic forces and non-linguistic variables.

This model represents the multidimensional system of FLP based on Spolsky's (2004) definition of language policy, which comprises three interrelated components: language practice (*de facto* language use – what people do with language),

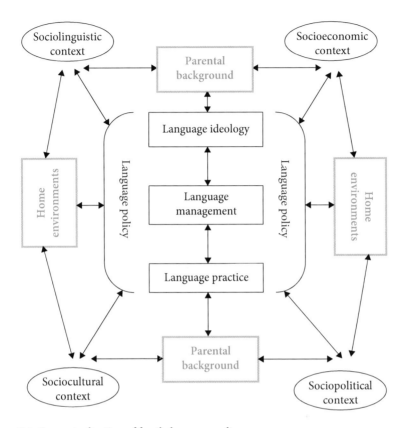

Figure 2.1 Conceptualization of family language policy

language ideology (what family members think about language), and language management (what they try to do about language). In the following section, I provide a brief discussion on these components and explain how they are integrated, linking political and ideological issues at the macro level with the family language situation at the micro level.

Language ideology

Language ideologies are the driving forces in FLP (King 2000), as they are "based on the perceived values, power and utility of various languages" (Curdt-Christiansen 2009, p. 354). According to Spolsky (2004), there are four major interrelated linguistic and non-linguistic forces, external to families, that co-exist with FLP: sociolinguistic, sociocultural, socioeconomic, and sociopolitical forces.

The sociolinguistic force provides sources for beliefs about what language is good/acceptable or bad/unacceptable. *The sociocultural force* provides reference for the symbolic values associated with different languages. *The socioeconomic force* is associated with the instrumental values that languages can achieve. For example, Chinese language, as a result of China's growing role in world trade, has gained considerable power in providing access to economical advantageous job possibilities. *The sociopolitical force* has a very powerful influence on individuals' language behavior as political decisions on language policy, especially language-in-education policy, can provide or constrain access to sociopolitical 'equality'. The ideologies underpinning what language should be given the official status, which variety should be considered the 'standard', and which language should be used as MoI reflect the conscious or subconscious assumptions of language as a problem, a right, and a resource (Ruiz 1984). These assumptions give languages both symbolic and practical values which directly shape the language practices adopted by family members in their everyday moment-to-moment interactions (Curdt-Christiansen 2013b).

Language practice

Language practices refer to regular and predictable language behaviors which constitute the *de facto* language use in different contexts and for various purposes. *De facto* language use differs from language beliefs in that it is "what people actually do" rather than "what people think should be done" (Spolsky 2004, p. 4). Schwartz (2010) points out that language practice is the reflection of "sociocultural changes in intergenerational interaction" (p. 178) within families. It should be noted that the borderline between language practice and language management is somewhat blurred as parents may control or intervene in their children's discourse behavior in their everyday talk. So in this chapter, all moment-to-moment interactions, including deliberate efforts and observable measures (e.g. to correct/modify language code), are considered language practices.

Scholars working in this area have paid particular attention to parental discourse strategies (Curdt-Christiansen 2013c; Lanza 2004; Gafaranga 2010) and home language models (e.g. OPOL – one parent one language, L1 only at home) when looking into the process of parental decision making and choice of family language in everyday interactions. Taking societal contexts into consideration, the scholars have examined how parents and children translate their family language policies into moment-to-moment language exchanges. Lanza (2004) identified five types of discourse strategy, including *minimal grasp, expressed guess, repetition, move on,* and *code-switch.* In his study of language shift of Rwandans in Belgium, Gafaranga (2010) found that Kinyarwanda-French bilingual children constantly use 'medium request' to negotiate family language policies and influence the adults' language use. Examining what language inputs parents provide for their children in homework sessions, Curdt-Christiansen (2013c) showed how parental discourse strategies and language input may lead to children's compliance with or rejection of the parental language policy.

Language management

While Spolsky's (2009) theoretical model is insightful in identifying the underlying forces for language practices and language management in home domains, the discussion of the specific measures that FLP actors engage in their language management need to be enriched. To do so, scholars have now begun to incorporate *family literacy* as a language management measurement in theorizing FLP (Curdt-Christiansen 2013b; Gregory 2008; Li 2007; Mui & Anderson 2008; Stavans 2012).

Family literacy scholars focus on home environments, parental involvement and different forms of family capitals to explain the meaningful literacy practices of multilingual children. Home environments include literacy related resources such as books and e-resources; parental involvements include formal and informal literacy activities, such as shared book reading, explicit teaching reading, homework help, and discussing children's school work and experiences with them (Edwards 2007; Weigel, Martin & Bennett 2006). Family capitals consist of physical, human and social capitals that can be transformed into educational attainment of children (Coleman 1988; Li 2007). Research has shown that home literacy environment and home language related literacy practices are pivotal in heritage language maintenance and development (Curdt-Christiansen 2013b; Kenner et al. 2007; Stavans 2012).

The importance of children's home environments as contributors to their literacy development is evidenced through both quantitative and qualitative studies. For example, correlation studies have demonstrated that when parents or extended family members read books with children, and when a home environment is rich in literacy materials, children's literacy development is enriched (Burgess et al. 2002; Weigel et al. 2006). Qualitatively, studies have shown that habitual literacy practices at home in different languages are instrumental in establishing FLP (Curdt-Christiansen 2013b; Ren & Hu 2013). To enrich the research literature, scholars have also examined how parents seek external professional help, such as private tuition, as a means to manage family language policies (Curdt-Christiansen 2012; Ren & Hu 2013).

This broader framework attempts to provide explanations of how FLPs are formed with family literacy practices as the micro components and sociopolitical ideologies and economic implications as the macro components. Thus, this chapter seeks to address the following questions:

–   What types of language use patterns can be found in Singaporean bilingual families? In particular how do these families use Chinese in their everyday encounters?

–   To what extent do parental language ideologies, as they relate to broader polit-
     ical, economic, sociocultural and linguistic issues, inform their family lan-
     guage policy regarding Chinese language development?
–   What kinds of home literacy activity and language management do Singapor-
     ean parents provide for their children' Chinese development?

The linguistic and non-linguistic environments in Singapore

Singapore's linguistic landscape is characterized by the four official languages:
English, Mandarin, Malay and Tamil and by four major ethnic groups – Chinese
(76.8%), Malaysian (13.9%), Indian (7.9%), and Europeans (1.4%) (Singapore
Statistics 2010). The political decision to make these four languages official
was based on the ideology that English has wider communication value and
provides access to the international market whereas mother tongues serve
as repositories for traditional cultural values and provide indices to ethnic
identities.

To reinforce the state ideology, the government has adopted English as the
Medium of Instruction (MoI) across all subjects in all schools at all levels. Mother
tongues are taught as a subject through primary and secondary schools. The local
status of English as the language of high income together with its prestige as a
global *lingua franca* has resulted in an aggregation of political and social functions
in English in public. Inevitably under such conditions, a visible shift away from
MTs towards English has occurred among all ethnic groups (Li, Saravanan & Ng
1997). This language shift has been accompanied by a local variety of Singapore
English, known as Singapore Colloquial English (SCE) or Singlish. As such,
English language use has slowly penetrated private domains. Recently, scholars
(Zhao & Liu 2008; Zhao, Liu & Hong 2007) have reported that over 47% of Singaporean Chinese kindergartners use a mix of Chinese and English at home. Only
23% of them claim to use predominantly Chinese at home.

Within the Chinese community in Singapore, no less than eleven major
Chinese varieties (dialects) were spoken (Teo 2005). In order to unite the various dialect groups, the government has chosen to promote Mandarin as the
language of intra-communication and ethnic unity.

In schools, Mandarin is taught as a subject throughout primary and secondary education. At the primary level, Mandarin is an examined subject in the
national Primary School Leaving Examination (PSLE). Subsequently, curriculum time is allocated from 2.5 to 7.5 hours weekly depending on the students'
grade and stream levels. The goals of the curriculum are:

(1) 培养语言能力 (Developing language skills); (2) 提高人文素养 (Enhancing humanistic accomplishment); and (3) 培养通用能力 (Developing general ability) (MOE 2006: 5). Guided by the core values in national education, the focus of Chinese education is on basic oral skills and "认识并传承优秀的华族文化" (recognizing and transmitting Chinese culture).   (MOE 2006: 6)

At the secondary level, Chinese curriculum is at an average allocated 3.75 hours weekly (MOE 2010). Currently, the focus of Chinese education is on practical communicative skills whereas previous curriculum objectives were appreciation of literary works. Although MOE emphasizes the importance of motivating students to learn the language, Chinese (as all mother tongues) is not an examination subject required for junior college and university admission, which might otherwise have served as motivation. In general, the language shift has resulted in several Chinese curriculum reforms leading scholars to wonder whether Chinese educational policy is planning for development or decline (Curdt-Christiansen 2014).

Methodology

Participants

The participants in this study were parents from 20 bi/multi-lingual Chinese families. They were randomly selected from a larger study on home language practices of lower primary children (age 7–9) (Curdt-Christiansen 2012). Importantly, these families voluntarily gave permission for regular home observations.

This study took a holistic stance by using multiple factors to locate children's biliteracy practices, and the relationship between the official bilingual policy and FLPs. These factors included parental language use, educational level, and socioeconomic status; children's language input from parents, grandparents and domestic helpers; and children's language use with siblings.

Table 2.1 presents the participating parents' educational profiles and socioeconomic backgrounds. Indirect financial information, such as type of housing, was used to determine the family's socioeconomic status, as the HDB (Singapore's Housing Development Board) exercises a policy of property allocation based on income level.

According to the parents' self-report, they all speak at least two languages: twenty of them speak three languages or more. Their language proficiency in their MT and English varies, depending on years of education and the language used as medium of instruction in the school they attended. Of the forty parents, about 55% reported good literacy skills in English, less than 40% reported adequate MT literacy skills.

Table 2.1 Parental educational level and economic background

Education (highest level attained in the household) (n = 40)/Housing (n = 20)	Primary (3)	O-level (4)	A-level and poly (3)	Diploma (11)	B.A. and higher (19)
3-room HDB (1)	1	0	0	0	0
4-room HDB (5)	0	1	1	2	1
5-room HDB (7)		1	0	2	4
Executive HDB (3)	0	0	0	1	2
Condo and better (4)	0	0	0	1	3

Of the 20 families, 1 lived in 3-room HDB, 5 in 4-room HDB, 7 in 5-room HDB, 3 in executive HDB, and 4 in condos or better. The highest educational level attained by the 64 parents was: primary education 3, O-level 4, A-level 3, Diploma 11, and BA and higher 19.

Data sources

In this chapter, I focus on data collected through parental interviews and participant observations to understand the multiple dimensions of these families' social worlds.

Using a prescribed language information form, *language use patterns* were obtained to illuminate the *de facto* language practice of the families (Table 2.2). To specify the literacy activities in the homes, a survey was employed to identify the multiple *literacy resources*. The self-reported information was validated by regular home observations conducted weekly for a period of four months during a semester.

Two lengthy (30–60 minutes) interviews were conducted to elicit *parental ideologies*; one at the beginning of the semester on the parental *language beliefs*, and one in the middle of the semester on *language management*. Most interviews were conducted in the language preferred by the parents, although code-switching did occur. Of the twenty Chinese families, seven preferred English, the remaining Mandarin with some code-switching to English.

Data analysis

With focus on divulging the various contextual factors that influence parental beliefs, the recorded interviews were transcribed, translated, reviewed, coded and reflexively studied. The interview data were triangulated with field-notes, observations and surveys to avoid decontextualizing the interpretation of the parental beliefs, expectations and attitudes. Based on semi-structured questions, the parents' ideological convictions were thematically organized as they gave their opinions on the government's bilingual policy and expressed their concerns about the implications of such policy. Two common themes emerged concerning the values evoked by a language: economic and cultural.

Regarding parents' involvement in their children's Chinese language practices, the parental concerns about their children's education and the implications of the bilingual policy and educational policy in Singapore were elicited in accordance with the self-reported literacy practices. The triangulation of data illuminated the recurring issues of literacy resources at home and language tuition.

In the following section, the parental accounts of their family language policy are presented according to three components: language practices, language ideology, and management and home literacy practices.

The enactment of family language policy

Language practices

In order to capture the complexity of language use in Singaporean households, the current study considered the variety of modes used within a family for daily interactions between spouses, between parents and children, and between children and caregivers, as shown in Table 2.2.

Table 2.2 *De facto* language practice: In which language do you speak to each other?

Numbers	Almost always in English	In English more often than Mandarin	In English and Mandarin about equally	In Mandarin more often than English	Almost always in Mandarin	Dialect and Mandarin
Wife/Husband	4	3	4	4	3	2
mother/children	5	3	5	4	3	0
father – children	6	5	6	2	1	0
Brothers/Sisters	4	6	7	2	1	1
Grandparents/Parents			1	4	7	9
Grandparents/Grandchildren			1	6	8	5
Domestic helper/children	6			1	0	6 (other languages)

Table 2.2 presents the language repertoire of the twenty multilingual families. It shows a visible shift from Chinese to English among all generations. While there

are still parents who use dialects among themselves (two couples) and with grand-parents, there are no parents who speak dialect to their children. Both mothers and fathers tend to use more English than Chinese when interacting with their children. Although the children's language input comes from several sources, including Chinese varieties and Chinese only speaking grandparents and English speaking domestic helpers, the children's language preference for communication with their siblings tend to be English rather than Mandarin.

While the table shows the overall language use patterns reported by parents, the following dialogue provides a snapshot of the everyday linguistic practices of the participating families.

The conversation took place at the dinner table.

[Mrs Tang; C= Child; **Bold**: code-switched items; *Italics*: Singlish particles]

Mrs Tang:	辣椒给那么少。
	Chili give so little.
	[you] ask for so little chili.
C:	Give me a bit, a bit *lah*, a bit only.
	(*lah*: Singlish discourse particle)
Mrs Tang:	This one very hot *one*.
	This is a very hot type of [chili]
	(*one*: singlish particle similar to 'of')
C:	Put it in here, a bit, a bit, a bit. I only want the sauce *lah*.
Mrs Tang:	The sauce put where, put on your rice?
	Where do I put the sauce, put it on your rice?

As we see in this conversation, the mother opens the dialogue in Mandarin. The son, on the other hand, makes his conversation move in English. The mother then accepts her son's implicit 'medium request' (Gafranga 2010), continues the dia-logue in English sprinkled with Singlish expressions. It is similar to what Lanza (2004) called a *move on* strategy.

In Singaporean families, translanguaging (Garcia 2009) is a very common phenomenon. Consider the following language practice before homework.

Mrs Teo:	明天考试了，对吗？
	[you] have an exam tomorrow, right?
C:	**compo.**
	(compo: comprehension test)
Mrs Teo:	**compo**, *ah*. 考 **compo** 还有 **oral**, 是 *meh*?
	compo, *ah*. Exam in **compo**. There is also an **oral** [exam], isn't it?
C:	我知道，有 **compo**.
	I know, there is **compo**.

Mrs Teo:	很像是有 **oral** *leh*.
	I remember there is also an **oral**.
C:	**oral** 当然有啦。
	Of course, there is always an **oral** [exam].
Mrs Teo:	拜一，拜二，拜三？
	Monday, Tuesday or Wednesday?
C:	**I don't know, go ask my teacher tomorrow.**
	I don't know. I will ask my teacher tomorrow.

While this example of *de facto* language practice shows the flexible language resources that family members have at their disposal, it indicates a gradual shift from Chinese to English when parents often adopt a move-on strategy (Lanza 2004), showing that they understand the children's language without emphasizing the use of Chinese in the interactional moves.

Competing language ideologies: Values, culture, and competing priorities

Values: Pragmatic and cultural

With regard to the forces underlying the FLPs of the twenty families, data indicate a dominant ideology of pragmatism; however, cultural and sociolinguistic factors and, to a lesser degree, political factors also play notable roles in family language planning. The following sections illustrate how parents perceive Chinese and the different values attached to Chinese and English when voicing their opinions about Singapore's bilingual policy.

One of the prevailing discourses in the parents' perception of languages is the linguistic instrumentalism revealed in their conviction of the bilingual policy.

> I find our bilingual policy is a very good policy. I personally know three languages – English, Mandarin and Malay. Therefore, I am aware of the advantages of knowing multiple languages, such as being able to communicate and work with foreign colleagues more easily. For example, English is an international language that you can use anywhere. For Mandarin, China is developing fast and it would be an asset if you know the language. Many job opportunities will be available if you know these two languages.
>
> (Mr. Shih, O'level graduate, Mechanic, self-reported proficient bilingual)

Echoing what the government has advocated in its official language policy, Mr. Soh underlined the pragmatic values of multilingualism. The lexical choices – *advantages, communicate, easily, asset* and *opportunities* – signify a strong recognition of the 'commodity' values of the three languages he knows. With regard to Chinese, he highlighted the market value of Mandarin, indicating the increasing economic power that Mandarin evokes. Similar opinions have been expressed by most of the parents,

中国是个非常重要的市场 **in economy now.** 假如讲我 **a-boy** 去中国做工，**he must know how to speak Mandarin** *lah.*

China is a very important market **in the economy now.** If my son were to work in China, **he must know how to speak Mandarin.**

(Mr Goh, O'level graduate, Mechanic)

中国现在比较强大，所以我们要学华语 *loh.*

China is becoming [economically] stronger now, so we should learn Chinese.

(Mrs Tay, O'level graduate, homemaker)

While these positive views about Chinese language are strongly associated with the economic value, almost all parents acknowledge the cultural values and heritage roots of Chinese language as seen in the following excerpt with Mrs Wee. [R=researcher; Wee=mother; xx=child's name].

R: 学华文对 xx 有多重要？
        How important is it for xx to learn Chinese?

Wee: 中国现在崛起所以我们应该该学华语。而且我们是华人更应该学华文。
        China is on the rise so we should learn this language. After all we are Chinese, too.

Although it is a simple comment, it clearly shows that parents recognize the symbolic value of language for identity, the connection between language and inheritance, and between language and affiliation (see Li and Duff in this volume). For some parents, such as Mr Soh, "Mandarin is very important for us as it is our roots. If we cannot speak our own language, that would be very shameful!" Here Mr Soh sees language as a form of cultural representation that directly shapes the politics of recognition (see Duff & Li 2008; Duff this volume). Not to be able to speak one's own mother tongue brings shame and has consequences for people as they may be positioned as 'fake Chinese'. The symbiotic relationship between language and ethnic identity is a deeply rooted conviction – a socially constructed "positional concept" marking the boundaries between ethnic groups even though "ethnic identities shift across interactional contexts" (Reyes 2010: 399–400).

In addition to such overtly expressed beliefs, some parents also saw the value of Chinese language as mediational means.

> … Chinese proverbs and idioms, this is the beauty of the Chinese language. I think no other language in the world can match this beauty. In terms of Chinese, you can describe the whole story in just four characters. Which other language can do that? …I myself appreciate the beauty of the Chinese language, even though I am English-educated…

(Mr Song, MA holder, manager, English/Mandarin speaker)

Emphasizing the "beauty" of the Chinese language, Mr Song expressed his strong appreciation of the language. Contrary to the instrumental value expressed by other parents, Mr Song emphasized the linguistic value of Chinese language. In his view, "proverbs and idioms" contain not only beauty, but also knowledge of culture and literature. For him, Chinese has a mediational value that allows children to access literary work and (his)stories represented by idiomatic phrases.

Competing ideologies: Learning Chinese at odds with learning English
While recognizing the cultural and pragmatic values of learning Chinese language, parents also expressed a sentiment of insecurity about developing Chinese and English simultaneously. The concerns about losing out to English in a competitive society and meritocratic educational system are noticeable in conversations and dialogues.

R:	可是，你讲，学华语不是重要的吗？ But, you said it is important to learn Chinese?
Mrs Yee:	有重要。只是她学了那么多的华语，*next time where to study?* 我的 **nieces and nephews** 在马来西亚送他们的孩子读华校。**In the end ah, cannot study in Malaysia or Singapore because, ah, English no good. Have to go to Taiwan or China to study. I don't want that for M.**
	Yes, it is important [to learn Chinese]. But if she studies so much Chinese, **where will she study in the future? My nieces and nephews** in Malaysia sent their children to Chinese vernacular schools. **In the end ah, they cannot study in Malaysia or Singapore because their English is not good. So they have to go to Taiwan or China to study. I don't want that for M.**

In this dialogue, Mrs Yee (a home maker) seems to indicate that learning Chinese may bar her child from more advanced educational opportunities. Her attitude toward learning Chinese is tinted by her personal encounters and factual examples. Although a competent Chinese speaker herself, she sees little value in developing strong linguistic abilities in Chinese. Her personal experiences have taught her that developing Chinese at the cost of English is likely to create problems when the educational system is concerned. This view will inevitably affect parental expectations of their children's proficiency level. Even within the same family, parents can hold different opinions about their children's desirable language outcome, as the next excerpt shows.

R:	你们认为，Travis 讲英文过多的原因是什么？ Why do you think Travis speaks English too much [all the time]?
Mr Toh:	都是我们以前没有给他机会学华文和福建话。以前就开始跟他讲英语。没有平衡。很不应该。以前觉得英文很重要，学了华文和福建话会影响他的英文，所以就跟他讲华语掺英文。我们以前是不要他长大后像我们一样英文烂。可是变成他在学校家里都用英文，只有上华文的时候才用华语。

That's because we didn't give him enough opportunities to learn Mandarin and Hokkien. We started using English when speaking to him in the past. No balance [between Mandarin and English]. We shouldn't have done that. By then, we thought English was very important, and learning Mandarin and Hokkien could interfere with his English. So we started speaking to him in Mandarin mixed with English. That was because we didn't want him to grow up speaking bad English like us. It ended up with him using English both at school and at home. The only chance for him to use Mandarin is during his mother tongue lesson.

Mrs Toh: It's okay so long as he knows how to speak [Mandarin] *lah*. After all, despite the government talking about bilingual policy, everything is in English.

R: So it's okay for Travis to be less proficient in Mandarin?

Mrs Toh: I am okay with it. I will not stop him from learning English in favour of Mandarin. After all, English is still the dominant language in Singapore and the world. And English is becoming more and more important. This was why I decided that I will speak English to him. Even China is starting to speak English now. I will just make sure that he doesn't stop speaking Chinese.

Framing his view on Travis' limited use of Mandarin, Mr Toh acknowledged the important role that parents play in maintaining and developing the mother tongue language. Their FLP, however, was established against the backdrop of the socio-political reality in Singapore, where success in school and life is evaluated by a person's level of English proficiency. Mrs Toh directly pointed out the "unspoken, unwritten, unofficial, but powerful language" mechanisms (McCarty et al. 2011, p. 43) that are used in our everyday life and through which "ideologies are conveyed and translated into practices" (Shohamy 2006, p. 50). Although Singapore's bilingual policy assigns equal official status to English and mother tongues, the socioeconomic, political and educational power that English has gained overtly and covertly 'coerces' parents to make way for English. The negotiation they make between educational reality and linguistic continuity has resulted in their compromise for their children's Chinese language development and lower expectations for Chinese language proficiency. While Mrs Toh only asks Travis to "know how to speak Chinese", other parents accept an "F" grade in Chinese, considering it unimportant for their children's academic performance,

Chinese... as long as she can speak and understand then it's okay. She can fail Chinese in school, ha-ha. I just want to make sure her English is very good.

(Mrs Ng, BA, school counselor)

> My stand is very clear. I only expect her to learn English well. As for her Chinese, I don't mind her having a good command of it, but definitely not at the expense of her English.   (Mrs Chai, BA, primary school teacher)

These statements reveal that parents place a strong instrumental value on English. Worth noticing from these comments is the positioning of Chinese as a hurdle for developing English proficiency. The discourse choices related to Chinese language such as *fail, ha-ha, at the expense, in favor of* and *don't mind* reveal their concerns about and voice their struggle with the balance between Chinese and English in reality. Contrary to the official language policy, the unspoken reality has placed Chinese and English into a dichotomous position where they compete with each other for language space within the child's language capacity, for educational opportunity, for upward mobility, for economic advance and sociopolitical accessibility.

Language management: Home literacy and private tuition

The multidimensional ideologies about Chinese language and bilingual education held by these parents profoundly influenced their investment and involvement in their children's language and literacy development. In what follows, I present two specific efforts made by these parents to improve their children's Chinese language proficiency – home literacy environment and private tuition.

Home literacy environment

Becoming literate in any given language entails a socialization process that involves learning to use language and controlling the linguistic code effectively and efficiently. To facilitate their children's literacy development, parents in this study enact myriad ways to engage in a variety of activities, including frequent library visits, reading of books and provision of rich literacy resources. Half of the families engage in reading practices at home and visit libraries as part of the fabric of daily life, as informed by the Lims,

> I take her to the library. On weekdays, when my husband is at work, I'll be the one accompanying her. Samantha enjoys reading a lot. I know that reading is a good way to improve both her English and her Chinese. Samantha often tells me how much she likes reading because she imagines herself playing different characters in books.   (Mrs Lim, diploma holder, homemaker, Chinese/English speaker)

> Reading also helps improve her creativity and her imaginative skills. When she was about five, she began borrowing more Chinese books as compared to younger days when she borrowed only English books. We can see how much she has grown to help herself improve in both languages.
> (Mr Lim, BA, engineer, English/Chinese Speaker)

Visiting the library and encouraging reading have long been recognized as effective ways for developing children's literacy skills. The Lims confirmed that reading not only offered their daughter an imaginary world, but also provided her with opportunities to "improve her English and Chinese language skills". Such positive perceptions of literacy practices, however, tend to come mainly from parents with at least some tertiary education and who in most cases have been educated in English.

With regard to book resources, seven families had more than 20 children's books in Chinese. Three families reported having more than 60 books. Through interviews with the parents, it transpired that these books were used for Chinese reading activities at home and were resources for literacy related talks. Their commitment to Chinese language education is demonstrated in the following excerpt:

R:	C 也会借华文书吗?
	Will C also borrow Chinese books?
Mrs Sun:	一般来说不会。但是我们有买很多华文书给他，每次我老公去台湾和中国公干，都会带书回来。台湾的华文书质量好。所以我们很少借华文书。
	No, not really. But we buy a lot of Chinese books for him. Whenever my husband goes to Taiwan or China for business, he brings books back. Chinese books from Taiwan are really good in quality. So we seldom borrow Chinese books.
R:	那如果要读华文的话，读什么。。.
	Then what do you read if need to read Chinese…?
Mrs Sun:	读这些 loh. (pointing at the books on the shelf).
	Read these book loh.
R:	C 读过 **all these books?**
	Has C read **all these books?**
Mrs Sun:	差不多。但是字太多的书要我帮他读。有拼音就可以自己读。
	Almost. But I have to read for him if there are too many characters. If the books have Pinyin, then he can handle it by himself.

The excerpt shows that parents may choose to buy books instead of borrowing them from the library. Either way, the Sun family makes sure that Chinese literacy resources are available and are utilized in literacy events.

It is noticeable, however, that most families have more than twice as many English books as they have Chinese books. The stark contrast between the numbers of English and Chinese books available exemplified the status and values that English and Chinese, respectively, enjoy in Singapore. This is understandable when parents have to face the reality of Singapore's educational system, where English proficiency is required for all school subjects and high stake examinations. These parents have little choice but to give Chinese lower priority, leading to more provision of literacy recourses in English. More critical is that FLP is constantly interacting with and shaped by language-in-education policy.

Tuition

A dominant feature of the home literacy practices is that all parents were convinced of the value of private tuition as one of the best ways to ensure successful acquisition of bilingualism. Justifying their decisions, the parents provided different accounts,

> I send my children for tuition at a language centre for English on Saturdays and Chinese on Sundays. Because I find that languages are hard to teach so I prefer them to go for extra classes.
>
> (Mrs Yim, BA, University Lab technician, Chinese/English speaker)

> 他是那种比较不认真，比较懒散。那现在的书跟我们的，　　我们以前读的又不同噢，所以啊，多数是很像给人家教会比较好。。。 他的华语是比较 **OK** 啦。因为他们现在的 **textbook** 很难啊，所以怕他跟不上。

> He [my son] is a type – less serious, less conscientious, a bit lazy. And the books are different from the ones we had then, so it is better to leave the teaching to other people… His Chinese is relatively **OK**. But because their **textbook**[s] is very difficult, we are worried that he can't keep up with [his study].
>
> (Mr. Wee, 'O'Level graduate, self-employed)

It is evident from the above statements that parents prefer to outsource language learning to private tutors/tuition centers – a noticeable and widespread phenomenon in Singapore (Curdt-Christiansen 2012 ; Toh 2008). Mr Wee acknowledges that the purpose of sending his son to tuition is not that the child is weak in his academic performance but that he is concerned about "怕他跟不上" (fear not able to keep up).

Singapore is built upon a meritocratic system which encourages competition and determines an individual's social position by his level of education. This socio-cultural practice is best reflected by the frequently used term *kiasu*, a word in Hokkien that literally means 'the fear of losing out'. While the parents' primary goal for their children is academic success, extra tuition in Chinese language has proven useful to compensate for the insufficient Chinese input children receive in school, as expressed by Mr Yim,

> Well, we have a tutor come to house for Chinese. In fact, he is in higher Chinese, 高级华语. But too little time is given to Mandarin lessons. On most days, they have Mandarin lesson for about an hour, and one or two days for two hours. That is not enough, in my opinion.

Here Mr Yim's concern about his son's Chinese goes beyond the academic results. Despite the son is in higher Chinese, he worried that the school's limited curriculum hours in Chinese language would not provide sufficient exposure. His emphasis on "ONLY" an hour that children are given to learn Chinese critically pointed out the implicit message conveyed through Singapore's language-in-education policy. His reflexive language management decision was a conscious reflection on how this policy may affect his child's Chinese language development. To counter against the potential risks of the imbalance between Chinese and English, parents like Mr Yim seek private tuition to enrich their children's language repertoire.

Conclusion

This inquiry documents how a group of Singaporean parents develop their theoretical position and linguistic practices about Chinese language development through their FLPs. All parents indicated unambiguous belief in the benefits of developing Chinese language, both in terms of cultural identity and in terms of providing overt socioeconomic opportunities.

The benefits, however, are only relative when comparing to English. The "English-knowing bilingual policy" (Pakir 2008) at the institutional level, the overt language planning implemented and covert language practice in public, and the overriding weight of the socioeconomic value of the English language have positioned Chinese as having less "value" and little "utility". Such a relativist view inevitably affects parents' FLPs resulting in the conflictual decisions about extra investment in English literacy resources, lower expectations for their children's Chinese proficiency and, finally, a language shift from Chinese to English. Most importantly, learning Chinese is for most of the parents at odds with learning English. The conflicting language ideologies and practices confirm that the "MoI is the most powerful means of maintaining and revitalizing a language and a culture" (Tsui & Tollefson 2004, p. 2).

Although Chinese has gained more recognition and has increased its economic value in recent years, and although bilingual education is a cornerstone of Singapore's education system, evidence from this inquiry suggests that FLP is often competing with unspoken and implicit language policies that compromise the value of Chinese. Despite the moral support and the efforts parents made for their children's Chinese language development, the lower expectations and inadequate exposure will inevitably affect the children's attitude toward Chinese. In fact, we often encounter cases in schools where children openly claim that "my parents say it's okay that I don't need to learn Chinese well". The study raises important questions with regard to language awareness in the current language policy in Singapore where English is given the preferential status as L1. What are the consequences of the "English-knowing bilingual policy"? And how effective is the bilingual policy with regard to developing bilinguals for socioeconomic and socio-political participation? Answers to these questions require policy makers at all levels – government, school and family – not only to understand the power of languages in society but also take measures to raise the status of MTs by implementing content teaching (Lo Bianco 2010) and raising stakeholders' critical awareness of their language's future and status (Canagarajah 2011).

Thus, the tensions between politics of language and economic forces, linguistics and culture, MTs and language rights as well as institutional policy and private policy require us to be responsive to and constantly engaged with questions of power, differences, access, disadvantages and sociocultural norms.

References

Burgess, S.R., Hecht, S.A. & Lonigan, C.J. 2002. Relations of the home literacy environment (HLE) to the development of reading-related abilities: A one-year longitudinal study. *Reading Research Quarterly* 37: 408–426.

Canagarajah, A.S. 2008. Language shift and the family: Questions from the Sri Lankan Tamil diaspora. *Journal of Sociolinguistics* 12(2): 143–176.

Canagarajah, A.S. 2011. Diaspora communities, language maintenance, and policy dilemma. In *Ethnography and Language Policy*, T.L. McCarty (ed.), 77–97. London: Routledge.

CLCPRC (Chinese Language Curriculum and Pedagogy Review Committee). 2004. *Report of the Chinese Language Curriculum and Pedagogy Review Committee*. Singapore: Ministry of Education.

Coleman, J.S. 1988. Social capital in the creation of human capital. *American Journal of Sociology* 94: 95–120.

Curdt-Christiansen, X.L. 2009. Visible and invisible language planning: Ideological factor in the family language policy of Chinese immigrant families in Quebec. *Language Policy* 8(4): 351–375.

Curdt-Christiansen, X.L. 2012. Private language management in Singapore: Which language to practice and how? In *Communication and Language*, A.S.Yeung, C.F.K. Lee & E.L. Brown (eds), 55–77. Scottsdale AZ: Information Age Publishing.

Curdt-Christiansen, X.L. 2013a. Editorial: Family language policy: Realities and continuities. *Language Policy* 13(1): 1–7.

Curdt-Christiansen, X.L. 2013b. 潜移默化 – Implicit learning and imperceptible influence: Syncretic literacy of multilingual Chinese children. *Journal of Early Childhood Literacy* 13(3): 345–367.

Curdt-Christiansen, X.L. 2013c. Negotiating family language policy: Doing homework. In *Achieving Success in Family Language Policy: Parents, Children and Educators in Interaction*, M. Schwartz & A. Verschik (eds). Dordrecht: Springer.

Curdt-Christiansen, X.L. 2014. Planning for development or decline? Education policy for Chinese language in Singapore. *Critical Inquiry in Language Studies* 11(1): 1–26.

Duff, P. & Li, D. 2008. Negotiating language, literacy and identity: Chinese heritage learners' language socialization. World Congress of Applied Linguistics, Essen, Germany, August.

Edwards, P.A. 2007. Home literacy environments: What we know and what we need to know. In *Shaping Literacy Achievement: Research We Have, Research We Need*, M. Pressley (ed.), 42–76. New York NY: Guilford Publications.

Fishman, J.A. 2004. Language maintenance, language shift, and reversing. In *The Handbook of Bilingualism*, T.K. Bhatia & W. Ritchie (eds), 406–436. Oxford: Blackwell.

Garcia, O. 2009. *Bilingual Education in the 21st Century: A Global Perspective*. Malden MA: Wiley/Blackwell.

Gafaranga, J. 2010. Medium request: Talking language shift into being. *Language in Society* 39(2): 241–270.

Gregory, E. 2008. *Learning to Read in a New Language: Making Sense of Words and Worlds*, 2nd edn. London: Sage.

Kenner, C., Ruby, M., Gregory, E., Jessel, J. & Arju, Y. 2007. Intergenerational learning between children and grandparents in East London. *Journal of Early Childhood Literacy* 5(2): 219–274.

King, K.A. 2000. Language ideologies and heritage language education. *International Journal of Bilingual Education and Bilingualism* 3(3): 167–184.

King, K.A., Fogle, L., & Logan-Terry, A. 2008. Family language policy. *Language and Linguistics Compass* 2(5): 907–922.

Lane, P. 2010. We did what we thought was best for our children: A nexus analysis of language shift ina Kvan community. *International Journal of Social Language 202*: 63–78.

Lanza, E. 2004. *Language Mixing in Infant Bilingualism: A Sociolinguistic Perspective*. Oxford: OUP.

Li, G. 2007. Home environment and second language acquisition: The importance of family capital. *British Journal of Sociology of Education* 28(3): 285–299.

Li, W., Saravanan, V. & Ng, J. 1997. Language shift in the Teochew community in Singapore: A family domain analysis. *Journal of Multilingual and Multicultural Development* 18(5): 364–384.

Lo Bianco, J. 2010. Language policy and planning. In *Sociolinguistics and Language Education*, N.H. Hornberger & S. McKay (eds), 398–426. Bristol: Multilingual Matters.

McCarty, T.L., Romero-Little, M.E., Warhol, L. & Zepeda, O. 2011. Critical ethnography and indigenous language survival: Some new direction in language policy research and praxis. In *Ethnography and Language Policy*, T.L. McCarty (ed.), 77–97. London: Routledge.

MOE, 2006. *2007 Syllabus Chinese Language Primary*. Singapore: Curriculum Planning & Development Division.

MOE, 2010. *2011 Syllabus Chinese Language Secondary*. Singapore: Curriculum Planning & Development Division.

Mui, S. & Anderson. J. 2008. At home with the Johars: Another look at family literacy. *The Reading Teacher* 62(3): 234–243.

Pakir, A. 2008. Bilingual education in Singapore. In *Encyclopedia of Language and Education: Bilingual Education*, J. Cummins & N. Hornberger (eds), 191–204. Dordrecht: Springer.

Ren, L. & Hu, G.W. 2013. Prolepsis, syncretism, and synergy in early language and literacy practices: A case study of family language policy in Singapore. *Language Policy* 12: 63–82.

Reyes, A. 2010. Language and ethnicity. In *Sociolinguistics and Language Education*, N.H. Hornberger & S. McKay (eds), 143–173. Bristol: Multilingual Matters.

Ruiz, R. 1984. Orientations in language planning. *NABE Journal* 8(2): 15–34.

Schwartz, M. 2010. Family language policy: Core issues of an emerging field. *Applied Linguistics Review* 1(1): 171–192.

Shohamy, E. 2006. *Language Policy: Hidden Agendas and New Approaches*. London: Routledge.

Singapore Statistic. 2010. Census of population 2010. ⟨http://www.singstat.gov.sg/pubn/popn/c2010asr/10A1.pdf⟩ (17 March 2010).

Stavans, A. 2012. Language policy and literary practices in the family: The case of Ethiopian parental narrative input. *Journal of Multilingual and Multicultural Development* 33(1): 13–33.

Spolsky, B. 2004. *Language Policy*. Cambridge: CUP.

Spolsky, B. 2009. *Language Management*. Cambridge: CUP.

Tsui, A. & Tollefson, J.W. 2004. The centrality of medium of instruction policies in sociopolitical processes. In *Medium of Instruction Policies: Which Agenda? Whose Agenda?*, J.W. Tollefson & A. Tsui (eds), 1–18. Mahwah NJ: Lawrence Erlbaum Associates.

Teo. P. 2005. Mandarinising Singapore: A critical analysis of slogans in Singapore's "Speak Mandarin" campaign. *Critical Discourse Studies* 2(2): 121–142.

Toh, M. 2008. Tuition Nation. ⟨http://newsgroups.derkeiler.com/Archive/Soc/soc.culture.singapore/2008–06/msg02235.html⟩ (30 October 2013).

Weigel, D., Martina, S. & Bennett, K. 2006. Contributions of the home literacy environment to preschool-aged children's emerging literacy and language skills. *Early Child Development and Care* 176(3–4): 357–378.

Zhao, S.H. & Y.B. Liu. 2008. Home language shift and its implications for language planning in Singapore: From the perspective of prestige planning. *The Asia Pacific-Education Researcher* 16(2): 111–126.

Zhao, S.H., Y.B., Liu & H.Q. Hong. 2007. Singaporean preschoolers' oral competence in Mandarin. *Language Police* 6(1): 73–94.

PART II

Complementary/heritage Chinese schools in diasporas

CHAPTER 3

Chinese complementary schools in Scotland and the Continua of Biliteracy

Andy Hancock
University of Edinburgh

This chapter employs Hornberger's Continua of Biliteracy as an analytical framework to critically engage with the Chinese complementary school phenomena in Scotland. It begins with an historical and up-to-date overview of the Chinese diaspora in Scotland. This is followed by a discussion of each of the Continua's four spheres of influence in turn. In particular, attention is paid to how prevailing language policies shape children's biliteracy experiences, including a shift towards learning Mandarin (Context); how texts are frequently used by teachers to guide children to an appreciation of Chinese cultural values (Content); how teachers sometimes deviate from traditional and 'mundane' practices in order to generate an interest in learning Chinese literacy (Media); and how children draw on their biliterate resources to support their Chinese learning (Development). Finally, the implications for Chinese complementary schools in Scotland are outlined.

Introduction

In this chapter, the Continua of Biliteracy (Hornberger 2003) model is applied as an analytical framework to gain insights into the Chinese complementary school sector in Scotland. The term 'complementary' schools has replaced 'community' and 'supplementary' schools in the United Kingdom (UK) in order to illustrate the positive complementary function of teaching and learning between voluntary schools and mainstream schools (Creese et al. 2006) and their potential to enhance educational achievement (Strand 2007).

In the Scottish context, this type of provision for the Chinese community occurs only at weekends with the most common arrangement being for children to attend classes for two hours on a Saturday. Research has shown that the scope and nature of such provision are very varied (McPake 2006). While there are some very successful initiatives, and the level of commitment among providers is high, much of the provision suffers from a paucity of resources. For example, the Chinese schools have to rely on the campaigning strength of community members to self-fund or lobby for support from local councils (such as making available school accommodation rent free) or pursue subsidies from the Chinese Consulate in Scotland.

The last two decades have seen a wave of research activity acknowledging the key educational, cultural and social role of Chinese schools in the United Kingdom. These studies provide insights on issues such as language choice (Li Wei 1994, 2000), code-switching (Li Wei & Wu 2009), approaches to teaching and learning (An Ran 1999; Chen 2007; Gregory 2008; Mau et al. 2009); the fusion of cultures of learning (Wu 2006; Li Wei & Wu 2010), literacy practices (Kenner 2004; Li Wei & Wu 2010) and children's socially and culturally constructed diasporic learner identities (Francis, Archer & Mau 2009). However, all of these qualitative studies have been located in urban areas in England whilst research examining the Chinese school phenomena in Scotland is scarce by comparison.

The data presented in this chapter draw on previous studies (Hancock 2006, 2010, 2012). The chapter takes a situated socio-historical approach that envisages Chinese schools as ecologies of practice where both teachers and children attempt to make sense of and navigate prevailing pedagogical ideologies. It views complementary classrooms as secure social spaces for children to negotiate their emerging learner identities and positionings relative to Chinese literacy learning. In this way importance is placed on both the collective socio-cultural educational experiences in diasporic communities and the individual histories with multiple identifications and distributed ways of viewing the world.

The chapter begins with a description of the Chinese school at the centre of the research. This is followed by historical and current overview of the Chinese community in Scotland to counter the myth of a homogeneous diasporic community. The next section uses the Continua of Biliteracy to assist the explanation and interpretation of the Chinese complementary school phenomena. In particular, it illustrates how prevailing language policies shape children's biliteracy experiences including a shift towards learning Mandarin (*Context*); how texts are frequently used by teachers to guide children to an appreciation of Chinese cultural values (*Content*); how teachers sometimes deviate from traditional and 'mundane' practices in order to generate an interest in learning Chinese literacy (*Media*); and how children draw on their biliterate resources to support their learning (*Development*). Finally, the implications for Chinese complementary schools in Scotland are examined.

The Chinese school and the community

The Central Chinese school at the centre of the research was founded in 1985 and has its premises in a mainstream secondary school. It is a registered charity but is self-funded through tuition fees and supported by an active parents' committee. Instruction is provided for two hours on a Sunday morning for over 90 children and young people of school age from a wide geographical area. A team of eight teachers and the head teacher make up the teaching team and their identities vary a great deal in terms of age, employment, linguistic histories, qualifications and teaching experience. Only one of the teachers is male. Two of the teachers have taught in Hong Kong, but only the head teacher teaches in mainstream education. None of the teachers has a community language qualification. As noted by Tsow as far back as 1984 (Tsow 1984), and more recently by Wu (2006), one of the main challenges of part-time Chinese schools is finding suitably experienced and trained teachers. The Chinese school in this study is no exception and relies heavily on volunteer parents (especially mothers) and postgraduate university students to fill the posts. The teachers' views expressed during semi-structured interviews remain anonymous following requests for confidentiality.

The school follows the curriculum developed by the United Kingdom Federation of Chinese Schools (UKFCS) and the eight classes are structured around the core UKFCS textbooks. Classes range from Year 1 to Year 7. There are also two Mandarin classes and an adult class. These classes also include a growing number of dual heritage children and white Scottish children whose parents want them to learn Mandarin. Detailed observations and field notes were drawn from the Grade 4 class.

As a result of wide-ranging language proficiency children are allocated to classes according to literacy-related ability rather than age which leads to the common occurrence of siblings being in the same class. This practice of mixed-age grouping can have detrimental effects on an older child's self-esteem but it can also promote positive learning relationships as this type of vertical learning environment supports scaffolding by peers and siblings.

The Chinese represent the third largest minoritised[1] community in Scotland, after those of Polish and Pakistani heritage. While Chinese communities developed earlier in England, it was not until the 1960s that Chinese neighbourhoods

---

1. The term 'minoritised' is used in preference to the more usual 'minority ethnic' because the former draws attention to the social processes by which particular groups are defined as lesser or outside the mainstream (Gillborn 2010).

were first established in Scotland as economic uncertainty in Hong Kong caused workers from the rural New Territories to look for work opportunities abroad. This migration pattern was characterized by high numbers of unemployed males with many spouses and family members arriving independently at a later date. A very high proportion of these early migrants started their own small family-run food catering businesses or became employees in existing restaurants. The vast majority of the Scottish-Chinese are still involved in the service industry but some scholars have acknowledged the limitations of drawing conclusions between socio-economic status and employment within the Chinese diaspora as the nature of the Chinese communities' association with the food catering business challenges traditional British understandings and applications of social class (Archer & Francis 2007).

Now almost 30% of the Chinese inhabitants are born in Scotland (see Table 3.1) and census data by ethnic group reveals that more Chinese migrants were born outside China itself than on the mainland, although it is difficult to say from this type of data how many of these migrants were from Hong Kong.

The first Chinese school was opened in 1973 in Glasgow whilst others were set up later in the other main cities of Scotland (Edinburgh, Aberdeen and Dundee) that contained the largest concentrations of Chinese population. However, the demographic nature of Chinese community shows that it is also scattered across Scotland. This geographical isolation means many Chinese children attend mainstream schools where they and their siblings may be the only Chinese enrolled. Consequently, complementary schools play a vital cohesive role by acting as a focal point to support the construction of children's cultural capital through social networking and by providing sheltered spaces so children can explore their dynamic and open-ended biliteracy learner identities and notions of 'Chineseness' among like-minded peers of Chinese heritage.

Table 3.1 Country of birth for Chinese people in Scotland, 2001 Census (source Bell 2011: 30)

Country of birth	Percentage of Chinese community
Far East (excluding China)	44.9%
Scotland	29.7%
China	18.0%
England	4.0%
Other	0.5%
South Asia	0.5%
Other EU Countries	0.5%
Total	16,310

The established 'settled' Chinese community, so long dominated by Cantonese and Hakka speakers from Hong Kong, have recently been joined by Mandarin-speakers from mainland China who have come to Scotland for further and higher education. Some of these students and their families have benefited from the Scottish Government's Fresh Talent Initiative to encourage people to extend their stay in Scotland to bridge the skills gap as a consequence of a declining working-age population (Rogerson, Boyle & Masonet 2006). Furthermore, political and economic instability in mainland China, particularly in the aftermath of the Tiananmen Incident in 1989, has seen the arrival of a meaningful number of refugees and asylum-seeking families to Scotland.

Another group within the Chinese community consists of Chinese women, mainly graduates and professionals, who have come to Scotland after their marriage to white Scottish men, resulting in a significant number of dual heritage children attending complementary schools. Taking into consideration the migratory factors above, the Chinese diaspora in Scotland can be characterised by the notion of 'super-diversity' distinguished by a dynamic interplay of variables among scattered, multiple geographical-origin, socio-economically differentiated and legally stratified migrants (Vertovec 2007). Both Hancock (2006) and Bell (2013) have pointed to the challenge of writing about the Chinese families in Scotland given the diversity of places of origin, levels of education, and language affiliations. All of these factors make homogeneous understandings of Chinese children attending complementary schools problematic.

The heterogeneous nature of the Chinese diaspora in Scotland has precipitated a range of Chinese schools serving the diverse needs of the community. For example, Edinburgh hosts four Chinese schools: two for Cantonese and Hakka-speaking children with heritage ties to Hong Kong; one for Cantonese and Hakka-speaking children with heritage ties to Hong Kong and affiliated to the True Jesus Church and one set up by academics and professional parents for Mandarin-speaking children from mainland China who often have short-term residences. This chapter draws on research from the first type of provision outlined above and therefore acknowledges that the arguments made in this chapter may not be generalisable to all Chinese schools in Scotland as the various schools have their own unique histories, pedagogical orientations and resources and, sometimes, faith orientations.

Scottish education system

Chinese complementary schools across the globe may have common goals, motivated by a need to retain parents' heritage language and their cultural identity but Chinese children are also influenced by their situatedness in diverse socio-political and cultural contexts. With this in mind it is important to make the point that the Scottish education system has historically remained distinct from the other countries of the United Kingdom (England, Northern Ireland and Wales) and political devolution in Scotland in 1999 has led to further divergences in educational ideologies and policy discourses across the four nations (Gunning & Raffe 2011).

This process of divergence and Scotland's educational autonomy is reflected in the organisation of schools, the curricular content, assessment regimes and qualification frameworks. For example, Scotland's new *Curriculum for Excellence* aims to transform school practices by placing an emphasis on a teacher-developed curriculum and situating the learner and learning at the centre of the process – including active, interdisciplinary and personalized learning approaches (Priestley 2010).

This type of mainstream school experience means Chinese children and young people who also attend Chinese schools have to encounter two educational regimes and engage with two institutionalised approaches to teaching and learning as they negotiate dispositions toward acquiring and using their heritage language and literacy in relation to English and its literacy which is central to power, mainstream education and upward social mobility. This chapter, therefore, illustrates how a Chinese school creates permissible spaces for not only traditional and routine literacy practices frequently associated with learning the Chinese script but also a less rigid pedagogy where teachers' and children's perceptions of teaching and learning come into contact. These activities around reading and writing are often not only a product of the teachers' own diverse experiences of education but are also influenced by the children's understandings of two ideological school environments. As a result children can draw on a range of bilingual and biliterate resources at their disposal to support their learning as they attempt to make sense of their dual learner identities and biliteracy development.

Continua of biliteracy

In this section, the Continua of Biliteracy (Hornberger 2003) is used to assist the explanation and interpretation of the Chinese complementary school phenomena in Scotland and their impact on children's biliteracy experiences. The model uses the concept of power differentials inherent in the framework to demonstrate the notion of dominant discourses and their relationship to the importance of contexts, content, media and development through which biliteracy is acquired (see Figure 3.1). While there are twelve features of the continua, my purpose in this section is to use specific data from my research in a Chinese school in order to shed light on each of the four components in turn: Context, Content, Media and Development.

	(less powerful)	⇔	(more powerful)
Context			
	micro	⇔	macro
	oral	⇔	literate
	bi(multi)lingual	⇔	monolingual
Content			
	minority	⇔	majority
	vernacular	⇔	literary
	contextualized	⇔	decontextualized
Media			
simultaneous exposure		⇔	successive exposure
dissimilar structures		⇔	similar structures
divergent scripts		⇔	convergent scripts
Development			
	reception	⇔	production
	oral	⇔	written
	L1	⇔	L2

Figure 3.1 Power relations in the continua model (Hornberger & Skilton-Sylvester 2003, p. 39)

Contexts of biliteracy

The *context of biliteracy* for Chinese children in Scotland is constructed and controlled by prevailing language-in-education ideologies. In terms of the continua model, English currently holds power (at the macro and monolingual level of context) as the dominant language of education and wider society. This is at the expense of Chinese literacy acquisition which finds itself relegated to the less powerful micro contexts of use.

An illustration of the policy discourses emanating from the Scottish Government, is encapsulated in the following clause contained within the draft document *A Strategy for Scotland's Languages*, circulated for consultation in 2007: 'We do not bear the same responsibility for the development of other world languages which are used by communities with their roots now in Scotland' (page 5 paragraph 5). This ideological opt-out clearly absolves the Government from any responsibility for the intergenerational retention of Chinese and other heritage minority languages.

The prevailing language ideologies cited above and tilting towards privileging of the traditional more powerful macro and monolingual continua means it has been left to the efforts and resourcefulness of concerned Chinese parents to establish and organise Chinese schools themselves in order to develop their children's heritage languages as it is integral to their identity, home literacy practices and cultural traditions (Hancock 2006). The expansion of this type of grass roots provision can be conceptualised in terms of Bourdieu's (1990) notion of agency and the capacity of parents to act independently and make their own choices as a direct consequence of institutional structures and a system of 'linguistic apartheid' (Li Wei 2006).

An alternative perspective is to move away from the polarised positions on the continuum about linguistic rights and the dominance of English and recognise that Chinese minority communities have a desire to maintain control and ownership of their community-initiated schools. Consequently, this type of bottom-up provision has a role in providing 'safe spaces' (Creese et al. 2006) for children and young people's exploration of self and learner identity shaping. There is an argument here that Chinese schools do not represent backward-looking traditions, but may be allied to global youth culture and urban sophistication in an increasingly interconnected world (Martin-Jones et al. 2012).

But social reality is never fixed, and the Chinese community in Scotland will encounter a number of contradictory discourses currently being played out within political and educational forums. For example, the status of community languages is also frequently determined by changing ideologies mediated through socio-politico-economic considerations which see shifting power relationships along the bi (multilingual)-monolingual continua context of biliteracy. This is illustrated through China's re- emerging position of strength within world global trading systems which has fuelled requests from political and business circles for Chinese to be taught in Scottish schools to support Scotland's commercial economic activity with China (Scottish Executive 2006). This new era of educational cooperation between China and Scotland has seen the creation of Confucius hubs in Scottish schools to support the teaching of Mandarin Chinese. In terms of the macro-micro continua, this means the divide in power is lessened as the status of Chinese in education and society continues to grow.

Mandarin is also gaining in popularity amongst the Hakka and Cantonese-speaking parents at the Chinese School, and teachers report that an increasing number of parents want their children to learn Mandarin. The most common reasons given for this decision include future employment prospects and enhanced life-chances available to their children through learning Mandarin. This privileging of the language is also allied to the changing language policies in Hong Kong (Davison & Lai 2007) and Mandarin's international standing as a result of China's increasingly important economic position in the commercial world. The following quotes are typical of parents' responses:

> Mandarin is a language that is becoming important around the world. I know from the television. Even my daughter's school is teaching Mandarin. It gives [*you*] a better chance.

> It is difficult to get a job here [*Scotland*]. Mandarin is an upcoming language and very important around the world. They can find a job in China. Even Hong Kong companies expect people to know Mandarin and Cantonese.

> It is important to learn the national language of China. All schools in Hong Kong now teach Mandarin. In the future children may work in China. I read in the newspaper about a British car company in Shanghai. There are job opportunities.

With regard to context along the oral-literate continua, it is worth stressing the distinctiveness of the Chinese orthography which provides a symbol for minoritised Chinese communities and a glue for cultural solidarity. The prestigious nature of Chinese literacy is frequently stressed in Chinese children's lives in Scotland and knowledge of the writing system is viewed as an intrinsic part of their cultural identity (Hancock 2006). According to Ingulsrud and Allen (1999: 133) "to learn Chinese characters is to be identified as Chinese and true Chinese literacy is literacy in Chinese characters…that constitute a tradition that is largely unbroken for over three millennia".

The Chinese parents interviewed by Hancock (2006) supported their children's Chinese literacy at home and encouraged their children's attendance at Chinese schools in developing these skills. For the Chinese parents, learning Chinese literacy was also closely bound to the maintenance and transmission of their culture. This view was expressed by Mr. Chang:

> It is important to learn Chinese. When they have their own family, they need to teach their children the language: they need to pass it on to the next generation. It is important for our heritage.

Literacy and cultural identity were profoundly interwoven for many of the parents and there was a perceptible resistance to what was regarded as cultural impoverishment. When asked what her attitude was towards her children not learning Chinese literacy, Mrs. Leung replied: 'Poor Chinese, poor Chinese person'.

As such, it is not surprising that a survey of secondary school students in Scotland (McPake 2004) indicated that students of Chinese heritage (compared with other minoritised groups) were the most likely to attend complementary schools. In addition, the Chinese schools have a custom of providing extracurricular activities after classes to support the transmission of Chinese cultural knowledge. Some of these learning experiences are allied to traditional literacy skills, such as brush calligraphy, memorizing and reciting Chinese poetry, and preparation for choral speaking competitions.

In terms of the influential oral to literate continuum, there are not just issues of linguistic dominance of English within Scottish schools at the more powerful end of the continuum, but thought also needs to be paid to disparities associated with learning Chinese. This includes differentiated scripts (traditional and simplified), alphabetic transcriptions to support reading, and a wide range of spoken varieties of Chinese as a consequence of political history and the diverse socio-linguistic landscape of Hong Kong and mainland China (Cheung & Ng 2003). These different spoken language varieties are closely tied to social group marker boundaries (Li Wei 1994), particularly amongst Hakka speakers concentrated in the west of Scotland, which adds a further dimension towards expressing forms of language affiliation and identity. For some parents their spoken language defined their sense of ethnic identity within a diverse sociolinguistic landscape. As Mrs. Tse stated:

> 'I am a Hakka person'.

The multilingual worlds that children live in were described in the following way by Mrs. Tsang:

> Hakka is our first language, English because of the children, Cantonese is used at the Chinese school, and we speak Putonghua to the kitchen staff. My daughter is going to dance classes and the teacher only speaks Putonghua so I have to teach her that language.

For these children from Hakka speaking homes, learning to read Chinese in Cantonese (or Mandarin) at the Chinese schools, represents an additional language-like phenomenon due to the mutually unintelligible nature of the spoken varieties of Chinese. This is where the Continua framework is valuable as it allows for multi-positioning along the oral-literate continua to encapsulate the particular complex socio-linguistic circumstances of the Chinese community in Scotland.

Content of biliteracy

The *content of biliteracy* concentrates on the meanings that texts express, and ideological perspectives imbued within texts (which can be deep or subtly loaded) continue to be a major influence in Chinese heritage schools (Curdt-Christiansen 2008). Central to this is the role of Confucian heritage teachers as moral cultivators and modelling a social conscience (Hui 2005).

Some Chinese schools in Scotland source materials from outside the UK or are donated textbooks from the Chinese government through its Consulate in Edinburgh. For example, the textbook designed by Ji Nan University in China and popular in the US and Canada, have simplified Chinese characters and pinyin as used in mainland China rather than the traditional characters familiar to people from Hong Kong. According to Bell (2011) the texts are tailored to present a favourable view of the People's Republic of China (PRC) and are an ingredient of the PRC government's strategy to exert 'soft power' in the world (Ding 2008).

The Central Chinese School uses textbooks designed by the UK Federation of Chinese Schools (UKFCS) to reflect the dual identities of British-born Chinese children living in the U.K. With this in mind, the literature aims to legitimise their images and cultural experiences and seeks to provide opportunities for building self-esteem. Using Louie and Louie's (2002) classification of contemporary children's literature criteria, the content of one of the textbooks written by UKFCS covers many examples of culturally inscribed texts, including transmitting and renewing aspects of cultural heritage (stories about cultural celebrations such as the Mooncake Festival), establishing appropriate Chinese moral values and socially accepted norms (the traditional folktale of Li Po 'reducing an iron rod to a sewing needle'), expanding knowledge of environmental studies (sight-seeing in Hong Kong), sharpening thinking skills (guessing cultural artefacts from clues in the text) and enhancing language development (how to write a Chinese letter and poetry). As such, the children are exposed to a wide range of genres and gain an appreciation of different literary conventions, but the cultural knowledge anchored in texts remains transparent.

Observations at the school show that at times teachers guide children to an appreciation and comprehension of texts. A common view held among teachers was that literature, especially traditional tales, offered opportunities to 'read beyond the lines' and this acts as a stimulus to communicate moral qualities and social norms. One class teacher encapsulates this outlook:

> Establishing moral values is part of the Chinese children's character development. It is part of our culture. Some of the stories are written with this in mind. It is up to the teacher how to explore this, and some say it is very important.

The traditional Han Chinese tale, studied by the children *Reducing an Iron Rod to a Sewing Needle* (from the textbook above), is a fitting example of how teachers mediate a wider culture of learning in their lessons by placing an emphasis on Confucian beliefs, such as perseverance and a commitment to learning. The text tells the story of Li Po, who disliked the books of classics and history that his teacher made him read. He thought they were difficult and boring. He slipped out of class one day and encountered an elderly woman who was honing a rod of iron into a needle. Li Po learnt from her that if you persist and are determined to work hard, you will always get the required result.

As the class teacher explains:

> I use the story of Li Po to encourage the children to persevere at their studies. Children can learn from this. The story tells them that so long as you do not give up, you can complete what seems to be an impossible task. But it needs hard work. Philosophy comes from language.

A number of other scholars have shown how it is common practice in Chinese schools for teachers to place emphasis on the symbolic value of folktales and fables to socialize children into particular ways of seeing the world (Curdt-Christiansen 2008), but also how the learners position themselves in terms of embracing or resisting these essentialised views of their heritage literature and cultural messages (Creese et al. 2009; Li Wei & Wu 2010).

With reference to minority-majority continua, Chinese texts are in competition with dominant English texts where Chinese children are exposed to majority language print media, gained from schooled literacy, as well as informal learning expressed through literacy practices associated with contemporary popular culture, new technologies and changing multimodal texts (Marsh 2005). Interviews with parents indicate that a challenge for Chinese families is the paucity of suitable Chinese literature for reading for pleasure matched to Scottish-Chinese children's reading ability with age appropriate content.

Media of biliteracy

The *media of biliteracy* highlights the relationship between the two writing systems in a child's biliteracy repertoire in terms of exposure and degree of similarity. In the case of such diverse scripts as Chinese and English, the nature of the debate tends to concentrate on the structural-visual principles of Chinese, syllable awareness and the challenge of mapping spoken morphemes onto a large number of characters. This can be compared to the role of the phonological awareness associated with grapheme-phoneme mapping in English (McBride-Chang 2004). These features and orthographic divergences are associated with differences in instructional methods and help shape classroom practices, learning styles and behaviour (Bialystok et al. 2005).

As children acquire literacy through the media of Chinese, much has been made of the institutionally led culture of learning in Chinese schools and preference for literacy practices with an emphasis on teacher-centered approaches (Cortazzi & Jin 2002) and the 'four Rs' – passive reception, repetition, recitation and reproduction (Hu 2002). Thus, learning the Chinese script is to participate in deeply rooted historical and cultural practices, and both parents and teachers interviewed articulated a pride in being able to master the writing system, including memorising a vast number of complex character configurations and rote learning texts. Parents and teachers alike also emphasised the importance of learning radicals, explaining the pictorial origins of characters to their children to support the memorisation process, practicing stroke order rules and the aesthetics of 'beautiful writing'.

Lesson observations at Chinese Schools have revealed that a significant proportion of the teaching is orientated around the core textbook and preparation for tests. Furthermore, the lessons are dominated by teacher talk in an expository and explanatory format employing traditional question-and-answer formats (Curdt-Christiansen 2006). When interviewed, many of the teachers report that they rely solely on the textbook and appreciate the prescriptive nature of the curriculum. The following response sums up the attitude of the majority of the teachers:

> Most of us are not professional teachers, so the textbooks give us the structure and guidelines.

Whilst different scripts require different ways of learning I have argued elsewhere that there is a need to unpack some of the taken-for-granted pedagogical approaches in Chinese schools (Hancock 2012). Observations also highlight how some teachers, when faced with the challenges of engaging and motivating Scottish-Chinese children, reflected on the efficacy of some of the traditional and 'mundane practices' (Li Wei & Wu 2010).

The following teaching episode, from the Grade 4 class, illustrates that there are instances when the teachers deviate from the textbook and incorporate literacy-related group activities into lessons to stimulate the children's interest and promote learning:

> Can we do the dictionary game, Ma Lao Sze (Teacher Ma)? Y calls out. T replies 'yes' and divides the class into three groups. Children congregate around three desks. T writes the character ('good') on chalkboard. T asks the children to pronounce the character. The children, with heads down, excitedly trace their fingers down pages of the Chinese dictionary, rapidly turning pages. One child calls out 'yur wrang' [*your wrong*]; another jumps up and down, 'hurry hurry', 'page two three five'. T observes the class smiling and goes to support one group which is experiencing difficulty in locating the character in the dictionary. The children's involvement and enjoyment is evident.

As a result of a child's request, the teaching methodology in the class shifts and the extract above shows how the teacher and the children create an environment which values talking and listening as the children borrow discourses from mainstream classrooms. The subsequent peer-group interaction provides opportunities for scaffolding learning by encouraging collaboration between more and less expert partners in dialogue, and some of the characteristics of dialogic teaching as set out by Alexander (2006) are present.

Some of the teachers reflected on their blended practices and the children's evolving learner identities. These pedagogical adjustments to teaching in the complementary school are encapsulated in the following responses:

> We don't know what happens in the children's schools. I know they have more active learning in the primary schools, which means some of the children find it boring here as it is all from the textbook. I try to make the lessons more enjoyable and fun or the children will not want to come.

> Western education is for speech and expression. Ours is another angle. However, I also taught English in Hong Kong and I have adapted some interesting activities and approaches used in the English lessons to teach Chinese. I think the children like the lessons as more and more children join in. Some of the other teachers are also interested in the way I teach.

These different approaches to instructional practices are explicitly related to the teachers' belief systems and pedagogical knowledge (Lau 2007). That is, teachers' knowledge, attitudes and values, gained from their own lived experiences, shape the decisions they make about their own teaching behaviour, orientations to literacy learning, and perceptions of the children in the classroom. As the head teacher sums up:

> Many of the teachers are not given professional training. They are just interested. In this school, there are eight Chinese teachers using eight different ways of teaching. Some use the traditional way, others a different method.

This phenomenon echoes the 'locally tailored' approaches to teaching and learning explained by Pantazi (2010, p. 112) who described teachers in a complementary school modifying their pedagogical approaches in order to accommodate the variety and complexity of learning needs of children in diasporic contexts.

Development of biliteracy

The *development of biliteracy* allows for variability as children make choices about their allegiances and affiliations to the different languages and literacies they come into contact with in diasporic communities (Leung et al. 1997; Maguire & Curdt-Christiansen 2007). Consequently, literacies are not fixed but syncretic, where cross-cultural encounters and negotiations characterized by power differentials coexist to create children's new and creative biliterate learner identities (Gregory et al. 2004; Curdt-Christiansen 2013). Although the Chinese schools in Scotland have an implicit one-language-only ideology to encourage learners to use the heritage language (Li Wei & Wu 2009), observations at the Central Chinese school reveal classrooms as sites where children are involved in languaging (García 2009; Creese & Blackledge 2010) as they draw on their bilingual and biliterate resources for a variety of purposes.

The following teaching episode, from the Grade 4 class, not only points to another example of collaborative group work, but also shows how the teacher supports the construction of written sentences while allowing opportunities for children to draw on their flexible bilingualism. From the field notes, the following entry is recorded:

> T divides class into groups. T writes characters on the board 'sun' [太陽] and 'women' [女人]. Children work together to make a sentence, giving instructions

to each other. One child in the group acts as a scribe, writing the sentence. Children call out 'copy it quickly', 'rub it out', 'no it's this', 'put it there'. When ready, the team shouts out 'finished' and teacher checks the sentence [那女人在晒太陽], meaning 'the woman is sunbathing'. T often replies, corrects children's syntax using the correct model and asks the children to repeat the sentence using the appropriate structure. When a team wins, T adds a character stroke on the board until it eventually forms the character [正] 'correct'.

From the above extract, it is clear that code switching is part of the children's naturally occurring discourse and is an integral part of their identity formation. It is also evident that their flexible bilingualism performs an important function as a tool for thinking and literacy learning. That is, the teacher taps into the children's prior knowledge and bilingual skills to support the learning of new characters. For example, in the lesson above, the teacher writes the Chinese character [海] 'sea' on the board and asks: 'What is this in English?' By using equivalence, the teacher reinforces the meaning of new characters and hence the vocabulary is extended in both languages. As the teacher explains:

> If I can teach them how to say it both ways, it leads to a better understanding. They can translate from Chinese to English and English to Chinese. I may say: 'What does that mean in English?' For some children, it may be more practical to remember in English.

The teacher's explanation here suggests that for many of the children, English has become the dominant language of education and literacy learning. As such, this merging and synthesizing of children's bilingual resources is used as a device to build a bridge between the two writing systems, and it promotes both the teaching and the learning of literacy.

Another illustration of children drawing on their bilingual resources is also from the Grade 4 class where many of the children annotate the new characters introduced in the lesson, using English transliterations to support the pronunciation and memorization of Chinese characters. This echoes Wong's (1992) study, which discovered that this literacy-learning technique was employed by the vast majority of students in the Chinese schools in England. It is clear from this lesson that the children drew on their English phonic skills, learnt in the mainstream primary school to map onto the sound of Chinese characters. Goh (2007, p. 128) argues that this bilingual approach enhances the children's language awareness skills as they gain an appreciation of the relationship between the two distinct writing systems. When asked about using this transliteration device, Ca Mei (aged 9) stressed the importance of listening skills and phonological knowledge, as her explanation suggests:

> I just listen to the teacher and write it as it sounds in English. It helps me remember how to say it.

Furthermore, a difference between the teachers' and the children's linguistic proficiency and preferences means that children skillfully employ code-switching as a tool for thinking and learning. There is also evidence of children engaging in multiple discourses in classrooms, including the use of Scots which adds a further intriguing ingredient to children's notion of self and the multifaceted understandings of identity formation in the Chinese diaspora in Scotland.

Li Wei (2011) takes the discussion further and draws on classroom transcripts to capture how children also use their proficiency in English in Chinese schools creatively and strategically not only in the learning process but also as an act of identity to rebel against the one-language-only policy and expectations about traditional ways of Chinese teaching.

Researching biliteracy development among the Chinese children in diasporic communities is a tricky enterprise as the learners' first and second-literacy is still evolving and the writing systems are learnt under different circumstances, and empirical studies of bilingual development in Scotland are rare. Cummins (2000) cautions against 'romanticising' the learning of community languages which are not used to teach subject content and thus lack academic rigour. Indeed, a number of analysts, including Wong (1992), Li Wei (2000) and Hancock (2010) have pointed to challenges of learning Chinese literacy part time in terms of the difficulties children face with stroke order rules, homophone detection, tonal differentiation, use of classifiers, and the use of colloquial Cantonese expressions in writing.

Conversely, it may be argued that the Chinese children, in comparison to other minoritised groups, have at their disposal enhanced cultural capital as a result of the extreme high value placed on education (regardless of their social class and gender), which is transmitted by Chinese parents to their children (Francis & Archer 2005). Whilst statistics indicate that Chinese young people are outperforming all other ethnic groups, including their white peers in Scottish schools in their examination results (Scottish Qualifications Authority 2011), this attainment is measured in English only. At the same time Francis and Archer (2005) warn of the dangers of resorting to ill-conceived stereotypes of Chinese children as hard working and conforming to Confucian values without exploring the richness of human reality and diversity within minority communities. Despite this complexity, a systematic investigation of how children use their multilingual resources in and out of the classroom is a worthwhile pursuit for further research.

Conclusion

This chapter has outlined how the Continua of Biliteracy can be effectively used as a flexible and analytical tool in which to critically engage with the Chinese school phenomena in Scotland. The power differentials inherent in the framework can also shed light on how policy and practice can enhance the bilingual learning experiences of Chinese children in diasporic communities.

The *Context of biliteracy* is shaped by monolingual ideologies but there is a need to build on recent Language Policy developments in Scotland and a growing educational and business interest in learning Chinese. The Scottish Government response to Report *The Language Learning in Scotland: A 1+2 Approach* (Scottish Government 2012: 24) includes a shift in discourse and a more inclusive approach to language learning, involving "teaching the community languages of pupils in schools", a commitment to further develop links involving "cultural organisations" and to derive maximum benefit from "foreign language communities in Scotland". In order to be effective, these new classes need to have suitably qualified staff of Chinese heritage, evidence-informed approaches to teaching and assessment for progressive learning (including planning for differentiation when native and non-native speakers are learning side by side), and community support. The result of these initiatives will be to raise awareness of languages among the monolingual school population and thus have a positive impact on intercultural encounters and education for citizenship initiatives.

At the same time it is important to acknowledge that complementary schools have a strong desire to maintain their independence, and they can build on the popularity of learning Mandarin by creating further spaces for a variety of learners (from Chinese and non-Chinese heritages), where Mandarin and English bilingualism is a an asset in a globalised world economy. Opening up Chinese schools in this way plays to the current political community cohesion agenda.

Therefore it is important to recognize the need for a mixed landscape of provision with a variety of opportunities to encourage the study of Chinese literacy in order to cater for the diversity of needs within the Chinese community, and the different motivations which individual parents continue to have for learning different spoken varieties of Chinese and for sending (or not sending) their children to Chinese schools.

The *Content of biliteracy* concentrates on the ideological meanings imbued within texts and it has been illustrated that teachers at the Central Chinese school are keen to use folk stories to communicate traditional cultural values to the children, beliefs which they consider to be missing from the dominant society. However, it has been documented elsewhere that tensions can exist between teachers and children in Chinese schools when their ideological worlds collide (Francis et al. 2009; Li Wei 2011). With this in mind it is important that folk stories continue to provide a context for Chinese children to play and display knowledge of languages, literacies and critically engage with their understandings of cultures.

The *media of biliteracy* acknowledges that diverse literacies are learnt in different ways, and pedagogic approaches in Chinese schools often depend on individual teachers' culturally embedded conceptions of teaching and learning literacy.

Many of the teachers at the Central Chinese school are volunteering parents and their attitudes and beliefs about learning are drawn from their own knowledge and varied experiences of education in different cultural contexts, but are also influenced by a need to motivate Scottish-born Chinese children to learn their heritage literacy.

The *Our Languages Project's Toolkit for Partnership* (*The National Centre for Languages* [*CILT*] *2008*) outlines a number of ways in which complementary school teachers' can reflect on their practice-based knowledges by more collaboration with mainstream schooling. Suggestions include promoting joint training and opportunities for reciprocal visits with paired observations of teaching and learning. The aim here is not for Chinese schools to replicate mainstream practices but these visits should be conducted in the spirit of respectful dialogue and, where conflicting pedagogies exist, these contentions can be used as a stimulus for critical reflection and professional enquiry.

The *Continua of Development* model has drawn attention to children as competent users of a variety of languages – including local vernaculars, registers and diverse orthographies and how these bilingual resources can be utilized to establish and consolidate concepts and skills. However, complementary and mainstream schools continue to act as two educational silos, each adopting implicit one-language-only policies (Hancock 2009).

Kenner and Ruby (2012) have shown how teachers from primary and complementary schools working together as equal partners can build a rapport with children and draw on their bilingual resources in an holistic way by making curricular links. They provide evidence that when children's lives are interconnected, their learning thrives. At the same time some researchers (Creese & Blackledge 2010; Li Wei 2011) have asserted that complementary schools need to move away from their one-language-only policies and view classrooms as authentic learning terrains with the potential for multiple practices and making educational use of translanguaging to enhance children's biliteracy development.

How children's varied understandings and lived experiences of biliteracy learning impact on their biliteracy development and complex learner identities is an intriguing field for further research. Studies of this type will build on an interest in high-achieving Chinese young people in Scotland and the role of complementary schooling in contributing to their mainstream academic achievement.

References

Alexander, R.J. 2006. *Towards Dialogic Teaching*, 3rd edn. York: Dialogos.
An Ran. 1999. Learning in Two Languages and Cultures: The Experience of Mainland Chinese Families in Britain. Ph.D. dissertation, University of Reading.

Archer, L. & Francis, B. 2007. *Understanding Minority Ethnic Achievement: Race, Gender, Class and 'Success'*. London: Routledge.

Bell, E. 2011. An Anthropological Study of Ethnicity and the Reproduction of Culture among Hong Kong Chinese Families in Scotland. Ph.D. dissertation, London School of Economics.

Bell, E. 2013. Heritage or cultural capital: Ideologies of language in Scottish family life. *Asian Anthropology* 12(1): 37–52.

Bialystok, E., McBride-Chang, C. & Luk, G. 2005. Bilingualism, language proficiency, and learning to read in two writing systems. *Journal of Educational Psychology* 97(4): 580–590.

Bourdieu, P. 1990. *The Logic of Practice*. Cambridge: Polity Press.

Chen, Y. 2007. Contributing to success: Chinese parents and the community school. In *Multilingual Learning: Stories from Schools and Communities in Britain*, J. Conteh, P. Martin & L. H. Robertson (eds), 63–86. Stoke on Trent: Trentham.

Cheung, H. & Ng, L.K.H. 2003. Chinese reading development in some major Chinese societies: An introduction. In *Reading Development in Chinese Children*, C. McBride-Chang & H–C. Chen (eds), 3–19.Westport CT: Praeger.

Cortazzi, M. & Jin, L 2006. Changing practices in Chinese cultures of learning. *Language, Culture & Curriculum* 19(1): 5–20.

Creese, A., Bhatt, A., Bhojani, N. & Martin, P. 2006. Multicultural heritage and learner identities in complementary schools. *Language and Education* 20(1): 23–43.

Creese, A., Wu, C.J. & A. Blackledge. 2009. Folk stories and social identification in multilingual classrooms. *Linguistics and Education* 20(4): 350–65.

Creese, A. & Blackledge, A. 2010. Translanguaging in the bilingual classroom: A pedagogy for learning and teaching? *The Modern Language Journal* 94: 103–115.

Cummins, J. 2000. *Language, Power and Pedagogy: Bilingual Children in the Crossfire*. Clevedon: Multilingual Matters.

Curdt-Christiansen, X.L. 2006. Teaching and learning Chinese: Heritage language classroom discourse in Montreal. *Language, Culture and Curriculum* 29(2): 189–207.

Curdt-Christiansen, X.L. 2008. Reading the world through words: Cultural themes in heritage Chinese language textbooks. *Language and Education* 22(2): 95–113.

Curdt-Christiansen, X.L. 2013. 潜移默化-Implicit learning and imperceptible influence: Syncretic literacy of multilingual Chinese children. *Journal of Early Childhood Literacy* 13(3): 345–367.

Davidson, C. & Lai, Y.W.A.Y. 2007. Competing identities, common issues: Teaching(in) Putonghua. *Language Policy* 6: 119–134.

Ding, S. 2008. *The Dragon's Hidden Wings: How China Rises with its Soft Power*. Lanham MD: Lexington Books.

Francis, B. & Archer, L. 2005. British-Chinese pupils' and parents' constructions of the value of education. *British Educational Journal* 31(1): 89–107.

Francis, B., Archer, L. & Mau, A. 2009. Language as capital, or language as identity? Chinese complementary school pupils' perspectives on the purposes and benefits of complementary schools. *British Educational Research Journal* 35(4): 519–38.

García, O. 2009. *Bilingual Education in the 21st Century: A Global Perspective*. Oxford: Blackwell.

Gillborn, D. 2010. The colour of numbers: Surveys, statistics and deficit-thinking about race and class. *Journal of Education Policy* 25(2): 253–276.

Goh,Y.S. 2007. English language use in Chinese language teaching. In *Language, Capital and Culture: Critical Studies of Language and Education in Singapore*, V. Vaish, S. Gopinathan & Y.B. Liu, (eds), 119–31. Rotterdam: Sense Publishers.

Gregory, E., Long, S. & Volk, D. (eds). 2004. *Many Pathways to Literacy. Young Children Learning with Siblings, Grandparents, Peers and Communities*. London: Routledge Falmer.

Gregory, E. 2008. *Learning to Read in a New Language*. London: Sage.

Gunning, D. & Raffe, D. 2011. 14–19 Education across Great Britain. Convergence or divergence? *London Review of Education* 9(2): 245–257.

Hancock, A. 2006. Attitudes and approaches to literacy in Scottish Chinese families. *Language and Education* 20(5): 355–73.

Hancock, A. 2009. Synergy or two solitudes? Chinese children's experiences of biliteracy learning in Scotland. Multilingual Europe Seminar: Multiple Spaces, Multiple Languages, Multiple Literacies. University of Strasbourg, 28 March.

Hancock, A. 2010. Chinese Children's Experiences of Biliteracy Learning in Scotland. Ph.D. dissertation, University of Edinburgh.

Hancock, A. 2012. Unpacking mundane practices: Children's experiences of learning literacy at a Chinese Complementary School in Scotland. *Language and Education* 26(1): 1–17.

Hornberger, N. (ed.). 2003. *Continua of Biliteracy. An Ecological Framework for Educational Policy, Research, and Practice in Multilingual Settings*. Clevedon: Multilingual Matters.

Hornberger, N. & Skilton-Sylvester, E. 2003. Revisiting the continua of biliteracy: International and critical perspectives. In *Continua of Biliteracy. A Ecological Framework for Educational Policy, Research and Practice in Multilingual Settings*, N. Hornberger (ed.), 35–67. Clevedon: Multilingual Matters.

Hu, G. 2002. Potential cultural resistance to pedagogical imports: The case of communicative language teaching in China. *Language, Culture and Curriculum* 15(2): 93–105.

Hui, L. 2005. Chinese cultural schema of education: Implications for communication between Chinese students and Australian educators. *Issues in Educational Research* 15(1): 17–36.

Ingulsrud, J.E. & Allen, K. 1999. *Learning to Read in China: Sociolinguistic Perspectives on the Acquisition of Literacy*. Lampeter: Edwin Mellen Press.

Kenner, C. 2004. *Becoming Biliterate: Young Children Learning Different Writing Systems*. Stoke on Trent: Trentham Books.

Kenner, C. & Ruby, M. 2012. *Interconnecting Worlds: Teacher Partnerships for Bilingual Learning*. Stoke on Trent: Trentham Books.

Lau, K.-L. 2007. Chinese language teachers' orientation to reading instruction and their instructional practices. *Journal of Research in Reading* 30(4): 414–28.

Leung, C., Harris, R. & Rampton, B. 1997. The idealised native speaker, reified ethnicities, and classroom realities. *TESOL Quarterly* 31(3): 543–560.

Li Wei 1994. *Three Generations, Two Languages, One Family: Language Choice and Language Shift in a Chinese Community in Britain*. Clevedon: Multilingual Matters.

Li Wei 2000. Extending schools: bilingual development of Chinese children in Britain. In *Bilinguality and Literacy: Principles and Practice*, M. Datta (ed.), 176–189. London: Continuum.

Li Wei 2006. Complementary schools: Past, present and future. *Language and Education* 20(1): 76–83.

Li Wei 2011. Multilinguality, multimodality, and multicompetence: Code-and modeswitching by minority ethnic children in complementary schools. *The Modern Language Journal* 95(3): 370–384.

Li Wei & Wu, C.-J. 2009. Polite Chinese children revisited: creativity and the use of code switching in the Chinese complementary school classroom. *International Journal of Bilingual Education and Bilingualism* 12(2): 193–211.

Li Wei & Wu, C.-J. 2010. Literacy and socialization teaching in Chinese complementary schools. In *Sites of Multilingualism. Complementary Schoolsin Britain Today*, V. Lytra & P. Martin (eds), 33–44. Stoke on Trent: Trentham Books.

Louie, B.Y. & Louie, D.H. 2002. Children's literature in the People's Republic of China: Its purposes and genres. In *Chinese Children's Reading Acquisition: Theoretical and Pedagogical Issues*, W. Li., J.S. Gaffney & J.L. Packard (eds), 175–193. London: Kluwer.

Maguire, M.H., & X.L. Curdt-Christiansen. 2007. Multiple schools, languages, experiences and affiliations: Ideological becomings and positionings. *The Heritage Language Journal* 5(1): 50–78.

Marsh, J. (ed.), 2005. *Popular Culture, New Media and Digital Literacy*. Oxon: Routledge/Falmer.

Martin-Jones, M., Blackledge, A. & Creese, A. 2012. Introduction: A sociolinguistics of multilingualism for our times. In *The Routledge Handbook of Multilingualism*, M. Martin-Jones, A. Blackledge & A. Creese (eds), 1–26. Oxen: Routledge.

Mau, A. Francis, B. & Archer, L. 2009. Mapping politics and pedagogy: Understanding the population and practices of Chinese complementary schools in England. *Ethnography in Education* 4(1): 17–36.

McBride-Chang, C. 2004. *Children's Literacy Development*. London: Arnold.

McPake, J. 2004. *Mapping the Languages of Edinburgh*. Stirling: Scottish CILT.

McPake, J. 2006. *Provision for Community Language Learning in Scotland*. Edinburgh: SEED/ Stirling: SCILT.

Pantazi, E. 2010. Teachers' developing theories and practices in Greek community schools. In *Multilingual Learning: Stories from Schools and Communities in Britain,* J. Conteh, P. Martin & L.H. Robertson (eds). 111–112. Stoke on Trent: Trentham.

Priestley, M. 2010. Curriculum for Excellence: Transformational change or business as usual? *Scottish Educational Review* 42(1): 23–36.

Rogerson, R., Boyle, M. & Mason, C. 2006. *Progess Report on the Fresh Talent Initiative*. Edinburgh: Scottish Executive.

Scottish Executive. 2006. *Scotland's Strategy for Stronger Engagement with China*. Edinburgh: Scottish Executive.

Scottish Government 2012. *Language Learning in Scotland: A 1+ 2 Approach. The Scottish Government's Response to the Report of the Languages Working Group*. Edinburgh: Scottish Government.

Scottish Qualifications Authority (SQA). 2011. *Scottish Qualification Authority Annual Statistical Report*. ⟨http://www.sqa.org.uk/sqa/47250.html⟩ (16 October 2012)

Strand, S. 2007. Surveying the views of pupils attending supplementary schools in England. *Educational Research* 49(1): 1–19.

The National Centre for Languages (CILT). 2008. *A Toolkit for Partnership: Our Languages Project*. Reading: CILT.

Tsow, M. 1984. *Mother Tongue Maintenance: A Survey of Part-Time Chinese Language Classes*. London: Commission for Racial Equality.

Vertovec, S. 2007. Super-diversity and its implications. *Ethnic and Racial Studies* 30(6): 1024–1054.

Wong, L.Y.-F. 1992. *Education of Chinese Children in Britain and USA*. Clevedon: Multilingual Matters.

Wu, C.-J. 2006. Look who's talking: Language choices and culture of learning in UK Chinese classroom. *Language and Education* 20(1): 62–75.

CHAPTER 4

Chinese heritage language schools in the United States

Chan Lü

Loyola Marymount University

Chinese heritage language schools in the United States have been playing a critical role in supporting the education of children of Chinese descent. This chapter first delineates the historical background and current sociopolitical environment of Chinese heritage language schools in the U.S. Then, a case of a Chinese heritage language school, including its structure, curriculum and pedagogical practices, is examined. Implications and suggestions for enhancing the school in the current context are discussed.

Introduction

In recent years, Chinese has become a popular language in both K-12[1] schools and universities in the U.S. (Asia Society & College Board 2008; Furman, Goldberg & Lusin 2010). A rapidly increasing number of students of Chinese descent are also taking Chinese language in a variety of Chinese programs within the U.S. educational system at public or private schools. However, more than 70% of Chinese learners in the U.S. are actually attending classes in Chinese heritage language (CHL) schools (McGinnis 2005a). Even though such schools have been functioning outside of the mainstream education system since they were first established in Chinese communities during the Gold Rush era (1848–1855), they are regarded as legitimate stakeholders in the development of Chinese language educational resources in the U.S. (e.g. McGinnis 2005a). In this chapter, I first briefly describe the background of CHL school, contextual Chinese as a heritage language in the U.S., and then provide a specific case description of such schools. Finally, I provide

---

1. K-12 in the U.S. refers to kindergarten to 12th grade, which is the last year of high school. K-16 refers to kindergarten to the end of a 4-year university program.

several concrete suggestions for CHL schools based on the current context and the issues within.

Background of Chinese heritage language schools in the U.S.

The U.S. is undoubtedly linguistically diverse: more than 150 languages other than English are used in this country (Brecht & Ingold 2002). In the U.S. context, the term *heritage language* has been used to refer to languages of immigrant, refugee and indigenous groups (e.g. Cummins 2005; Fishman 2001). Others have suggested a broader definition, referring to *heritage language* as languages other than English, spoken by groups known as linguistic minorities (e.g. Hornberger & Wang 2008).

Chinese immigrants also brought their language (or dialects) with them to the U.S. The earliest Chinese heritage language schools were established in the San Francisco area during the Gold Rush era. During that time and up until World War II, the Chinese in America were heavily discriminated against by mainstream American society and were denied access to many public services including education. For example, in California, school-age Chinese children were denied admission to public schools in 1870; public education only re-opened to them in 1885, when a successful lawsuit forced San Francisco authorities to open a Chinese public school for Chinese immigrant children (Lai 2000). Lai (2000) estimated that in the 1870s, there were about a dozen Chinese teachers, and a number of privately established schools in operation, teaching Chinese language using textbooks traditionally used in China such as *Sanzi Jing* (三字经) (Trimetrical classic), and arithmetic. Therefore, historically, community-based CHL schools played a vital role in educating school-age Chinese children and in developing an ethnic awareness and pride in them when they were excluded by the mainstream society.

After WWII, mainstream American society became more tolerant towards Chinese immigrants. The establishment of the Immigration and Nationality Act in 1965 reopened the doors to Chinese immigrants, and the subsequent immigration laws in 1970 and 1976 allowed more skilled professionals to enter the U.S., which changed the demographics of the Chinese in America. Since then, Chinese immigrants were no longer settled only in urban Chinatown areas in major cities, but spread out all over the U.S. (e.g. Wang 2007).

The continuous influx of immigrants from Chinese-speaking areas have supported and shaped CHL schools in the U.S. Broadly speaking, there are currently three major types of CHL schools (e.g. Wang 2010): (1) those which teach

Cantonese, Taishanese or Fukienese in classrooms located in Chinatowns in major cities, (2) Chinese schools established by parents of Taiwanese or Hong Kong origin, and (3) Chinese schools run by parents who mostly emigrated from Mainland China after the 1980's. According to Lai (2004), there are few programs of the first type. The Heritage Language Programs Database (http://www.cal.org/heritage/), maintained by Center for Applied Linguistics, lists 16 Cantonese programs, but the database does not have information on programs teaching other Chinese dialects.

The second type of Chinese schools is typically comprised of members of the National Council of Associations of Chinese Language Schools (NCACLS), founded in 1994. It has more than 400 member schools that usually teach Zhuyin Fuhao, a syllabary-alphabetic sound-annotating symbol system, and traditional characters. Information on its website shows that its member schools are spread across 47 states of the U.S., with a total of over 100,000 students. The textbook which most of the schools have adopted is *Meizhou Huayu Keben* (Chinese textbook: American Version, distributed by Overseas Compatriots Affairs Commission, Republic of China).

The third type of Chinese schools are generally under the umbrella organization of the Chinese School Association of the United States (CSAUS), and are mostly formed by Chinese from the mainland who came to the U.S. for higher education and settled down afterwards following China's reform and opening policy in the early 1980's. According to the information on CSAUS's website, this organization was founded in 1997 and has over 400 member schools in most major cities of 41 states across the U.S. The total number of students enrolled in these schools sums up to 80,000. These schools usually teach pinyin and simplified characters and use the textbook series *Zhongwen* (中文). This textbook series was edited by Jinan University under the leadership of the Overseas Chinese Affairs Office of the State Council of the People's Republic of China and are distributed at a very low cost to member schools with subsidy from the Chinese government.

Regardless of their organizational affiliation, CHL schools typically offer both Chinese language and cultural classes from kindergarten level to 12th grade. In some cases, for example, an NCACLS-affiliated school would offer classes teaching simplified Chinese in order to meet the needs of local residents. Although their main goal is to serve the Chinese community, many schools also started programs teaching Chinese to non-Chinese community members as well as Chinese children adopted by American families (e.g. Wang 1996, 2010).

CHL schools generally operate outside of the K-12 mainstream educational system. Nevertheless, in recent years, due to the fact that many current or former CHL students choose to continue learning Chinese beyond their community schools, the heritage sector, high schools and universities have begun to work together on inter-institutional articulation (McGinnis 1999, p. 332). Inter-institutional articulation refers to the vertical connection among all levels within K-16, i.e. whether a student who has completed his/her course in a CHL program can be assessed and placed appropriately into his/her university without repeating or recycling old materials. Recently, CHL programs and university Chinese programs have begun to collaborate on this issue especially through the Advanced Placement (AP) Chinese Curriculum & Test[2] (McGinnis 2005a). Another effort on this front is that mainstream high schools and CHL schools have begun to align their curricula to assist students in their progress, especially in foreign language learning. The typical process is that upon application from a CHL school to a local school district and upon approval by the school district, the Chinese classes that a high school student takes at a CHL school can be recognized to fulfill his/her foreign language requirement towards high school graduation. For example, the Los Angeles Unified School District recognizes the foreign language credits its students receive from district-approved CHL schools if the minimum amount of instructional time is 120 clock hours for 10 credits, with a maximum of 40 credits (Liu 1996).

While learning Chinese in mainstream American schools has become increasingly popular since 2004 (see next section), CHL schools are being challenged, particularly with regard to student retention and recruitment. It has been reported that nationally NCACLS-affiliated school enrollment has decreased from over 100,000 in 2002 to 70,000 in 2009 (Liu, Musica, Koscak, Vinogradova & López 2011). One reason for this may be that as Chinese becomes available in more and more world language[3] programs or through AP Chinese class in mainstream schools, CHL learners may choose to study in such programs instead of a weekend program (Liu et al. 2011). But it has been quite well documented that despite parents' hopes and actions to help their children to learn and maintain Chinese, children fail to see the relevance and thus resist such efforts (e.g. Zhang & Slaughter-Defoe 2009). In addition, as children grow older, they also become

---

2.   Advanced Placement (AP) tests are taken by students at participating high schools after yearlong AP courses. Although not a requirement of college admission, universities grant credits based on AP test scores. In most cases, universities require a minimum of 3 or higher on an exam to grant college credits or to waive course prerequisites.

3.   In recent years, the term "world languages" is being used instead of "foreign languages" to eliminate the implied connotation of otherness.

busier with other after-school or weekend extracurricular activities such as sport clubs, which could lead to their dropping out of a CHL school.

The issue of teacher recruitment and retention is also a challenge for CHL schools. Teachers at CHL schools are almost exclusively parent-volunteers (e.g. Chao 1997). On the one hand, given limited school funding and busy schedules of working professionals, it is not easy to retain parent-volunteer teachers to stay committed for an extended period of time. On the other hand, this group of volunteer teachers is also the group from which university teacher credential programs recruit. Based on my personal experience with several students in Chinese teaching credential programs, once these teachers had acquired the necessary credentials and secured positions in mainstream schools, they gave up their volunteer work in CHL schools. Therefore, the Chinese community and CHL schools have to come up with timely strategies to face these challenges. I will return to these issues in the discussion section below.

Current environment for Chinese heritage language schools in the U.S.

The language-as-resource (Ruiz 1984) attitude towards language education has had a deep impact on the current discourse around heritage languages in the U.S., especially after the event of September 11, 2001 (e.g. Bale 2010). The National Security Language Initiative has identified Chinese, along with several other non-European languages, as one of the most "critical languages" in an effort "to further strengthen national security and prosperity in the 21st century through education, especially in developing foreign language skills" (Powell & Lowenkron 2006). With catalysts such as substantial amounts of funding from both Chinese government (e.g. Hanban) and U.S. governmental agencies (e.g. Departments of Education and Defense) for programs such as Confucius Institutes, Confucius Classrooms, the Foreign Language Assistance Program (discontinued in 2012), StarTalk and the Language Flagship programs (K-16), along with news that China has replaced Japan as the second largest economy in the world, the general public in the U.S. is becoming increasingly aware of the presence of China as a competitor and have realized the importance of learning Chinese. There has been a boom in recent years: K-12 schools offering Chinese as a world language grew from 264 in 2004 to almost 800 in 2008 (Asia Society & College Board 2008). Over 70 schools across 20 states in the U.S. also began offering Chinese immersion programs (Center for Applied Linguistics 2011), which cater mostly for non-heritage learners. In higher education, Chinese enrollment reached 60,976 in 2009; this number is an 18.2% increase since 2006, which makes Chinese one of the fastest growing languages in the U.S. higher education sector (Furman et al. 2010).

In this positive environment, researchers and educators have rationalized that the linguistic resources possessed by heritage language learners should be capitalized on in order to fill the need for individuals with highly developed language competencies in languages other than English (Brecht & Ingold 2002). Therefore, heritage language learners, in the current discourse, are theorized and depicted as an "untapped" reservoir of linguistic competence for the nation (Peyton, Ranard & McGinnis 2001; Brecht & Ingold 2002). As such, various initiatives have been put forth to form alliances with heritage language schools, to promote research on heritage language learners, to produce materials for heritage language programs, and to provide professional development for heritage language teachers. It seems, however, that such efforts are mostly taking place in the higher education and heritage language school sectors, as is evident in a series of recent publications (e.g. Brinton, Kagan & Bauckus 2008; He & Xiao 2008; Kondo-Brown 2006; Kondo-Brown & Brown 2008). K-12 schools, public or private, seem slow to catch on. Especially, with the passage of the No Child Left Behind Act (NCLB 2001), public schools have become increasingly pressured by the law-mandated high-stake tests taken in English only. Therefore, the non-English language and literacy skills are often viewed as a problem, not an asset, in the process of students' English learning. Teachers in mainstream schools, even if they are aware of the additional linguistic competence some of their students have, often do not know what to do to capitalize on such linguistic resources (e.g. Pu 2010). Furthermore, some scholars are pessimistic about K-12 systems in relation to heritage language programs. Cummins (2005, p. 587) opined that

> [I]n this highly pressured and almost paranoid educational context, heritage and foreign languages are of relatively low priority for policy-makers, educators, and the general public. Thus, there appears to be little hope in the immediate future for expanding the range of heritage and foreign language programs within the regular public school system.

Therefore, the current environment for heritage language programs in the U.S. is promising, yet with no clear agenda. McGinnis (2005b) described the situation as ironic in that even though visionary members of the language education profession have been promoting heritage language and their communities as a precious national resource for many years, no coherent policy has been made in relation to heritage languages. In the sections that follow, I will first describe a case of a CHL school and then outline some specific suggestions for CHL program improvement based on the current situation in the U.S.

A case of Chinese heritage language learners in the U.S.

Methods

The study took place in the 2007–2008 school year as part of a larger study on biliteracy learning at the Hope Chinese School (pseudonym). The school was located in a mid-sized city in Pennsylvania. Although the larger biliteracy project was quantitative in nature, to contextualize the study, I observed five teachers in the Kindergarten (1 teacher), Grade 1 (2 teachers) and Grade 2 (2 teachers) classes, respectively. I also interviewed the principal and two school staff members. In addition, a survey (Lü & Koda 2011) on home language and literacy environment was distributed among Grades 1 and 2 parents (N=37) since their children participated in the biliteracy project. Therefore, the current study has three sources of data: field notes, classroom videotaping, and survey. In addition, I also documented the environmental print input given its importance in literacy learning (e.g. Hiebert 1981).

However, the information I gathered in this process was to contextualize the biliteracy study rather than for the purpose of an ethnographic study; therefore, in the sections below, I provide a summary of my data as a case description of a CHL school.

The City

In recent years, the city where the school is located has gradually transformed itself into a leader in science and technology. Big knowledge-based industries such as health care, high-tech, and finance have been attracting more and more international professionals and students to the region.

Two major waves of immigration formed the Chinese community. The first wave, consisting of mostly graduate students from Taiwan, came in and settled down around the 1960's. During the 1980's, many immigrants from Mainland China came in and settled. The 2007–2011 American Community Survey 5-Year Estimates for the city (U.S. Census Bureau, 2007–2011) estimated that 1.4% of the population, or 4444 (±630) people, are Chinese. This small but growing population mostly consists of well-educated professionals such as professors, medical doctors, engineers, and finance experts. The majority of these families, unlike earlier immigrants who tended to settle in urban ethnic enclaves such as Chinatowns, mostly resides in suburban areas and newly established middle-class communities.

As might be expected with a small and dispersed population, environmental input in Chinese is extremely scarce. The city has no Chinatown or concentrated areas with Chinese businesses. There are two major Chinese grocery stores in the city where Chinese newspapers and packages labeled in Chinese are available.

Only one university library in the area has a significant number of Chinese books, but this Chinese collection is mostly for research purposes. Likewise, oral language use in the community is almost all in English. There are only a few Chinese restaurants scattered in the region where Chinese could be used, and two major Chinese churches in the area where services in Chinese are provided. Other than these venues, there is no other significant source of environmental and oral input in Chinese.

Therefore, the community literacy environment can be described as English-only with extremely restricted input in Chinese. Such an environment, although not the best condition for heritage language learning, is highly representative of most regions in the U.S. outside of the few regions with large Chinese populations.

The Chinese school

The Chinese school, like many other such schools in the U.S., is a grassroots non-profit organization initiated, operated and supported by parent volunteers outside the U.S. K-12 education system (Chao 1997). The school is one of the two Chinese weekend schools in the region. The school meets on Sundays at a local high school from which classrooms are rented. The first two hours are for Chinese language arts classes and the third hour for optional culture classes.

All classes are taught in Mandarin Chinese; students learn Pinyin and simplified characters. At the time of this study, the textbook series *Zhongwen*, which includes workbooks, was used throughout all grade levels. One volume per year was taught at each grade level. At the time of the study, the school had 14 weeks of classes in each of the spring and fall semesters. There were three tracks of language classes:

(1) Heritage language classes from Kindergarten to Grade 12, for students from Chinese-speaking families. Students in this track usually had well-developed oral proficiency in Chinese.
(2) English-Chinese bilingual classes (four levels) for students from non-Chinese-speaking families and/or families in which only one parent speaks Chinese and adopted Chinese children from English-speaking families.
(3) An adult-Chinese class for any interested adult non-native Chinese learners.

For heritage language classes, students were placed into a grade level according to their age, English grade level, and Chinese language proficiency. The school also placed non-heritage students who finished the last level at the English-Chinese bilingual class into Grade 1 of the heritage language class, irrespective of their age.

According to my interview with one of the school administrators, the school had no formal written goals in terms of students' achievement at each grade.

Therefore, articulation between grades seemed to rely mainly on the coherence of the textbooks. That is to say, the school and the teachers had no specifically clear idea of what the logical progression of learning objectives from one grade level to the next should be, and they relied on the content of the textbooks at each grade to determine what their students should learn at each grade level.

Each teacher had to make their own syllabus and submit it to the school at the beginning of each academic semester. Mandatory assessment at each grade level included weekly homework assignments, weekly quizzes, a mid-term and a final exam. Teachers were required to notify parents about the weekly homework assignments and the content for the quiz one week in advance in a formal report card fashion in order for the parents to help their children prepare for the quiz. By the end of the semester, final scores for each student were reported to the school. A mock SAT[4] Chinese test was also offered to high school students. In the past few years, the school has organized high school students to participate in the SAT Chinese test. However, at the time of this study, this CHL school could not grant any high school foreign language credits to their students.

Students' profiles

In the 2007–2008 school year, there were altogether 266 students registered at the school, which was estimated to be quite a high enrollment rate when compared against the Chinese population living in the area;[5] 27 (10%) of the students (including nine adult learners) were from non-Chinese-speaking families. Among the Chinese heritage language learners, 34 (13%) were kindergarteners, 144 (54%) were in Grades 1–5, 42 (16%) were in Grades 6–8 and 20 (7%) were in Grades 9–12. Besides learning Chinese on weekends, they all studied at mainstream English-speaking schools during weekdays.

According to the survey (Lü & Koda 2011), Grades 1 and 2 students were born in the U.S. into Chinese-speaking families; most of the students also went through

---

4. The Scholastic Aptitude Test (SAT) and SAT Subject Tests are a set of standardized tests designed to assess students' academic readiness for college. The SAT test assesses critical reading, mathematics and writing. The SAT Subject Tests measure students' knowledge and skill in a particular subject, such as Chinese, Italian, World Literature, Biology, etc.

5. According to the 2007–2011 American Community Survey 5-Year Estimates for Pittsburgh, PA (U.S. Census Bureau 2007–2011), there were 4444 people who identified themselves as Chinese. Within the same region, the total percentage of people between 5–9, 10–14, and 15–19 years old was 17.4%, which suggests an estimate of about 770 school-age Chinese students. Given that there were two Chinese schools of similar size in the region, the enrollment rate was about 70%, i.e. 70% of the Chinese immigrant children enrolled in Chinese weekend schools.

kindergarten classes at this school during weekends while they attended English-speaking kindergartens on weekdays.

Parents' profiles

Most of the parents in the school were immigrants from Mainland China; there were several Caucasians with Chinese spouses and one English-speaking couple who had adopted a Chinese child. Nine of the ten students in the adult class had no special affiliation with China or Chinese people, but one of them had moved to the U.S. from China with her family when she was a child.

The Chinese parents were all speakers of Mandarin Chinese and/or another Chinese dialect. In contrast to earlier immigrants, parents in this Chinese school tended to be well-educated professionals who settled in the Pittsburgh area after finishing their graduate studies in the U.S. All the Grade 1 and Grade 2 parents (N = 35) who responded to the survey had received education at high school level or higher: 10% reported that they held bachelor's degrees, 30% held master's degrees, and 50% had earned doctoral degrees. All parents reported that they and their spouses had sufficient English oral proficiency for work and daily communication.

Teachers' profiles

At the time of my observation, there were about 50 teachers in this school. These 50 teachers were of two kinds: Chinese language arts teachers and Chinese culture teachers, though some of them taught both classes. Chinese culture teachers taught classes that focused on particular aspects of Chinese culture, such as Chinese chess, calligraphy, dance, or paper cutting. Among the teachers, one was becoming a certified math teacher in Pennsylvania, and two other teachers held degrees in Education (teaching language arts) in China; the rest of the teachers did not have formal training in Chinese teaching, but all had bachelor's degrees or higher. With respect to teacher training, the school itself did not offer teacher-training workshops; however, the school supported teachers to attend workshops on Chinese pedagogy organized by the regional Chinese school association (Association of Chinese Schools). According to the website of this organization, the content of these workshops varied; some were offered by university lecturers or experienced teachers from other schools and focused on classroom teaching, some were invited talks by specialists from the College Board on Chinese AP Test, and a few workshops were held by private companies as a way to promote their learning-related products. According to school administrators, the teachers found these workshops oftentimes useful, especially those directly targeted at heritage language classroom teaching, and those which offered first-hand methods, materials, and class designs to teachers. Up to the point of the observation, most of the teachers from the school had been to such workshops, and some had gone more than once. However, according to the principal, teachers were increasingly reluctant to go to future workshops.

Curriculum, instruction and assessment

I observed Kindergarten and Grades 1 and 2 classes during the 2007–2008 school year. I discovered that the focus of these classrooms was almost exclusively on Chinese language and literacy, and not on teaching content (such as mathematics or history) through Chinese. Although all the teachers spoke in Chinese exclusively in their classes, the focus of teaching differed between kindergarten and the other two classrooms. Kindergarten classroom teaching mostly consisted of language games, nursery rimes, holistic character recognition and stroke-by-stroke writing of simple characters; Pinyin was not yet taught at this level. By contrast, Grade 1 and 2 classroom teachers spent most of their time helping students learn how to read characters with the help of Pinyin, write characters in correct stroke order, and expand characters into words and phrases. Grade 2 teachers also helped students differentiate homophonic syllables with different meanings. Although teachers emphasized writing accuracy and recognition of subtle differences between graphically similar characters, students were not expected to analyze morphological structures of characters except for characters with very frequently used radicals. The teachers did help their students compare new characters with those previously learned. Such comparison, however, was mostly for the purpose of distinguishing characters with graphic similarity.

The classes were characteristic of the teacher-centered classroom (e.g. Hancock, Bray & Nason 2003). Although the Kindergarten teacher used a variety of games, songs and other activities in her class, the teacher still dominated the class by direct questions, and by modeling correct language use and monitoring students' involvement actively. The main focus of Grades 1 and 2 classes was to finish the text from the textbook *Zhongwen* according to their syllabi. The teachers dominated the class most of the time, students talked when they were answering the teachers' questions; few opportunities were given to students to raise questions. When introducing a new text, the teachers used methods such as direct instruction (explaining language forms and meanings) with guided practice. For example, students would read a text aloud either individually or together, and the teachers would provide corrective feedback on their pronunciation or intonation, or the teachers would lead the students to write out a new character stroke by stroke. After introducing the new content of the day, some teachers tried to incorporate activities to make the classroom more fun and lively such as word games or tongue twisters. I also observed that one of the Grade 2 teachers tried to wind down the class by reading a story related to the text of that day to students. Before the classes were dismissed, the teachers assigned materials for review and preview for next week, and assigned homework from the *Zhongwen* workbook. Some teachers provided extra homework for their students, typically such homework involved copying new characters, or creating new sentences with given words.

Discussion and suggestions for enhancing CHL schools

Combining the national trend and my observations at this school, one obvious suggestion to make would be to provide teacher training to equip the teachers with student-centered language pedagogy. Learning to teach, however, is a long and arduous process, affected by a number of factors (e.g. Freeman & Johnson 1998). While it should be a long-term goal for all Chinese language programs, CHL schools included, in this section, I would like to offer several immediate steps that can be taken by CHL schools similar to the one described in this chapter.

First, the school faculty and staff should work together to specify their learning goals and objectives, student learning outcomes, assessment plans, and a formalized curriculum. Given that such work requires a substantial amount of professional expertise in curriculum design and assessment, I recommend that CHL schools reach out for assistance from educational professionals at local educational institutions.

Secondly, once the learning goals and objectives, assessment plan and curriculum are in place, the school should work on articulation and collaboration with local K-12 schools to make sure that students' time spent at a CHL school and credits earned can be transferred back to their home mainstream schools. Having this credit-transfer mechanism in place could be a motivation for CHL learners to complete their study at a CHL school. Chen (1996:53) outlined the process for establishing credit transfer in California, which could be a model for CHL schools elsewhere. The process begins with a CHL school submitting a proposal to a local school district, which should include information regarding the school, the teaching staff, the courses for which students should receive credits, as well as a credit-hour plan to demonstrate how additional activities through the CHL school beyond regular instructional hours could fulfill the requirement. Chen (1996) also suggested that the proposal should explain how the school would report students' records back to their home school or school district. Chen (1996)'s article included several sample application documents, which should be helpful for CHL schools to initiate the process.

In addition, CHL schools could work with local universities, especially through their service organizations, office for community outreach or service learning courses (e.g. Polansky 2004) to involve undergraduate students (especially those enrolled in university Chinese courses and/or former CHL school students) at local universities to volunteer as teacher assistants, or to lead school-based projects.

Thirdly, to address the challenge of teacher retention and recruitment, I recommend that CHL schools reach beyond members of the Chinese community who send their children to the schools. Currently teachers are mostly recruited among parents; however, CHL schools, especially those in smaller cities with a small Chinese population, could tap into local universities for graduate students who may not have children enrolled in the school, but are interested in serving the community as volunteers.

In a long run, CHL schools could also consider concentrating on K-6 education rather than stretching to K-12 (McGinnis personal communication). In this case, administrative pressure due to limited resources (such as insufficient space and teacher shortage) can be alleviated to a certain extent. In this case, CHL schools could look into the possibilities of collaborating with local mainstream schools to provide courses for CHL learners in their middle school or high schools, much like the Spanish-for-Native-Speakers (SNS) courses in secondary and postsecondary courses.[6] This approach has the additional benefit of fostering public awareness and interest by making Chinese language programs more visible in mainstream public schools outside of the Chinese community.

In addition, trained Chinese instructors at all levels of educational institutions should work together with teachers of heritage schools to create textbooks that are more relevant to CHL learners' experiences in the U.S. In an analysis of the textbook series widely used among Chinese heritage language schools in Canada, Curdt-Christiansen (2008) analyzed the social and cultural knowledge embedded in the texts. She problematized not only the advocacy of teacher-centered approach, but also, more importantly, the culture- and moral-laden texts, which often incorporated notions such as conformity and obedience that were at odds with mainstream ideology in Canada. Another aspect that CHL textbook developers and designers should consider is the quality and quantity of characters to introduce to CHL learners, who rely on these textbooks as the major source of print input. Koda, Lü and Zhang's (2008) study found that, compared to the print input native Chinese children receive through textbooks, the amount of characters introduced in CHL textbooks is not only substantially less in quantity, the

---

6.   For more information, visit ⟨http://www.cal.org/resources/pubs/sns_brochure.pdf⟩

distribution and the quality of the characters also do not allow CHL students to develop sound morphological awareness in Chinese.

Last but not least, CHL schools should serve as a resource center for parents who want to enable their children to become proficient bilingual speakers and readers but may not necessarily have realized what they could do at home. Lü and Koda (2011)'s study revealed that although half of the surveyed parents of Grade 1 and 2 children indicated that they speak Chinese to their children 80% of the time at home, almost 40% of their children never read books in Chinese at home. Information, resources and workshops regarding how to create a supportive home environment for language and literacy learning could be disseminated throughout the school.

Conclusion

This chapter presented a specific case of a CHL school in the U.S. in the current socio-political environment regarding learning Chinese as a heritage language. I have also put forth a few suggestions for CHL schools to consider in order to meet the challenge brought about by the new environment in which Chinese enrollment in other instructional settings has expanded exponentially. Many of the suggestions require significant collaboration and coordination by the CHL schools with local educational institutions; however, in my view, it is only through opening up to the outside that we can make our century-long educational effort better recognized. Working with other schools, organizations and communities provides us with great opportunities to address the issue of limited funding and resources, and to learn and improve our own practices based on other people's expertise.

Acknowledgements

The author acknowledges the guidance from Drs. Keiko Koda and Dick Tucker throughout this project.

References

Asia Society & College Board 2008. *Chinese in 2008: An Expanding Field*. New York NY: Asia Society.

Brecht, R.D. & Ingold, C.W. 2002. *Tapping a National Resource: Heritage languages in the United States*. Washington DC: Center for Applied Linguistics. ⟨http://www.cal.org/resources/digest/0202brecht.html⟩

Bale, J. 2010. International comparative perspectives on heritage language education policy research. *Annual Review of Applied Linguistics* 30: 42–65.

Brinton, D., Kagan, O. & Bauckus, S. (eds). 2008. *Heritage Language Education: A New Field Emerging*. New York NY: Routledge.

Chao, T.H. 1997. *Chinese Heritage Community Language Schools in the United States*. ⟨http://www.cal.org/resources/digest/chao0001.html⟩ (15 January 2009).

Center for Applied Linguistics. 2011. *Directory of Foreign Language Immersion Programs in U.S. Schools*. ⟨http://www.cal.org/resources/immersion/⟩

Chen, R.S. 1996. Obtaining credit from local school districts. In *A View From Within: A Case Study Of Chinese Heritage Community Language Schools in the United States*, X. Wang (ed.), 51–57. Washington DC: National Foreign Language Center.

Cummins, J. 2005. A proposal for action: Strategies for recognizing heritage language competence as a learning resource within the mainstream classroom. *Modern Language Journal* 89: 585–592.

Curdt-Christiansen, X.L. 2008. Reading the world through words: Culture themes in heritage Chinese language textbooks. *Language and Education* 22(2): 95–113.

Fishman, J. 2001. 300-plus years of heritage language education in the United States. In *Heritage Languages in America: Preserving a National Resource*, K. Peyton, D. Ranard & S. McGinnis (eds), 81–98. McHenry IL & Washington DC: Delta Systems & Center for Applied Linguistics.

Freeman, D. & Johnson, K.E. 1998. Reconceptualizing the knowledge-base of language teacher education. *TESOL Quarterly* 32: 397–417.

Furman, N., Goldberg, D. & Lusin, N. 2010. *Enrollments in Languages Other Than English in United States Institutions of Higher Education, Fall 2009*. New York NY: Modern Language Association.

He, A.W., & Xiao, Y. (eds). 2008. *Chinese as a Heritage Language: Fostering Rooted World Citizenry*. Honolulu HI: University of Hawai'i Press.

Hancock, D.R., Bray M. & Nason, S.A. 2003. Influencing university students' achievement and motivation in a technology course. *The Journal of Educational Research* 95: 365–372.

Hiebert, E.H. 1981. Developmental patterns and inter-relationships of preschool children's print awareness. *Reading Research Quarterly* 16: 236–259.

Hornberger, N.H. & Wang, S.C. 2008. Who are our heritage language learners? Identity and biliteracy in heritage language education in the United States. In *Heritage Language Education: A New Field Emerging*, D.M. Brinton, O. Kagan & S. Bauckus (eds), 3–35. New York NY: Routledge.

Koda, K., Lü, C. & Zhang, Y. 2008. Properties of characters in heritage Chinese Textbooks and their Implications for Character knowledge development among Chinese Heritage Language Learners. In *Chinese as a Heritage Language: Fostering Rooted World Citizenry*, A.W. He & Y. Xiao (eds), 125–135. Hawaii HI: University of Hawaii Press.

Kondo-Brown, K. (ed.). 2006. *Heritage Language Development: Focus on East Asian Immigrants* [Studies in Bilingualism 32]. Amsterdam: John Benjamins.

Kondo-Brown, K. & Brown, J.D. (eds). 2008. *Teaching Chinese, Japanese and Korean Heritage Language Students: Curriculum Needs, Materials, and a Assessment*. New York NY: Lawrence Erlbaum Associates/Taylor & Francis.

Lai, H.M. 2000. Retention of the Chinese heritage: Chinese schools in America before World War II. *Chinese America: History and Perspectives* 14: 10–31.

Lai, H.M. 2004. *Becoming Chinese American*. Lanham MD: AltaMira Press.

Liu, J. 1996. Awarding credit through testing – The case of the San Francisco Unified School District. In *A View from Within: A Case Study of Chinese Heritage Community Language Schools in the United States*, X. Wang (ed.), 59–61. Washington DC: National Foreign Language Center.

Liu, N. Musica, A. Koscak, S. Vinogradova, P. & López, J. 2011. Challenges and needs of community-based heritage language programs and how they are addressed. *Heritage Brief Collection.* ⟨www.cal.org/heritage/pdfs/briefs/challenges-and%20needs-of-community-based-heritage-language-programs.pdf ⟩ (1 May 2013).

Lü, C. & Koda, K. 2011. Impacts of home language and literacy support in English-Chinese biliteracy acquisition among Chinese heritage language learners. *Heritage Language Journal* 8: 44–80.

McGinnis, S. 1999. Articulation. In *Mapping the Course of the Chinese Language Field* [Chinese Language Teachers' Association Monograph Series 3], M. Chu (ed.), 331–344. Bloomington IN: CLTA.

McGinnis, S. 2005a. Heritage Language Preservation: Chinese as a model for intersector collaboration. ⟨http://www.international.ucla.edu/languages/article.asp?parentid=20146⟩

McGinnis, S. 2005b. More than a silver bullet: The role of Chinese as a heritage language in the United States. *Modern Language Journal* 89: 592–594.

No Child Left Behind (NCLB) Act of 2001 2002, Pub. L. No. 107–110, §115, Stat. 1425.

Peyton, J.K., Ranard, D. & McGinnis, S. 2001. *Heritage Languages in America: Preserving a National Resource*. McHenry IL & Washington DC: Delta Systems & Center for Applied Linguistics.

Powell, D. & Lowenkron, B. 2006. *National Security Language Initiative Briefing.* ⟨http://web.archive.org/web/20080306151344/⟩ ⟨http://www.state.gov/r/pa/prs/ps/2006/58733.htm⟩ (30 May 2013).

Pu, C. 2010. Bridging for biliteracy development: Instructional needs of community-based heritage language schools and public schools. Paper presented at the First International Conference on Heritage/Community Languages, Los Angeles.

Polansky, S. 2004. Tutoring for community outreach: A course model for language learning and bridge building between universities and public schools. *Foreign Language Annals* 7: 367–373.

Ruiz, R. 1984. Orientations in language planning. *NABE Journal* 8: 15–34.

U.S. Census Bureau. 2007–2011. *American Community Survey.* ⟨http://factfinder2.census.gov/faces/tableservices/jsf/pages/productview.xhtml?pid=ACS_11_5YR_DP05⟩ (30 May 2013).

Wang, S.C. 2007. Building societal capital: Chinese in the US. *Language Policy* 7: 27–52.

Wang, S.C. 2010. Chinese language education in the United States: A historical overview and future directions. In *Teaching and Learning Chinese: Issues and Perspectives*, J. Chen, C. Wang, & J. Cai (eds), 3–32. Raleigh NC: Information Age Publishing.

Wang, X.Y. (ed.). 1996. *A View from Within: A Case Study of Chinese Heritage Community Language Schools in the United States*. Washington DC: The National Foreign Language Center.

World Affairs Council of Pittsburgh, 2005. from ⟨www.worldpittsburgh.org⟩ (20 January 2009).

Zhang, D. & Slaughter-Defoe, D.T. 2009. Language attitudes and heritage language maintenance among Chinese immigrant families in the USA. *Language, Culture and Curriculum* 22: 77–93.

CHAPTER 5

Learning and teaching Chinese in the Netherlands

The metapragmatics of a polycentric language

Jinling Li & Kasper Juffermans
Tilburg Uniersity / University of Luxembourg

This paper is concerned with the metapragmatics of Chinese as a polycentric language. Based on ethnographic observations and interviews in and around a Chinese complementary school in the Netherlands, this paper describes an ongoing shift along with demographic, economic and political changes, in what counts as Chinese: a shift from Hong Kong and Taipei to Beijing as the most powerful centre of Chinese in the world. Migration makes communicative resources like language varieties globally mobile and this affects the normativity in the diaspora classroom. A clearer understanding of the metapragmatics of Chinese is useful because it provides a key to understanding social identities in contemporary Chinese migration contexts and to understanding language within contexts of current globalisation.

Introduction

Mobility has become one of the key notions in the field of sociolinguistics (Blommaert 2010; Heller 2011; Pennycook 2012; Canagarajah 2013). In an ever more globalised world, the movements and migrations of people become increasingly important to understand their communicative practices. People move across spaces and bridge distances between spaces in their communication. These spaces are not empty but filled with norms, with conceptions of what counts as 'proper' and 'normal' language use and what does not count as such. The mobility of people therefore involves the mobility of linguistic and sociolinguistic resources. This mobility creates inequalities, overlaps and contrasts between languages as produced in different spaces. We find that such spaces are not equal or flat, but hierarchically ordered, and that language practices orient to one or more of such spaces as centers of communicative practice.

This paper focuses on learning Chinese in one of the oldest diasporas in Europe, the Netherlands. It examines the subtle ways of speaking about and referring to Chinese and explores the implicit and more explicit meanings that are carried with it in metapragmatic discourses. We suggest that we need to consider Chinese as a polycentric language, i.e. as a language that operates on various scales and has multiple centers, and that these centers are unstable and shifting as a result of political and historical changes.

In what follows, first we shall look at the key theoretical notions and contextualize these against the linguistic backgrounds of China in relation to Chinese complementary schooling in the Netherlands. Second, in order for us to understand the ongoing processes of change within the Chinese community in the Netherlands, it is necessary to trace its historical, linguistic and demographic development. After that, we shall focus on empirical data collected in and around a Chinese complementary school in the city of Eindhoven, the Netherlands. The theoretical notions will be deployed in the paper for interpreting and analyzing the empirical data.

Theoretical framework: Metapragmatics, polycentricity and Chinese

Metapragmatics as coined by Silverstein describes how the effects and conditions of language use themselves become objects of discourse (Silverstein 1993). Metapragmatics has to do with meta-language, i.e. language about language. More precisely, it refers to the pragmatics, i.e. the meanings in use or the processes of social signification in praxis, that are applied in relation to varieties of language or ways of speaking, including accents, dialects/languages, etc.

Metapragmatics is thus concerned with the meanings or indexicalities that are attached to the use of a particular language variety. Such meanings may vary from (in-) appropriate, (un-) civilized, (un-) educated, (in-) authentic, (non-) standard, (ab-) normal, (im-) polite, (in-) correct, (im-) proper, to right/wrong, good/bad, backward/modern, old/young, rude/elegant, beautiful/ugly, etc. Metapragmatic meanings are mappings of social categories on the basis of the language use of a particular individual or group. Often language use generates multiple and competing and partially overlapping meanings along several parameters. Someone's language may for instance be considered educated but inauthentic, or standard but too polite or old-fashioned for a particular context. Such meanings are applied to individuals' idiosyncratic ways of speaking, as in statements such as 'my English is a bit rusty' or 'she has a fake accent when she speaks dialect'; but often also to the types of language associated with whole groups of speakers as in (*cliché*) statements such as 'French is a romantic language', 'Japanese sounds aggressive' or 'dialect speakers are dumb'.

Polycentricity is used in various disciplines of the humanities and social sciences, including geography, political sciences and sociolinguistics. It refers to the multiplicity of centres of gravity (or centering forces) in social or spatial configurations. Whereas monocentric configurations are regulated according to a single reference point in space (and/or time), polycentric configurations are regulated by multiple, competing centers with unequal power.

Sociolinguistically, whether languages (in their nominal, countable form) are seen as species of ideolects with family resemblance (Mufwene 2008), as artefacts created by linguists (Blommaert 2008) or as historical constructs that emerged as by-products of nation-building projects (Makoni & Pennycook 2007), they may be recognized to have a centre and periphery. The centre of a language is where speakers recognize that the language is 'best', 'most correctly' or 'most normally' spoken and often corresponds to the most populated middle class areas and to where the best or the highest number of educational institutions and publishers are or were established (think of Cambridge English, Florentine Italian, Île-de-France French, Randstad Dutch). The periphery of a language is where speakers (from the center) recognize the language is 'hardest to understand', 'most corrupted' or 'least civilised' and often corresponds to those areas with (historically) lower access to (higher) education and printed language.

To say that a language is polycentrically organized is to say that it has multiple, more or less powerful centers that compete with each other. These centers may differ along the metapragmatic parameters that are considered. What may be the center of educated speech or of 'the standard' language is not necessarily (often not) also the center for authentic or cool speech; and what counts as center for such evaluative norms may change over time and be replaced by other centers. Polycentricity is not entirely the same as pluricentricity as used by Clyne (1992) because the latter term emphasizes plurality of varieties within a language, i.e. plurality of relatively stable self-contained linguistic systems that together make up a language. This is the case when 'the German language' is defined in terms of its German, Austrian and Swiss counterparts; or when 'the English language' is represented in terms of concentric circles consisting of a small number of native and a larger (growing) number of second and foreign language varieties. Polycentricity emphasizes the functional inequality between such varieties and the simultaneous links to the various centering powers language practices are simultaneously subject to. Whereas a pluricentric language is the sum of its varieties, a polycentric language is a dynamic, socially ordered system of resources and norms that are strongly or weakly associated with one or more centers.

Although all languages are polycentrically organized, Chinese presents an extreme case of polycentricity. The Chinese language groups a higher number of people, a vaster geographical area and a larger continuum of variation beyond mutual intelligibility than any other language in the world, while at the same time upholding a meaningful sense of unity among its speakers through a common writing system. For this reason, the Ethnologue (2009) recognizes Chinese in their list of languages of China not as *a* language, but as a macrolanguage, i.e. 'multiple, closely related individual languages that are deemed in some usage contexts to be a single language'. As a macrolanguage, Chinese has thirteen 'member languages', listed alphabetically as Gan, Hakka, Huizhou, Jinyu, Mandarin, Min Bei, Min Dong, Min Nan, Min Zhong, Pu-Xian, Wu, Xiang and Yue.

The official discourse in China, however, is that there is only *one Chinese language* that comprises variation in the form of many *fangyan* or dialects on the level of informal, spoken language. The Chinese language is unified by a homogeneous writing system that enables communication across a wide geographical area and among speakers of widely varying and mutually largely unintelligible vernaculars. This unification has a long and complex history, dating back to the third century BCE when Qin Shi Huang, the first Chinese emperor passed a series of major economic, political and cultural reforms, including the unification of the Chinese writing system. DeFrancis (1984) explained the situation of Chinese and its internal diversity, translating it to the European context with the hypothetical situation as if the greater part of the European continent, from Italy to the Iberian peninsula and France with their many language varieties (Italian, French, Catalan, Corsican, etc.) would be united in single state and would have only Old Latin as a common language of literacy and of education, despite the differences and unintelligibility that exists between the language varieties spoken in such places as Rome, Paris, Geneva, Barcelona and Milan.

In order for us to understand the changing polycentricity of Chinese in the Netherlands, it is necessary to trace the historical, linguistic and demographic development of the Chinese diaspora. After that, we shall focus on empirical data collected in and around a Chinese complementary school in the city of Eindhoven, the Netherlands.

China and the Chinese diaspora in the Netherlands

The Chinese are one of the oldest established immigrant communities in the Netherlands, and they form one of the largest overseas Chinese populations in continental Europe. In July 2011 the Chinese community celebrated its centennial: one hundred years of Chinese in the Netherlands (Wolf 2011). The first Chinese immigrants were seamen from the southern part of China who settled in harbor cities like Rotterdam and Amsterdam where they built Chinatowns. Later, Chinese immigrants and their children spread all over the county. Figures of the number of Chinese residing in the Netherlands vary a lot depending on the source and on the definition of 'Chinese'. According to the Dutch Central Bureau of Statistics, there were in 2011 around 78,500 Chinese in the Netherlands (i.e. persons who were born or one of whose parents were born in mainland China or Hong Kong). Among them, 51,000 are first generation. In official statistics third and subsequent generation migrants are invisible and are registered only in terms of citizenship and country of birth.

During the Mao Era (1949–76), a series of reforms in the Chinese language were introduced in the People's Republic of China, including the introduction of a new, simplified Chinese writing system and a new romanisation system ('*pinyin*') – reforms that were not followed in Hong Kong and Taiwan (where traditional characters continued to be used). During this period, migration from and to, or foreign contact, including business, with the People's Republic was by and large impossible. The Chinese variety of the mainland, Mandarin or *Putonghua*, played only a marginal role in the Chinese diasporas until sometime after the Economic Reforms of 1978. Because migration from and contacts with Hong Kong (and Taiwan) remained possible all along this period, the Hong Kong Chinese, together with the earlier migrated Guangdong Chinese – both Cantonese-speaking – became the largest group of Chinese immigrants in the Netherlands. Together they represented some seventy percent of the Dutch Chinese around 1990 (CBS 2010:6). Consequently, Cantonese was the dominant language and lingua franca of the Dutch Chinese diaspora.

However, this has changed since the 1990s because of the political and economic transformation in China in the last three decades. In the period of 1991–2000, immigration by people from mainland China, especially from Zhejiang province has increased dramatically to over 50 percent (CBS 2010:4). After 2000, more and more Chinese students have come to the Netherlands to study at Dutch universities and they have consequently become the second largest group of foreign students (after Germans) in the Netherlands. From this period onwards, Chinese immigrants have originated from all over China. This increase of diversity in the Chinese diasporic population has meant a dramatic change of the status of Cantonese from the main language of the diaspora to only one of the dialects. The Chinese variety of the north, Mandarin or *Putonghua* has steadily gained importance, both in China itself as well as in the diaspora.

After the turnover of Hong Kong and Macau to China, in 1997 and 1999 respectively, *Putonghua* became increasingly important there as well. In the course of the events recounted above, we are witnessing a language shift within language, or the making of the world's biggest language. This account suggests how little languages as we identify them by their names are natural givens and how much languages are the result of political and historical contingencies and of strategic decisions and promotion campaigns designed to create national unity/identity or to boost national economies.

In short, the current flow of Chinese migration to the Netherlands is multi-layered and highly diverse in terms of the place of their origin, individual motivations and personal or family trajectories. The demographic changes in the constitution of the Chinese diaspora and their linguistic changes have far-reaching consequences for people's language and identity repertoires.

A Chinese complementary school in the Netherlands

Many young persons of Chinese heritage attend Chinese language schools on weekends. Most of these so-called 'complementary schools' gather on Saturday mornings, often on the premises of mainstream schools. They are community-run schools operating outside of the mainstream education system and offering a community-specific curriculum complementary to the mainstream educational contents. While much recent applied linguistics research exists on Chinese and other complementary education in the UK (Francis, Archer & Mau 2009; Li Wei & Wu 2009; Blackledge & Creese 2010), not much has been published about the Dutch context.

The first officially registered Chinese school in the Netherlands was established in the late 1970s. At the moment of our research (2010–2011), in all major cities in the Netherlands there was at least one Chinese school offering complementary education in Chinese language and culture for children with Chinese parents. The *Stichting Chinees Onderwijs Nederland* [Foundation Chinese Education The Netherlands] lists more than forty schools ⟨www.chineesonderwijs.nl⟩ (accessed March 2013).

The research reported here takes place primarily in a Chinese complementary school in Eindhoven in the Dutch province of North Brabant. The school is one of the oldest registered Chinese schools in the Netherlands, initially established in 1978 by the Chinese Protestant Church of Eindhoven. It originally provided Cantonese lessons to children of Cantonese origin in a café-restaurant. There were only about twenty students at the time. With the changing composition of Chinese immigrants in the Netherlands and the geopolitical repositioning of PRC in the globalized world system, lessons have gradually shifted from Cantonese to Mandarin in the last decade. Since 2006, there have been only Mandarin classes left.

At the time of our research, the school had around 280 students, and like many other Chinese community schools, the Chinese school in Eindhoven rents classrooms from a Dutch mainstream secondary school. This happens mostly on

Saturdays when students and teachers are free from their daily education and/or work, and when the school premises are available for rent. Classes in the Chinese school run from 9.15 to 11.45 in the morning and include a 20-minute break, during which there are regular staff meetings for the teachers. The school has classes starting from kindergarten and progressing to level 1 through level 12. The lower grades typically have double classes of up to twenty pupils whereas the higher grades usually only a handful in combined classes. In addition, there are four levels of adult language classes on offer to non-Chinese speakers who wish to learn Chinese. There is also a Dutch class for people of Chinese origin that is attended by, among others, teachers that are not yet proficient in Dutch.

Students in the school are mainly from the area of Eindhoven, but some students also travel considerable distances to attend the school, including from across the border in Belgium. Altogether there are 25 teachers, including teachers for calligraphy, music and *Kong Fu*. Many of the teachers are long-term residents in the local area. Both teachers and students at the School come from a wide range of social and linguistic backgrounds. Some of the teachers are well-paid professionals working at the High Tech Campus or for one of the hospitals in the city. Others are housewives or househusbands or they work in the catering business, running or working for a Chinese restaurant. Yet others are researchers or doctoral students who have recently arrived in the Netherlands from Mainland China. Recruitment of teachers is mainly from the community through personal introductions, or through the school website. Student recruitment, likewise, is through word of mouth, the website, and advertisements in local Chinese supermarkets and restaurants.

Since the classes have gradually changed to Mandarin, the school no longer uses textbooks prepared in Hong Kong but by Ji Nan University in Mainland China. The textbooks that are donated by the Chinese embassy in the Netherlands, are written especially for 'overseas Chinese' and were originally targeted at overseas Chinese children in the United States and Canada. Therefore, the language of instruction in the textbooks used is English. Teachers often speak English in addition to, or sometimes instead of Dutch, and *flexibly* switch in an out of Chinese, Dutch and/or English in the classroom.

Methodology

We adopted a sociolinguistic ethnographic perspective (Blommaert 2005; Rampton 2007; Heath & Street 2008; Blackledge & Creese 2010; Heller 2011) in our study of discourses of multilingual identity and inheritance among young people with families of Chinese migration background.

Our fieldwork started from the institutional context of the Chinese language and culture classroom at the Chinese school in Eindhoven, but we also see the school as deeply situated in a wider context, and as a non-autonomous sociolinguistic space anchored in the wider Chinese community of Eindhoven. Thus we move from what happens inside the classroom to what happens outside the classroom and outside the school, involving e.g. observations in both on- and offline Chinese communities (Qingfeng tea-room, Chinese restaurants and other organized community celebrations and activities such as *tai chi* and *ping pong* as well as in online social network sites (e.g. the Asian and proud forum on Hyves). The ethnographic perspective thus includes on the one hand the 'traditional' objects of ethnography (sound recordings, observation of situated events, interviews), but it adds to this two other dimensions: attention to visuality in the field of language; and attention to macro-sociolinguistic aspects influencing and constraining micro-events.

Before entering the field as researcher, Jinling was a teacher in the Eindhoven Chinese school giving a practical course of Chinese as a foreign language for Dutch adults. Access to the Chinese school was therefore not problematic. After four years of involvement as a teacher and as a first-generation migrant herself, Jinling was regarded as a member of the teaching staff and a member of the Chinese community more generally. As an outsider to this community and only working part-time on this project, Kasper had a secondary role in the ethnographic fieldwork and joined only some of the weekly visits.

Together we worked as a team complementing each other's strengths and weaknesses and combining in our ethnography an insider's with an outsider's perspective – both in terms of membership of the school community and the wider Eindhoven Chinese community and with respect to our multilingual repertoires. We discussed and analyzed pieces of data together, and drafted and revised internal research reporting as well as research papers for publication collaboratively, helping each other, in turns, to render the strange familiar and the familiar strange. The authorial 'we' used here reflects that collaborative research practice (see Creese & Blackledge 2012 for general discussion about ethnographic team research and Creese & Blackledge 2014 for reflexive researcher vignettes of us and other researchers in the project).

Our observations followed the school year and spanned the period between April 2010 and June 2011. During this time we regularly observed classroom practices, staff meetings and breaks in the school context and had many conversations with teachers, students, administrators and parents about complementary school life, diasporic identity, China, and Chinese language teaching in the Netherlands.

The metapragmatics of sociolinguistic transformation

The first extract we discuss is based on an observation in May 2010 in Mr. Zhou's combined grade 11/12 class, the final class in the school. Nine students aged 16 to 19 had officially registered in Mr. Zhou's class. The actual number of students attending his class, however, fluctuated considerably. At the moment of our observation there were only four students, all female. According to Mr Zhou, the low attendance was due to the fact that it was exam weeks in the mainstream schools.

Mr. Zhou's class is ethnolinguistically very heterogeneous. Two of the students present, Esther and Hil Wah, were of Hong Kong Cantonese background, one, Wendy, of Wenzhounese background, and Tongtong had a mixed Guangdong and Hong Kong background. According to Mr. Zhou, there were also students from Fujianese and Malaysian Chinese backgrounds. Seven of the nine students attended mainstream Dutch medium school, the two Malaysian students attended an English-medium international school from Monday to Friday. Six of the students in Mr. Zhou's class were born in the Netherlands, and the remaining three in mainland China and Malaysia.

Mr. Zhou is an earlier migrant from Guangdong province and is a speaker of Cantonese. The day when Mr. Zhou and the researcher (Li) arrived in the classroom, he greeted and chatted with the students in Cantonese. When the lesson started, Mr. Zhou switched from Cantonese to Mandarin as the language of instruction. During the lesson, Mr. Zhou and the students were practicing synonyms in the *Hanyu Shuiping Kaoshi* (HSK – 'Chinese proficiency test') for level 5. The HSK test is the Chinese equivalent of the TOEFL and IELTS tests for English. It is a Chinese language proficiency test designed and developed by the HSK Center of Beijing Language and Culture University to assess the Chinese proficiency of non-native speaking foreigners and overseas Chinese. HSK has in total six levels ranging from elementary level 1 to advanced level 6. What is interesting is that the term for Chinese in the name of the test is Hanyu (汉语) – the language of the Han, the majority nationality (zu, 族) in China. In practice this means Putonghua.

The classroom was organized in rows. All four students sat in the middle row. Wendy and Hil Wah were in the middle of the first row in the classroom with Esther and Tongtong sitting in the row behind them. There was a whiteboard in front of the classroom and the teacher sat between the whiteboard and the students. The researcher took position in the back of the classroom, making notes and video recordings at selected moments while audio recording the entire lesson. The lesson started with vocabulary training of what is known in the HSK exercise book as *tong yi ci* 同义词 'synonyms'. Extract 1 below is taken from the beginning of the lesson.

Extract 1. Tongtong correcting Mr. Zhou's accent (classroom observation, May 2010)

		Original in Chinese/Dutch	Translation in English
1	Mr Zhou	你们造句也行，把荷兰文的意思说出来也行，就过了。' 本质' [běn zhí]	You can make sentences or say the meaning in Dutch: 'Quality/nature' [běn zhí].
2	Tongtong	本质 [běn zhí]? 某某东西的本质 [běn zhí]] *eigenschap van* ×××?	Quality/nature? Something's nature? nature of ×××?
3	Mr Zhou	Eigenschap。	Quality/Nature.
4	Tongtong	不是本质 [běn zhì] 吗?	Should it not be [běn zhì?] (with falling tone)
5	Mr Zhou	((looks at the book again)) 本质啊，应该读第四声啊，对不起。	Běn zhì ah, should be pronounced with the fourth tone *ah*, sorry.
6	Mr Zhou	下一个，'比较' [bǐ jiǎo]。	The next one, 'comparing' [bǐ jiǎo]
7	Tongtong	比较 [bǐ jiǎo]? 比较 [bǐ jiào] 嘛?	Bǐ jiǎo? Should it not be bǐ jiào?
8	Class	((all four students correcting his pronunciation))	
9	Mr Zhou	((nodds in agreement, repeats the corrected pronunciation)) 比较啊，也读错了。	bǐ jiào *ah*. I made again a mistake.
10	Class	((students look at each other and laugh))	

Let us first take a look at what is happening here. The class was one month before the HSK exam. Mr. Zhou's assignment was to let the students practice synonyms. To achieve this, Mr. Zhou asked the students to make sentences with difficult words in Chinese or translate these words into Dutch. The students did not, however, just do the assignment by making sentences in Chinese or translating the words into Dutch but immediately turned the exercise into pronunciation training for the teacher. In line 4, Tongtong corrected Mr. Zhou's pronunciation of *bǐjiǎo*. In line 5, Mr. Zhou agreed with Tongtong that he had made a mistake. In line 7, Tongtong corrected Mr. Zhou's pronunciation again and in line 8, all four students corrected Mr. Zhou's pronunciation. Mr. Zhou kindly agreed with the students and admitted in line 9 that he had made yet another mistake. The extract ends with the students looking at each other and laughing at the situation and/or the teacher.

This example adds further evidence to Li & Wu's (2009) observations in the UK that despite the prevalent stereotypes of Chinese children being polite, passive subjects in the classroom, Chinese adolescents in fact regularly engage in ridiculing and mocking behaviour at the expense of the teacher. The resources for such 'linguistic sabotage' (Jaspers 2005) are located in the tension and conflict between the teachers and pupils' language repertoires and preferences. Whereas in Li & Wu's data, the participants are younger than the current research group, the tension manifests itself mainly in the children's more sophisticated proficiency in English compared to the teachers, in this example the tension also arises over ownership and expertise in Chinese, the target of learning and teaching in this community.

When we take a close look at the transcript, we see abundant features of non-nativeness in Mr. Zhou's speech. The classroom episode presents a serious deviation from the traditional Chinese language class where the teacher has all the 'knowledge' and is assumed to be a model language user, with respect to vocabulary, grammar, orthography and also pronunciation. However, in this classroom, we see another scenario. The language teacher's pronunciation is corrected by his students. From a traditional educational point of view, one might raise doubts about Mr. Zhou's qualification as a teacher of Chinese. Is he a qualified language teacher?

In order to answer this question from a sociolinguistic point of view, we need to look at what happens outside the classroom. Schools as institutions are non-autonomous sociolinguistic spaces and are deeply situated in a wider societal context. Chinese heritage schools are situated at the intersection of two or more different political, social, economic, linguistic and sociological systems or regimes. Our analysis sets out from a sociolinguistic perspective that involves different scale-levels. Different scales organize different patterns of normativity (Blommaert 2005; Collins & Slembrouck 2006; Collins 2009). The analysis of our classroom interaction requires a processual epistemology in which the classroom interactions at one level of social structure need to be understood in relation to phenomena from another level of social structure. Time and space are the two key concepts in understanding of what is happening here.

For a long time, Cantonese was taught at Chinese school overseas. Mr. Zhou is a first generation migrant of Cantonese background, who started his voluntary teaching career as a Chinese language teacher teaching Cantonese but had to re-educate himself to teach Mandarin. His re-education is self-taught, but also partly taken care of by his students as could be seen in Extract 1 above.

The point here is not about the pronunciation of *ben zhi*, but to document the emergent and problem-ridden transition from one language regime to another. This little classroom episode reveals big demographic and geopolitical changes of global Chineseness – i.e. changes in spatial configurations: (1) the language teacher becomes a language learner; (2) the school surrenders the old language regime to capture a (new) audience; (3) the traces of worldwide migration flows impact on the specific demographic, social and cultural dynamics of the Chinese presence in Eindhoven; (4) the Chinese philosophy of cultural, political and sociolinguistic 'harmony' is not strongly enforced in the diaspora, but is brought in – with force – by new immigrants from the PRC; and (5) on the whole we witness a geopolitical repositioning of China: the emergence of PRC as new economic world power.

This classroom episode triggered an interview with Tongtong's parents. The meeting took place at the restaurant of Tongtong's parents on a Saturday evening. The restaurant is located next to a supermarket, under a residential apartment in the north of Eindhoven. The name of the restaurant is written in Dutch (*Chinees-Indisch Restaurant*), traditional Chinese characters (富貴酒樓) and Cantonese romanisation (*fu kwei* 'prosperous'). The linguistic landscape of Chinese communities and the role of restaurants deserve a separate paper. This kind of Chinese restaurant is a typical Chinese restaurant in the Netherlands: established in the 1960-70s and serving Chinese-Indonesian (*Chinees-Indisch*) cuisine. The restaurant was a family business. For 20 years, the restaurant has been owned by Tongtong's parents, who inherited it from Tongtong's paternal grandparents.

Extract 2 is taken from a one-hour interview with Tongtong's mother in Tongtong's presence. The interview was an informal, although audio-recorded conversation about the family's migration history and their language use. In the extract, we can read the researcher inquire about the family's language policy.

Extract 2. Interview with Tongtong's mother about family's language policy

		Original in Chinese (Mandarin)	Translation in English
1	JLi	听彤彤她说她小时侯在家是说广东话，看广东话电视，后来你把广东话的电视频道删了？只让她看普通话电视节目？	I heard from Tongtong that she watched Cantonese channels at home when she was small, but later you deleted all the Cantonese channels and let Tongtong watch only Putonghua channels?
2	TM	是，因为我是在国内受的教育。我们国内都是讲普通话教学的嘛。来这里我就觉得奇怪，为什么要广东话教学。不过我们家都是讲广东话的，我们是广东人嘛，当然在家是讲方言啦。	Yes, because I was educated in China. In China, we all know about Putonghua teaching. When I came here, I felt it was very strange that Cantonese was taught at school. But at home, we speak Cantonese. We are Cantonese; of course at home we speak dialect.

3	JLi	方言？你是指广东话？	Dialect? You mean Cantonese?
4	TM	是，我们的方言是广东话。后来，后来中文学校我要求要那个普通话教学，要开普通话班，那时没有，那是14，15年前，彤彤，她5岁左右。后来读了两年小学幼稚园的课程，后来就有了(普通话班)，我就赶快给她转，她那时还哭。因为都是小朋友，都在一起玩，就把她一个人拽出来，到另外一个班上，她那时不适应，她不肯走，哎呀，连哄带骗的	Yes, our dialect is Cantonese. Then, then in the Chinese school I asked for Putonghua teaching, Putonghua class, but they didn't have. That was about 14 or 15 years ago, when Tongtong was about 5 years old. She started two years of Cantonese kindergarten class, and then there came the Putonghua class, so I immediately sent her there. She cried, because she had made friends in the class and didn't want to go to another one. I had to sweet-talk her into Putonghua class.
5	JLi	那是第一个普通话班？九几年的时候？	Was it the first Putonghua class? When did that happen?
6	TM	我估计她那时侯7岁左右，99年的时候。	When she was about 7 years old, around 1999.
7	JLi	你是什么时候来荷兰的？	When did you move to the Netherlands?
8	TM	我二十多年前来的荷兰，80年代末。	More than twenty years ago, in the late 1980s.
9	JLi	你来荷兰前生活在广东？在广东也是说粤语的，但是你还是觉得普通话很重要？	You were living in Guangdong before you came to the Netherlands? Cantonese is spoken in Guangdong. Do you think that Putonghua is very important?
10	TM	是的，因为你要是在中国跟其它省份联系，这是必须的桥梁来着.	Yes, if you want to communicate with people from other provinces in China. Putonghua is the bridge to enable that.

Tongtong's behaviour in the classroom (her correcting of the teacher's accent) needs to be understood against the background of the decision made by Tongtong's mother to transfer Tongtong from a Cantonese class to a Mandarin class as soon as this was possible in Eindhoven. This extract gives insight into Tongtong's 'family language policy' (Curdt-Christiansen 2013) as well as the macro political transformation at the highest scale-level. This is most clearly articulated by Tongtong's mother in line 10: Putonghua is a bridge to enable communication in a broader network of Chinese migrants. This rescaling of the community (from a local Guangdongese language community to a translocal or global Chinese community) is necessitated by the new waves of Chinese mobility from the PRC, causing a diversification of 'Chineses' and Chineseness.

This diversification of Chinese diasporas across the world is a result of political and economic changes in China over the last three decades. The language ideological effects of this geopolitical transformation can be read in Extract 2. For people who are educated in China such as Tongtong's mother, being educated is equal to speaking *Putonghua*. We read this quite literally in line 2 and 4. Tongtong's mother found it strange that Cantonese was taught at Chinese schools in the Netherlands, because for her, Cantonese is not a language, but a dialect. Tongtong's mother, who has been educated in China and has worked as an editor at a television station in Guangzhou before her emigration in the late 1980s, stresses the importance of speaking *Putonghua* for educational and general success in life. This ideology is shared with the majority of new migrants from the PRC, especially the university educated elite of *liuxuesheng* (Chinese international students).

This brings us to extract 3, an interview with a former teacher of the school, who was educated in Guangdong. The interview is conducted in 2011. Jessie migrated to the Netherlands in the late 1990s to study and was a voluntary teacher at the school from 1999 to 2003.

Extract 3. Interview with former teacher Jessie

1.	JLi	你以前在安多分的中文学校教过书?	You had been teaching Chinese in the Chinese school in Eindhoven?
2.	Jessie	教过，教粤语，教过4年。从99年开始。	Yes, I taught Cantonese for 4 years since 1999.
3.	JLi	那时中文学校粤语班多吗?	Were there many Cantonese classes?
4.	Jessie	有好几个，学校都是以说粤语为主。	Quite a few. Cantonese was the dominant language in the school.
5.	JLi	现在中文学校都没有粤语班了，都是普通话班。	There is no Cantonese class anymore in the Chinese school.
6.	Jessie	就是，早就该没粤语了。	Yes, should have done that earlier.
7.	JLi	Hmmm	Hmmm
8.	Jessie	知道吗，我那时候教得很痛苦。书是繁体字，教简体字。	You know, it was very painful for me to teach at that time, because the textbooks were in traditional characters but you had to teach the children simplified character writing.

9.	JLi	怎么有这种？	How come?
10.	Jessie	因为当时也可以教繁体字，但有些班里学生家长的意见，他们觉得简体字比繁体字有用。当时我们的课本都是台湾提供的，没有简体字的课本。	Because some parents requested for simplified character teaching, they thought it was more useful. But our textbooks were provided by the Taiwanese government, so they had no simplified characters.
11.	JLi	所以当时中文学校的课本都是台湾提供的。	So the teaching materials were provided by Taiwan at the time.
12.	Jessie	是，以前我们都是10月10号台湾的国庆节，我们都是去台湾的大使馆吃饭。有很多这样的活动。	Yes, We also celebrated the Taiwanese national day on the 10th of October by going to the Taiwanese embassy to have a meal there.
13.	JLi	这些年的变化很大。	Things have changed in the last decade.
14.	Jessie	是，我们以前教的都是广东，香港移民的孩子。现在都是大陆那边的。我以前没有接触香港那边的教材，其实台湾那边的教材用广东话教是教不出来的。有些国语的音用广东话教是教不出来的。所以教得很痛苦，用的是台湾的教材，教的是粤语的发音，写得是简体字。	Yes, my students were all Guangdong and Hong Kong origin. But now the students are from all over China. I didn't have experience with the textbooks provided by Hong Kong. What I experienced is the teaching material provided by Taiwan couldn't be used to teach Cantonese, because some pronunciations in these textbooks couldn't be pronounced in Cantonese. For instance, rhymes in the Mandarin poetry don't have the same effect in Cantonese. So it was very painful for me to teach Cantonese pronunciation while using the Taiwanese textbooks and teaching simplified character writing at the time.

In the interview, Jessie described her experience of teaching Chinese, the demographic composition of the students, and the teaching materials that the school used. In her teaching, she confronted with the strong 'polycentricity' of Chinese: Cantonese had to be taught using Taiwanese textbooks, raising linguistic and literacy issues that she found hard to manoeuvre, all the more since the parents demanded the teaching of simplified script to their children.

Intuitively, many people see the school teacher as the all-knowing repository and mediator of knowledge, as a stable figure whose input would always be directed towards the focus of the class activities and the curriculum knowledge he or she is supposed to transfer. In the context of our research, however, we came to see the teachers as a highly heterogeneous, 'unstable' group of people. The reason for this is twofold. First, the teachers themselves have a complex repertoire and a complex sociolinguistic biography, involving sometimes dramatic and traumatizing language shift during certain phases of their lives. As a consequence, language teachers themselves are, in actual fact, language learners. The second reason is that teachers from the PRC often arrive with a teaching style and a set of language-ideological assumptions that are at odds with those of the learners in the diaspora. This potentially results in mutual frustration and in incidents over class activities and interpretations of tasks.

Jessie's teaching experience dated to a decade ago, probably the very early stage of the process of language shift to Putonghua we currently see in full force. These observations show the fundamental aspects about language in the current globalised world. Chinese, or any language for that matter, is not a fixed object or entity that people can learn to make use of but is dynamic, changing, contested, in transformation. Languages are moving targets. Chinese as a language has a long history of export and mobility, of being exported 'to the world' by Chinese migrants from the late 19th Century until today. This has resulted in divergent configurations of language diversity overseas and at home, that are converging in the current wave of globalization characterized as superdiversity (cf. Blommaert & Rampton 2011). If we understand current globalization processes as the compression of time and space through increased flows of people, goods and images facilitated through technologies, then we can understand how developments in the diaspora are reflecting in intricate ways developments in the PRC. Researching Chinese language in the diaspora helps us look at "the world as one large, interactive system, composed of many complex subsystems" (Appadurai 1996, p. 41) and at processes that are of a larger scale than nations and states.

Conclusions

We began this paper by suggesting that we need to consider Chinese as a polycentric language in the context of migration and globalisation. Drawing on Silverstein's notion of metapragmatics, we have examined the specific Chinese diasporic context, namely the educational context of the Chinese complementary school in the Netherlands, through which this paper has demonstrated an ongoing shift along with demographic, economic and political changes, in what counts as Chinese: a shift from Hong Kong and Taipei to Beijing as the most powerful reference centre of Chinese in the world.

These ongoing language shifts in the Chinese diaspora reflect a series of language political changes in China and have to do with what Dong (2010) has called 'the enregisterment of Putonghua in practice', the processes in which Chinese is becoming an exclusive, monoglot, homogeneous entity that erases the diversity existing underneath it, the process that makes Chinese synonymous with *Putonghua* in an increasing number of contexts (Li & Juffermans 2012). Consequently, speakers in the diaspora such as Mr. Zhou, Tongtong and her mother, and Jessie have adjusted or are adjusting or catching up with this changing situation. Chinese language learning and teaching take place on shifting ground: the main foci of orientation – the normative 'centers' of language learning and teaching – are shifting and changing rapidly and intensely. The object of learning and teaching in this heterogeneous, polycentric community and the identities that emerge in the process are moving targets – unstable and changing sociolinguistic configurations. A better understanding of these is a key to understanding the complex and shifting social identities as they are shaped by and shaping various educational settings, both within and beyond the complementary school context.

Acknowledgements

The authors gratefully acknowledge support of Babylon, Center for Studies of the Multicultural Society at Tilburg University and HERA (Humanities in the European Research Area) which funded the data collection and analysis of this paper as part of a Collaborative Research Project, *Investigating Discourses of Inheritance and Identities in Four Multilingual European Settings* (IDII4MES), coordinated by Prof. Adrian Blackledge at the University of Birmingham and involving colleagues at the Universities of Stockholm and Copenhagen, see ⟨http://www.heranet.info/idi4mes/index⟩. An earlier version of this paper was discussed at an IDII4MES project meeting in Birmingham (May 2011) and presented at the 8th International Symposium of Bilingualism in Oslo (June 2011). We are indebted to the members of the IDII4MES team, the editors of this volume, as well as two anonymous reviewers for feedback, comments, and useful suggestions.

Transcription conventions

×××	:	inaudible word(s)
(( ))	:	the transcriber's comments
italics	:	Dutch
[běn zhí]	:	pinyin gloss of characters, with tone indication

References

Appadurai, A. 1996. *Modernity at Large: Cultural Dimensions of Globalisation.* Minneapolis MN: University of Minnesota Press.

Blackledge, A. & Creese, A. 2010. *Multilingualism: A Critical Perspective.* London: Continuum.

Blommaert, J. 2005. *Discourse: A Critical Introduction.* Cambridge: CUP.

Blommaert, J. 2008. Artefactual ideologies and the textual production of African languages. *Language & Communication* 28: 291–307.

Blommaert, J. 2010. *The Sociolinguistics of Globalization.* Cambridge: CUP.

Blommaert, J. & Rampton, B. 2011. Language and superdiversity. *Diversities* 13(2): 1–22.

Canagarajah, S. 2013. *Translingual Practice: Global Englishes and Cosmopolitan Relations.* London: Routledge.

CBS. 2010. Herkomst van Chinezen in Nederland. In *Bevolkingstrends: Statistisch Kwartaalblad over de demografie van Nederland. Jaargang 58, 1e kwartaal,* 6–6. Den Haag: Centraal Bureau voor Statistiek.

Clyne, M. (ed.) 1992. *Pluricentric Languages: Differing Norms in Different Nations.* Berlin: Mouton de Gruyter.

Collins, J. 2009. Social reproduction in classrooms and schools. *Annual Review of Anthropology* 38: 33–48.

Collins, J. & Slembrouck, S. 2006. 'You don't know what they translate': Language contact, institutional procedure, and literacy practice in neighborhood health clinics in urban Flanders. *Journal of Linguistic Anthropology* 16(2): 1055–360.

Creese, A. & Blackledge, A. 2012. Voice and meaning-making in team ethnography. *Anthropology & Education Quarterly* 43(3): 306–24.

Creese, A. & Blackledge, A. 2014. Researching bilingual and multilingual education. In *The Handbook of Bilingual and Multilingual Education,* W.E. Wright, S. Boun & O. García (eds). Hoboken, NJ: Wiley Blackwell.

Curdt-Christiansen, X.L. 2013. Family language policy: Sociopolitical reality versus linguistic continuity. *Language Policy* 12: 1–6.

DeFrancis, J. 1984. *The Chinese Language: Fact and Fantasy.* Honolulu HI: University of Hawaii Press.

Dong, J. 2010. The enregisterment of Putonghua in practice. *Language & Communication* 30(4): 265–75.

Ethnologue. 2009. In *Ethnologue: Languages of the World,* 16th edn, M.P. Lewis (ed.). Dallas TX: SIL International. ⟨www.ethnologue.com⟩

Francis, B., Archer, L. & Mau, A. 2009. Language as capital, or language as identity? Chinese complementary school pupils' perspectives on the purposes and benefits of complementary schools. *British Educational Research Journal* 35(4): 519–38.

Heath, S.B. & Street, B. 2008. *On Ethnography: Approaches to Language and Literacy Research.* New York NY: Teachers College Press.

Heller, M. 2011. *Paths to Post-nationalism: A Critical Ethnography of Language and Identity.* Oxford: OUP.

Jaspers, J. 2005. Linguistic sabotage in a context of monolingualism and standardization. *Language & Communication* 25(3): 279–97.

Li, J. & Juffermans, K. 2012. Chinese complementary schooling in the Netherlands: experiences and identities of final year students. In *Mother Tongue and Intercultural Valorization: Europe and its Migrant Youth,* F. Grande, J.J. de Ruiter & M. Spotti (eds), 61–80. Milano: Franco Angeli Publication.

Li Wei & Wu, C.-J. 2009. Polite Chinese children revisited: Creativity and the use of codeswitching in the Chinese complementary school classroom. *International Journal of Bilingual Education and Bilingualism* 12(2): 193–211.

Makoni, S. & Pennycook, A. (eds). 2007. *Disinventing and Reconstituting Languages.* Clevedon: Multilingual Matters.

Mufwene, S.S. 2008. *Language Evolution: Contact, Competition and Change.* London: Continuum.

Pennycook, A. 2012. *Language and Mobility: Unexpected Places.* Bristol: Multilingual Matters.

Rampton, B. 2007. Neo-Hymesian linguistic ethnography in the United Kingdom. *Journal of Sociolinguistics* 11(5): 584–607.

Silverstein, M. 1993. Metapragmatic discourse and metapragmatic function. In *Reflexive Language: Reported Speech and Metapragmatics,* J.A. Lucy (ed.), 33–58. Cambridge: CUP.

Wolf, S. 2011. *Chinezen in Nederland.* Utrecht: Forum: Instituut voor Multiculturele Vraagstukken.

CHAPTER 6

Language and literacy teaching, learning and socialization in the Chinese complementary school classroom

Li Wei & Zhu Hua

Birkbeck College, University of London

The Chinese complementary schools for overseas-born ethnic Chinese children provide an interesting, complex and forever changing context where the teaching and learning of the Chinese language, especially literacy, is intertwined with the teaching and learning of Chinese cultural values and ideologies. These values and ideologies, however, are not static but changing across the generations and with the on-going process of transnational movement and globalization. This article focuses on classroom interactions in Chinese complementary schools in Britain and aims to show how the teachers use the opportunity of language and literacy teaching to pass on cultural values and ideologies to the pupils, how the pupils react to this kind of socializational teaching and how the teachers and the pupils negotiate identities through the process of language and literacy learning. The findings of the study have implications for both policy and practice regarding the education and development of multilingual children.

Introduction

This chapter focuses on the teaching of Chinese, especially literacy, to the British-born Chinese children in a specific context, namely the Chinese complementary schools in Britain. We take teaching and learning as a socialization process – the dissemination and acquisition of knowledge and skills, as well as social norms and ideologies, to and by novices in order for them to become competent members of the society (Duranti, Ochs & Shieffelin 2011). In language and literacy teaching and learning, the social norms and ideologies are implicitly transmitted through explicit modeling of linguistic skills, for example, by the contents of the structures the teacher produces. The contents, as well as the interactional acts, i.e. the way teaching is done, reflect the teacher's attitude, ideology, stance and identity.

The learners, with their own personal histories, experiences, attitudes, ideologies and stances, may react to this kind of 'socializational teaching' in different ways; some may be more aware of the socialization dimension of the teaching than others. There may also be occasions when the teacher explicitly discusses issues of attitudes, beliefs, values, and identities with the learner, in connection with the linguistic structures being taught. Kramsch (1996) talked about this kind of discussion as part of what she called 'critical cross-cultural literacy', which is helping the learner realize the differences between the perspective of one community and another.

In this chapter, we will show that the Chinese complementary schools provide an interesting, complex and forever changing context where the teaching and learning of the Chinese language is intertwined with the teaching and learning of Chinese cultural values and ideologies. These values and ideologies, however, are not static but changing across the generations and with the on-going process of transnational movement and globalization. One of the consequences of the socialization process in the Chinese complementary schools is the emergence of new forms of multilingualism and transcultural identities of both the teachers and the pupils (Li Wei 2011).

The idea of 'socializational teaching' draws its inspiration from Language Socialization, which Ochs (2002, p. 106) describes as follows:

> The discipline articulates ways in which novices across the life span are socialized into using language and socialized through language into local theories and preferences for acting, feeling, and knowing, in socially recognized and organized practices associated with membership in a social group.

Most language socialization research has been conducted in non-formal settings. Though explicit modeling of linguistic behavior is abound, it has not been a focus of the analysis. Studies of second language socialization in schools by adolescents and adults by, for example, Duff (1996), Harklau (2003), and Rymes (2001) have also interpreted the processes of language socialization without reference to the explicit modeling that we see in socializational teaching. Working with heritage language learning in the US, He (2010) suggests that it is the interactional acts and stances that teachers do and take rather than the content of the teaching that socializes students to ways of acting and feeling. Whilst we agree with these language socialization researchers, we believe that the explicit modeling of language behavior also has important socialization effects. Thus, identities and attitudes are accomplishments or outcomes of not only interactional stances but also what is being taught and how it is taught in the classroom.

The chapter is structured as follows. We begin with an outline of the Chinese complementary schools in the UK, followed by a brief discussion of the changing hierarchies of the Chinese language and their impact on the teaching of Chinese to overseas-born ethnic Chinese children. The main body of the chapter is devoted to a detailed analysis of classroom interactions that show how the teachers use the opportunity of language and literacy teaching to pass on cultural values and ideologies to the pupils, how the pupils react to this kind of socializational teaching and how the teachers and the pupils negotiate identities through the process of language and literacy learning. The chapter concludes with a brief summary of the findings and implications.

Complementary schools for the Chinese diasporic communities

The Chinese diasporic communities across the globe have long been setting up schools and classes for their locally-born children. They are known as community language schools/classes, heritage language schools/classes, or complementary school/classes in different parts of the world. They have a strong cultural flavour in that they offer a variety of teaching that is associated with the traditional Chinese cultural practices, such as martial arts, folk dancing, paper folding and cutting, and calligraphy and ink painting. They are one of the three pillars of the Chinese diasporas – the other two being the townsmen associations and the community media – which provide an important social network where high quality information is being exchanged (e.g. school admission for the children, university and career choice, finding reliable workers and other services) between families who otherwise live dispersed from each other. However, the primary aim of these schools and classes is to teach the language, especially literacy, i.e. the reading and writing of Chinese characters, to the new generations of overseas Chinese children.

In Britain, the Chinese schools and classes are part of a major socio-political and educational movement which began in the 1950s with the establishment of community schools by the Afro-Caribbean communities as a means of tackling racism towards and under-achievement amongst black children. In the 1960s and 70s, the Muslim communities set up a number of faith schools, especially for girls. Some of these schools later received governmental recognition along with other faith schools. The vast majority of such schools in today's Britain, usually known as complementary schools, are cultural and language schools, usually run outside the hours of mainstream schools, i.e. at weekends (see Li Wei 2006 for a review of the historical developments of complementary schools in Britain). According to the national resource centre Contin You's register ⟨http://www.continyou.org.uk/⟩, there are over 2000 such schools. However, such figures are likely to be an underestimate, as these schools are voluntary organisations and many are very small and informal, and they may not wish to appear on official registers for a variety of reasons. According to the UK Federation of Chinese Schools and the UK Association for the Promotion of Chinese Education, the two largest national organizations for Chinese complementary schools, there are over 200 Chinese complementary schools in the United Kingdom.

Whilst the establishment of the complementary schools is sometimes seen as a challenge to the dominant ideology of uniculturalism in Britain, the ideology of the complementary schools themselves is rarely questioned. For instance, most complementary schools have an implicit one language only (OLON) or one language at a time (OLAT) policy, usually the minority ethnic language, of course. We have raised the question elsewhere (Li Wei & Wu 2009) about the implications of such policies. For us, OLON and OLAT policies are another form of the monolingual ideology. Although it is understandable that the complementary schools want to insist on using specific community languages in this particular domain, the long-term consequence of the compartmentalisation of community languages is an issue of concern (see also Martin et al. 2006; Creese et al. 2006; Blackledge & Creese 2010).

Changing hierarchies of the Chinese language and implications for Chinese complementary schools in Britain

As far as the overseas Chinese diasporas are concerned, the vast majority happen to be from the traditionally Cantonese-, Hokkien- and Hakka-speaking provinces of mainland China, hence the prominence of these language varieties among the overseas Chinese communities. One noticeable change in the past 20 years has been the increase of Mandarin-speaking Chinese among the new arrivals and of Mandarin classes for overseas Chinese children across the globe. In Britain, the Chinese are one of the largest and longest-established immigrant communities. The British Chinese community website (www.dimsum.co.uk) reports that the Chinese community is the fastest growing non-European ethnic group in the United Kingdom. It has an annual growth of approximately 11%. In 2006, the estimate was 400 000 Chinese people in total. The majority of the British Chinese have close connections with former British colonies, especially Hong Kong, and other Southeast Asian countries where there are large concentrations of Chinese people. People from mainland China and Taiwan and their descendants constitute a relatively minor proportion of the British Chinese community, although the most recent and ongoing growth of the British Chinese community is largely due to the increased number of mainlanders. As a result, the vast majority of the British Chinese use Cantonese as first or home language. According to the website ethnologue.com, Cantonese is spoken by

300 000 British Chinese as a primary language, while 10 000 speak Hakka and 6 000 speak Hokkien. Approximately 10 000 are believed to be Mandarin Chinese speakers, although the number may be significantly more if the Chinese students and other professionals who are in the United Kingdom temporarily are also included. Many of them speak Mandarin as a second or third, rather than the first, Chinese variety. The proportion of British Chinese people who speak English as a first or secondary language is unknown (Li Wei 2007).

As reported in Li Wei and Zhu (2010), the hierarchies of the different varieties of the Chinese language are changing within the Chinese diasporic communities as a result of the recent demographic changes in Chinese migration, globalization and the rising politico-economic power of mainland China. A concrete example of this change is that all the Chinese complementary schools in Britain that traditionally taught Cantonese as the main language now offer Mandarin classes and simplified characters, both represent the linguistic norms of mainland China. Yet, none of the Mandarin schools which have been set up in all major cities in Britain in the last ten years teaches Cantonese or the traditional characters. In this chapter we will see examples of how Cantonese-first-language pupils learning Mandarin react to the changes of the hierarchies of the varieties of Chinese.

The present study

The data for the present study come from a series of ethnographic studies of the multilingual practices by the pupils and teachers in Chinese complementary schools in a number of cities in England, especially in Newcastle, Manchester and London. In each case, we made extensive observations, field notes, and audio and video recordings of all the activities during the school hours. We also conducted interviews with teachers, parents and the pupils. Like most Chinese complementary schools, the classes are grouped according to the children's perceived proficiency in Chinese by the parents and teachers. In other words, children of different ages can be found in the same class, though in most cases the age difference is only between two or three years. In our fieldwork, we focused on the classes with age groups of between 8 and 14. This was done primarily for access reasons.

Ideological and literacy socialization

One of the most commonly occurring examples of socializational teaching that we observed in the Chinese complementary schools is when the teacher tries to relate the teaching of specific linguistic structures to some broader socio-cultural issues. For example, the following fieldnote was made during our observation of a Mandarin class in Manchester where the teacher, a university academic from mainland China in her thirties who was doing a postgraduate degree in Britain, was supposed to be teaching the modal verb 应该 (*should, must*). But the examples she chose in teaching it were all related to moral duties and behavioural norms, including "respect" and "working hard". What might have been a fairly basic grammatical drill became a socialization process.

Example 1 (A class of 12 year olds in Manchester. The teacher is female, from China.)
> The class teacher asked a boy to read out the sample sentence. Then asked them what the key word '应该 ⟨should, must⟩' '是什么意思啊 ⟨what does it mean⟩'.
> After a short pause, a girl answered (in English) '*Must*.'
> Teacher then asked pupils to make sentences using the key word.
> She gave examples such as '我们应该尊敬长辈。<We must respect members of older generation.>' '我们今年应该回中国。<We must go back to China this year.>' '我们应该写我们的作文。<We must write our compositions.>' …
> Other sentences were offered. '你应该好好学习。<You must learn well.>' '弟弟应该好好睡觉。<Younger brother must go and have a good sleep.>' '我应该做作业了。<I must do homework.>'
> (Taken from fieldnotes, hence not in dialogue format.)

This kind of examples is also very common in the textbooks the Chinese schools use. They are full of traditional folk tales and other stories that carry a moral message to the learner, usually about the traditional Chinese cultural values of respecting the elderly; family is the most important social unit; social advancement can only be achieved through academic studies and hard work, etc. We regard these as part of a process of cultural socialization, as the teachers make use of these stories to socialize the pupils into the Chinese cultural traditions and values.

Example 2 is taken from a recorded classroom interaction, also in Manchester, where the teacher moves from various Chinese folk festivals to the key phrase 盼望 (panwang), meaning *longing for*. But the examples she gives in collocation with it all concern higher socio-cultural ideals, such as having a united homeland and united family. In contrast, the pupils are all longing for the less "serious" things such as holidays, sporting events, and in an apparent act of rebellion, the end of the Chinese school.

Example 2 (T: Female teacher in her forties. Q and B are girls, the others are boys, all between 10 and 11 years old.)
> T: 那是第五个词了。第四个词? 盼望。盼望怎么说? 比如说，我们都盼望什么? 盼望，expect, look forward to. Write down the explanation beside the words, in case you forget it later. 盼望，the 4th one, means look forward to. 比如说，我们都盼望什么?
> *That's the fifth word. The fourth word? 'Panwang' (long for). How do you use 'panwang'? For example, what do we long for? 'Panwang' expect, look forward*

to. Write down the explanation beside the words, in case you forget it later. 'Panwang', the fourth one, means look forward to. For example, what do we 'panwang'?

P1: 过节.
Having festivals.

P2: 圣诞节。
Christmas.

T: 世界杯?
World cup?

P3: No.

P4: 吃月饼。
Eating mooncakes.

T: 我们都盼望吃月饼? Sounds a little strange.
We all long for eating mooncakes?

B: Birthday! My birthday!

T: 我们都盼望着圣诞节。B 盼望着过生日。盼望 can be a little big for all these occasions. 比如说，我们都盼望着祖国统一，对吧? 我们都盼望着祖国 get reunited.
We all long for Christmas. B longs for her birthday. 'Panwang' can be a little big for all these occasions. For example, we all long for our mother country to get reunited, right? We all long for our mother country to get reunited.

L: 盼望中文学校完了。
Long for Chinese school to end.
(All laugh.)

T: L, be serious, OK?

L: I am serious; I'm looking forward to it.

T: 比如说，我们都盼望家人团聚。
For example, we long for family reunion.

T: For example, if you are here in Manchester, your parents are back in China, and you have been separated for years, you are looking forward to the reunion of the family.

It is difficult to speculate about the specific reasons why this teacher wanted the pupils to use the phrase in connection to what seems to be high and lofty ideals whereas the pupils tended to associate the phrase with 'unserious' and personal events. In our interviews with the teachers, several of them expressed the view that some children 'did not take the Chinese school seriously'. They wanted to make the Chinese classes more formal and similar to schools in China, whereas the children took the complementary school as an opportunity to meet and talk with their friends. Some teachers said that they wanted to teach pupils 'proper Chinese' by which they meant standardized, textbook language, which they could use in writing essays on topics such as 'the motherland', 'unity', and 'tradition'. The pupils, on the other hand, appeared to be primarily interested in learning basic expressions for everyday communication and would produce much more interesting and fluent writing on topics such as friends and holidays. These conflictual literacy objectives are a reflection of the social positions the teacher and the pupils occupy in the community, as well as their migration history and personal ideologies. Very similarly, in Example 3, the teacher is making sentences with the phrase 期待 *qidai*, also meaning *longing for*, in collocation with a united motherland, family reunion, peace and friendship, while the pupils are making fun of each other as well as making light of the learning task. B deliberately transliterates his classmate's girlfriend's name, Jennifer, in a funny Chinese phrase literally meaning *real clay Buddha*, and the phrase *moon bathing* is clearly a parody of *sun bathing*.

Example 3. (From a Mandarin class of 13 year-olds in Newcastle. T: Female teacher in her forties. B, a boy.)

> T:　"期待"可以说什么？期待 祖国统一, 期待家人团聚, 期待和平友好。
> *What can you say with qidai (longing for)? Longing for a united motherland; longing for family reunion; longing for peace and friendship.*
> B:　xxx (name of another boy in the class) 期待真泥佛跟他晒月光。
> xxx is longing for Jennifer to go moon bathing with him.
> (All laugh.)

Another example that shows the discrepancy between what the values that the teacher wants to pass on to the pupils and what the pupils are interested in is Example 4 where the teacher makes sentences with the verb 团结 *tuanjie* (unity/unite) by citing examples of propaganda slogans from mainland China, while the pupils use the word in association with football.

Example 4. (T: Female teacher in her early thirties. B1 and B2: 11 year-old boys.)

> T:　团结 (tuanjie)。 团结就是力量，团结起来争取更大胜利。团结 (tuanjie), united.
> *Unity/Unite. Unity is strength. Unite to strive for greater success.*
> B1:　Manchester United.
> B2:　Yeah, United will win.

The teacher, given her age, could not have herself experienced the historical periods when such slogans were widely used – initially during the anti-Japanese wars in the 1940s and later during Mao's Cultural Revolution. She must have picked them up in her own reading. What is rather intriguing is the fact that she felt it appropriate to use such expressions for her teaching. But the most important point here is the sharp contrast between the teacher's use of the expression and the pupils' use, which cannot be further apart.

Shifting power, changing language

Let us now turn to an example which was recorded in a Cantonese school in London. The class consists of twelve 13–14 year-olds. The teacher is from mainland

China. She studied in Guangzhou (Canton) for a number of years and speaks good Cantonese. But she normally speaks Mandarin with her friends, as her native Chinese dialect is different from both Cantonese and Mandarin and she claims that she does not know many people in London who can speak her dialect. She is also a fluent speaker of English and is completing her postgraduate degree in education in a London college. She has set the class a task of writing a 100-character story in Chinese which must contain some dialogues. The pupils are working on their own but occasionally ask each other for help. Unlike some other teachers in Chinese complementary schools who seem to prefer the pupils doing their work silently and independently, this teacher does not mind the pupils talking in class and encourages them to solve any problems amongst themselves. The pupils sit around tables in groups of threes and fours.

Example 5

	B1:	How do you say 唔該 (m guai)?
	G1:	唔該啦 (m guai la).
	B1:	No, how do you write it?
	G1:	You can't.
5	B2:	writes down 五塊 (m faai, meaning *five dollars*)
		Laugh.
	G1:	That's five dollars (.) money.
	B2:	Yes.
	G1:	Yes.
10	T:	What's going on?
	B1:	唔該生 (*m guai sang*), how do you write 唔該 (*m guai*)?
		Excuse me, teacher.
		Laugh.
	B2:	唔該生唔該 (m guai sang m guai).
15		*Excuse me teacher excuse me*
	T:	You can't.
	B1:	What do you mean you can't?
	T:	冇啦 (mou la). 对不住 (dui m jiu).
		There isn't. Excuse me/Sorry.
20		Teacher writes down 对不住 and pronounces it *dui m jiu*.
	G2:	But is it the same?
	T:	係啦 (hai la). It's more formal.
		Yes.
	B1:	So you say 唔該 (m guai) and write this (pointing at the characters the teacher has written).
25	T:	Yes.
		Silence. Pupils looking confused.
	T:	When do you want to say it?
	B1:	What do you mean?
	T:	I mean you say it differently for different things.

30 Silence.

G1:   Oh so you can say 唔該 (m guai) when you want to call somebody, and 对不住 (dui mu jiu) when you are sorry.

T: No you don't say it. You write it.

Silence.

G2:   好难啊 (ho nan a).
       So hard.

35 T: I mean you write 請問 (cheng man) if you want to ask a question.
       Or 对不住 (dui mu jiu) if you want to say Sorry or Excuse me.

G1:   What about 唔該 (m guai)?

B1:   You don't write 唔該 (m guai).

Puzzled.

40 T: It's Cantonese.

G1:   So you don't write Cantonese.

T: That's right.

B2:   Cool.

B1:   Crap.

45 All laugh.

Teacher says B1's name.

G1:   Do we have to write Mandarin for everything then?

T: OK. Five minutes, OK?

The extract begins with one of the boys, B1, asking the girl sitting next to him, G1, how to write the characters for the Cantonese phrase for *Excuse me* which he wants to use to construct a dialogue in his story. He mistakenly asks "how do you say" rather than "how do you write". He evidently knows how to say the phrase in Cantonese. So G1 responds by repeating the phrase B1 has said himself. B1 corrects himself and asks G1 how to write the characters. G1 says "You can't." The Cantonese phrase, *m guai*, is a colloquial expression that is rarely written. Regional varieties of Chinese, of which Cantonese is a major one, have many unique words and phrases that usually exist in spoken form only. Sometimes people invent written characters for such words and phrases or use characters that have similar pronunciations to approximate them. Cantonese is amongst the few regional varieties of Chinese that have an elaborate set of written characters for the dialectal expressions. But this kind of advanced knowledge of register differences is rarely taught in heritage language learning context. G1, however, does seem to be aware of the fact that *m guai* is a colloquial Cantonese expression that does not normally get written. Another boy, B2, joins in the discussion by writing down two characters that have a very similar pronunciation as the phrase *m guai*. But the words he has written mean 'five dollars'.

It is at this point that the teacher comes over to the table and asks what is happening. B1 puts the question to the teacher. The question contains the very phrase, *m guai* or Excuse me, that he is asking for help with. The other pupils laugh because the way B1 constructs the question, with *m guai* used twice, sounds funny. The teacher's answer is exactly the same as G1's in her previous reply. B1 asks the teacher to clarify. The teacher uses an equally colloquial Cantonese expression in her elliptic reply, *mou la*, literally "have no", meaning there is no written form for *m guai*. She then gives another Chinese expression for Excuse me, 对不住. 对不住 is more formal and exists in Mandarin, thus has a written form that is commonly used. She writes it out in Mandarin and pronounces it in Cantonese, *dui m jiu*. The negation morpheme in the middle in Cantonese should be 唔 rather than the Mandarin 不. Another girl at the same table, G2, questions the teacher whether the two phrases are the same. The teacher says yes and explains that *dui m jiu* is more formal. In fact, the two phrases are not the same in terms of meaning and usage. *Dui m jiu* is more apologetic, whereas *m guai* has no such connotation. B1 tries to clarify the usage with the teacher in Line 24. But all the pupils look rather confused. The teacher then asks exactly what the pupils want to express, and explains that different phrases are used in different contexts. After a short pause, G1 offers her explanation and seeks the teacher's confirmation. But the teacher's response "*you don't say it. You write it.*" confuses them even more. G2 moans "*So hard*". The teacher offers further explanation of the usage of different expressions, introducing a new phrase 請問 (*cheng man*, or "please can I ask"). The real question the pupils have always had is how to write, and use, *m guai*. So G1 asks again. This time B1, who asked the question originally, offers his understanding that you just do not write the phrase *m guai* at all. The discussion then changes its focus when the teacher says, following B1's turn, that *m guai* cannot be written because it is a Cantonese phrase. G1's utterance "*So you don't write Cantonese.*" can be seen as a challenge to the teacher's explanation. The pronoun she uses "you" could mean either everyone or the teacher herself specifically. The two boys react seemingly differently; B2 probably feels that at last he understands the difference in usage, while B1 thinks that it is bad that one cannot write Cantonese. But it is B1's reaction and his rejection of B2's apparent acceptance of the teacher's explanation that gets the laugh from the others. G1 further challenges the teacher by asking if everything has to be written in Mandarin. The teacher puts a stop to the discussion by turning to the whole class and gives a five minutes warning to finish the task.

Two issues emerge from this example that interest us in particular. First, we can see that translanguaging is commonplace amongst the pupils and the teacher. They move seemingly freely between languages and between speaking and writing. They are genuinely engaged in learning and problem solving, and using translanguaging as a resource to facilitate that process. The teacher's struggle with the competing spoken and written forms and her production of a hybrid between Mandarin orthography and Cantonese expression is an example of the complex translanguaging they are engaged in. Second, and perhaps more important, is the gradual realization by the children of the status differential between different varieties of Chinese through the exchange. What started as an apparently simple question about writing two characters has turned into a discussion of the legitimacy of the language they speak and thereupon their linguistic and ethnic identity. As mentioned before, all Cantonese schools in Britain nowadays offer Mandarin classes, to both children and their parents, whereas no Mandarin school teaches Cantonese. Mandarin is being actively promoted in the Chinese community in Britain as a new Chinese lingua franca to connect with mainland China and is fast gaining currency, at least in formal settings. Official visits by the Chinese embassy staff to the local Chinese community organisations are always conducted in Mandarin, and cultural events such as Chinese New Year celebrations are increasingly done in Mandarin, as well. Mandarin has also replaced Cantonese in much of the satellite television and other entertainment media in Europe. Many Cantonese speaking parents realise the pragmatic potential of Mandarin and encourage their children to learn it at the Chinese school. Yet, enthusiasm for Mandarin is by no means universal in the Chinese diaspora. There are groups who feel a strong affinity to Cantonese and nostalgia for Hong Kong. They see the spread of Mandarin as another example of the increasing power and influence of mainland China. Even among people who are not directly linked to Hong Kong, there are those who see the spread of Mandarin as a threat to Cantonese cultural heritage. Of course, the fact that many colloquial Cantonese words and phrases have no written form has nothing to do with the changing hierarchy and socio-political values amongst the different varieties of the Chinese language, and Cantonese is certainly not the only regional variety of Chinese that lacks written form for its special expressions. Nevertheless, when the community one belongs to is already undergoing dramatic changes, a realisation that one's native tongue cannot be written must add to their feeling "crap". This realization is an outcome of socializational teaching where the teacher hints at the shifting power relations between Mandarin and Cantonese while responding to the challenges of the different orthographic and spoken forms.

Pedagogical tensions

Elsewhere we have discussed the tensions between the traditional way of teaching and what is appropriate for the British Chinese pupils in the complementary schools. Similar to Example 5, Example 6 below is taken from a recording of a

Mandarin session in a Cantonese school in Manchester. The majority of children in the school are Cantonese-English bilinguals. But since 2001, Mandarin is also offered to all children. In this example, the teacher has asked the class to make sentences with the Chinese adverb 就 (*jiu*). This is a particularly complex word, as it has several meanings, including *at once, as early as, just about, really, simply, exactly*, etc. and can be used with various functions. G1 responded to the teacher and made a sentence with the target word. The teacher asked the class whether or not G1 got the sentence right. This is a typical teaching method in Chinese classrooms where the teacher asks the pupils to point out each other's mistakes and correct them collectively. In written examinations, 'correcting mistakes' is often used as a method of assessing the learner's linguistic knowledge. However, as we can see in the example, the pupils think that this kind of pedagogical activity is picking on people, not just the language errors. There seems to be two kinds of cultural expectations and practices at work here.

Example 6. (G1: girl of 11 years old ; T: female teacher in her thirties; B1 and B2: boys about 11; in the Manchester Chinese school)

G1: 他就想睡觉 (*ta jiu xiang shuijiao*)。
    He really/just wants to sleep.

T: Good. Is there any mistake in what she said?

..... (no response from pupils)

T: (To B1) XXX, what do you think?

B1: *M ji la?*
    NEG. know PART.
    Don't know.

T: (To B2) XX, 你呢 (*ni ne*)?
            You PART.
            How about you?

B2: 我也 (*wo ye*) *mu ji.*
    I also
    I also don't know/(am) a hen.

All laughed loudly.

T: Stop it. 安静 (*anjing*)。 Be quiet.
        Silence.

B1: Can we do something else?

T: 先说完了这个 (*xian shuo wanle zheige*)。
    Let's finish talking about this first.

B2: Why 总要挑人家错啊 (*zongyao tiao renjia cuo a*)?
        always pick other people mistake PART.
        Why do we always pick on other's mistakes?

When the class did not respond to her initial question, the teacher specified B1 and asked him to say whether he thought G1 had produced a correct sentence with the target word. B1 responded in Cantonese as he is a Cantonese L1 speaker and he knew that the teacher also understood Cantonese. His response consists of a typical Cantonese negation marker *m*, a verb *ji* (know), and an utterance particle *la*. We have spelt these out in Roman letters as the pronunciation here is a crucial factor. When the teacher turned to B2 and asked for his opinion, B2 made a pun by simply adding a vowel to the Cantonese negation maker. However, *mu* in Mandarin means *female*, and *ji* in Mandarin means *chicken*. By changing the pronunciation from *m ji* to *mu ji*, B2 made the phrase into *I am also a hen*. Cantonese-Mandarin bilinguals would understand the pun easily, and the whole class laughed. G2 thus gained some authority, or at least popularity, in the classroom context. When the teacher tried to stop him making fun of the activity, both boys, B1 and B2, protested and asked the teacher to change the activity to something different. B2's direct question to the teacher challenges the pedagogical practice.

There is another even subtler, but perhaps more important, point of the two boys' responses to the teacher in this example. Let us remind ourselves that this is a Mandarin session to a group of children most of whom are Cantonese-English bilinguals. They are learning Mandarin as an additional language. Earlier we mentioned the increasing presence of Mandarin in the British Chinese community. Many Cantonese speakers see the spread of Mandarin as another example of the increasing power and influence of the Chinese government in Beijing. What we do not know is how the British-born generations of Chinese children and young people feel about the elevated status of Mandarin vis-à-vis Cantonese. Whilst we cannot be absolutely sure why B1 chose to respond to the teacher in the present example in Cantonese, his choice of language, and B2's making fun of it, certainly had the effect of undermining the purpose of the class which is to teach Mandarin. When we presented the case to the head-teacher of the school and asked if she thought the pupils were resisting Mandarin, she gave a very interesting answer. She told us that when the school first decided to teach Mandarin to the children on a voluntary basis in an extended period following the normal standard hours for Cantonese, i.e. the children could decide for themselves whether they wanted to stay for an extra hour for Mandarin, the take-up rate was very low, around 20 percent. So the school decided to incorporate Mandarin in the main teaching hours and made it compulsory to all. The head-teacher claimed that it had been a success, and the UK Association for the Promotion of Chinese Education, which is the main national advocate for Mandarin teaching, has held the school as an example of excellence in promoting Mandarin. The examples we have seen here in the pupils' actual responses in the classroom may show a different side of the story. The children may not be all that pleased with the imposition of Mandarin on them. Whether this is simply a concern of learning load or more of an ideological issue, one cannot be sure.

One may take this kind of resistance on behalf of the pupils as failure of the teachers' socializational teaching. However, the prerequisite of any resistance is awareness of the power relations and differentials. That awareness is developed by the teachers' socializational teaching. The pupils are not passive recipients of the socializational attempts. Once they realize what is going on and understand what the teaching is trying to explain to them, or at least hint at, they will decide their responses in their own way, as the examples show.

Socializational teaching and identity negotiation

Questions must be asked as to what impact the kind of socializational teaching which we see in the above examples have on the development of the pupils' identity. The examples show that the pupils in the Chinese complementary schools often resist the teachers' socializational teaching by posing challenging questions or making fun of the classroom activities (see also Li Wei & Wu 2009). Many of them associate China with food, music and everyday culture. While most of them are aware of certain aspects of the Chinese history, some of the old folk tales and archaeological artefacts, their primary interests in things Chinese are Chinese pop songs, comics and youth magazines and various card and computer games. Yet, little of what the young British Chinese seem to be interested in is reflected in the teaching in the Chinese complementary schools. For the schools and the teachers, and many of the parents for that matter, on the other hand, the emphasis seems to be on a set of traditional values and practices, many of which are imagined rather than real. They also tend to think of the children as primarily Chinese and they want them to be very much similar to those in China. The children, on the other hand, think of themselves primarily as British youths of Chinese heritage. The issue of identity is sometimes discussed explicitly in the Chinese complementary school classrooms, as the final example illustrates.

Example 7. (From the Mandarin school in London. T: Female teacher in her early thirties. G1 and G2 are girls and B1 and B2 boys, all between 11 and 12 years old.)

 T: 我们中国人。
   We are Chinese.
 B1: 我们不是中国人。
   We are not Chinese.
 T: 你不是中国人是什么人?
   You are not Chinese, what are you?
 B2: 英国人。
   British.
 G1: 英国华侨。

British Chinese.

T: OK.

G2:   海外华人。
      Overseas Chinese.

G1:   是华人还是华侨。
      Should it be huaren (*ethnic Chinese*) *or* huaqiao (*Chinese citizens residing outside China*).

T: 严格地说，应该是华人。
      Strictly speaking, it should be huaren (*ethnic Chinese*).

B1:   华人。
      Huaren (*ethnic Chinese*).

T: 对。你们是海外华人。
      Correct. You are overseas Chinese.

G1:   英国华人。
      British Chinese.

T: 也可以。
      Also correct.

B1:   那你呢？
      Then what are you?

T: 我？我是中国人。
      Me? I am Chinese.

B1:   So you don't have a British passport.

T: No.

B2:   Isn't your husband British?

T: Yes, I have permanent residence.

B1:   So you are not British.

T: 我可以说是华侨。
      I can say that I am huaqiao ((*Chinese citizen residing outside China*)).

B2:   British Chinese.

T: No. I am a Chinese living in Britain. You are British Chinese.

B1:   Or Chinese British.

B2:   Like they call it Chinese American or American Chinese.

B1:   ABC (American-born Chinese).

T: You are BBC (British-born Chinese).

Here, the Chinese phrase 中国人 (zhongguo ren) is linguistically ambiguous as it can refer to the general ethnic category or Chinese citizens or nationals. What the pupils object to is to be described as Chinese citizens or nationals. But the two terms often used to describe Chinese people living outside China are also confusing. 华人 (huaren) means persons of Chinese ethnic origin, and 华侨 (huaqiao) means Chinese citizens who are living outside China. However, when the English term Overseas Chinese is used, it often includes both groups of people. Many of the governmental and non-governmental organizations for overseas Chinese affairs do not make a clear distinction between the two groups and they are both invited to events in the Chinese embassy, for instance, Chinese National Day celebrations and Chinese New Year receptions. Remarkably, the pupils in the present example seem to be interested in the fine technical details and one of them asks the teacher directly what she is. The teacher first gives a cliché reply that she is Chinese. After the pupils' challenges, she has to reflect on it and gives a more precise answer. The pupils also begin to reflect on who they are. What starts as a technical discussion of some terminological issues has led to a meaningful discussion and enhanced awareness of their identities.

Summary and conclusion

The examples we have seen in this paper illustrate a number of dimensions of language and literacy teaching in the Chinese complementary schools context. What we have chosen to focus on here is its socializational dimension. The teachers and pupils alike seem to hold a belief that an ability to read and write Chinese characters is also an integral part of being Chinese. This complex association between language, especially literacy, and Chinese identity may have prompted the teachers to embed the teaching of language in cultural socialization. In addition to the focus on standard forms, especially standard written forms, the teachers incorporate a significant amount of cultural knowledge in the teaching, either through their choice of examples or through the use of historical stories and facts. In unpacking what we call "socializational teaching" of language and literacy, i.e. impressing socio-cultural traditions and values on pupils through what seems to be mundane pedagogical activities, in the Chinese complementary schools context, we hope to have demonstrated the competing notions of "culture" and "heritage" between the schools and the teachers on the one hand and the British Chinese children on the other.

In the meantime, we have seen that the pupils can and do resist this kind of socializational teaching by posing challenging questions to the teachers and making fun of the classroom activities. For them, China is a fast changing nation and an increasing world power, and not something that exists in the past, in old folk tales, archeological artifacts or textbooks. On an everyday basis, we see the pupils listening to Chinese pop songs, reading Chinese comics and youth magazines and playing various card and computer games. Many of these activities require an ability to read Chinese characters. Yet, none of what the young British Chinese seem to be interested in is reflected in the teaching in the Chinese complementary schools. For the schools, the teachers and the parents, the emphasis seems to be on a rather static notion of Chinese cultural heritage that lasted a very long time in history and exists in print, whereas the pupils think of themselves primarily as British youths of Chinese heritage. While accepting language and literacy as being an important part of being Chinese, they reject the simplistic association of Chinese culture with only the past. Whilst one may assume that these pupils' resistance is a natural part of adolescent behavior, the complementary schools provide a 'safe space' for them to contest outdated and backward looking pedagogical practices and challenge monolingual and unicultural ideologies (see Martin et al. 2006 on the notion of 'safe space').

Chinese complementary schools as a world-wide socio-educational institution have played a major role in the lives of thousands of Chinese diasporic families (see also Zhu 2008). Yet there has been rather little critical reflection on the policies and practices in the Chinese schools (cf. Curdt-Christiansen 2006, 2008; He & Xiao 2008). The Chinese complementary schools are an important site of multilingualism where different language ideologies, beliefs and practices are competing with each other. There is little doubt that through this competition a new set of diasporic cultural identities will emerge, which will have a long lasting impact on the Chinese diasporic communities and the individuals of different generations. It is hoped that the discussion of the examples in this chapter both contributes to the exploration of the multiple dimensions of this particular site of multilingualism and opens up further debates over the interculturality of diasporic communities.

Acknowledgements

We gratefully acknowledge the support of the Economic and Social Research Council of Great Britain for the project "Investigating multilingualism in complementary schools in four communities" (ESRC, RES-000-23-1180) from which this chapter draws some of its examples. Chao-Jung Wu was the Research Associate on the project and collected the data from the Manchester Chinese schools. The final version of the chapter benefited from the most constructive comments by two anonymous reviewers and the two editors of this volume.

References

Blackledge, A. & Creese, A. 2010. *Multilingualism: A critical perspective*. London: Continuum.
Creese, A. Bhatt, A., Bhojani, N. & Martin, P. 2006. Multicultural, heritage and learner identities in complementary schools. *Language and Education 20*(1): 23–43.
Curdt-Christiansen, X.L. 2006. Teaching and learning Chinese: Heritage language classroom discourse in Montreal. *Language, Culture and Curriculum 29*(2): 189–207.

Curdt-Christiansen, X.L. 2008. Reading the world through words: Cultural themes in heritage Chinese language textbooks. *Language and Education* 22(2): 95–113.

Duff, P.A. 1996. Different languages, different practices: Socialization of discourse competence in dual-language school classrooms in Hungary. In *Voices from the classroom: Qualitative research in second language education*, K.M. Bailey & D. Nunan (eds), 407–433. Cambridge: CUP.

Duranti, A. Ochs, E. & Schieffelin, B. (eds). 2011. *Handbook of Language Socialization*. Oxford: Wiley-Blackwell.

Harklau, L. 2003. Representational practices and multi-modal communication in US high schools: Implications for adolescent immigrants. In *Language socialization in bilingual and multilingual societies*, R. Bayley & S.R. Schecter (eds), 83–97. Clevedon: Multilingual Matters.

He, A.W. 2010. The heart of heritage: Sociocultural dimensions of heritage language learning. *Annual Review of Applied Linguistics* 30: 66–82.

He, Agnes & Xiao, Y. (eds). 2008. *Chinese as a Heritage Language: Fostering Rooted World Citizenry*. Honolulu HI: National Foreign Language Resource Centre and University of Hawai'I Press.

Kramsch, C. 1996. Stylistic choice and cultural awareness. In *Challenges of Literary Texts in the Foreign Language Classroom*, L. Bredella & W. Delanoy (eds), 162–184. Tübingen: Gunter Narr.

Li, Wei. 2006. Complementary schools: Past, present and future. *Language and Education* 20(1): 76–83.

Li, Wei. 2007. Chinese. In *Language of the British Isles*, D. Britain (ed.), 308–25. Cambridge: CUP.

Li, Wei. 2011. Multilinguality, multimodality and multicompetence: Code- and mode-switching by minority ethnic children in complementary schools. *Modern Language Journal* 95(3): 370–384.

Li, Wei & Wu, Chao-Jung, 2009. Polite Chinese children revisited: creativity and the use of codeswitching in the Chinese complementary school classroom. *International Journal of Bilingual Education and Bilingualism* 12(2): 193–211.

Li, Wei & Zhu, Hua. 2010. Changing hierarchies in Chinese language education for the British Chinese learners. In *Teaching and Learning Chinese in Global Contexts Multimodality and Literacy in the New Media Age*, L. Tsung & K. Cruichshank (eds), 11–27. London: Continuum.

Martin, P.W., Bhatt, A., Bhojani, N. & Creese, A. 2006. Managing bilingual interaction in a Gujarati complementary school in Leicester. *Language and Education* 20(1): 5–22.

Ochs, E. 2002. Becoming a speaker of culture. In *Language Acquisition and Language Socialization: Ecological Perspectives*, C.J. Kramsch (ed.), 99–120. London: Continuum.

Rymes, B. 2001. *Conversational Borderlands: Language and Identity in an Alternative Urban High School*. New York NY: Teachers College Press.

Zhu, Hua. 2008. Duelling languages, duelling values: Codeswitching in bilingual intergenerational conflict talk in diasporic families. *Journal of Pragmatics* 40: 1799–1816.

PART III

Bilingual Chinese educational models

CHAPTER 7

Chinese education in Malaysia

Past and present*

Wang Xiaomei
University of Malaya

This chapter reviews the evolution of Chinese education in Malaysia in the past 190 years. For each phase of the development, the medium of instruction, syllabus, curriculum allotment, and learning objectives are discussed against the sociopolitical background during that period. It starts with the introduction of old-style *Sishu* prior to the 20th century, followed by a description of new-style schools in early 20th century. Subsequently, the process of localization of Chinese education in the 1950s is highlighted as the third stage of evolution. In the 1960s and 1970s, the conversion of medium of instruction has a great impact on the development of Malaysian Chinese education. After the revival movement in the 1970s, Chinese education enters a new stage with the implementation of KBSR curriculum in the 1980s. The sixth section discusses the development of Chinese education in the 1990s when English was to be promoted by the government in response to the global economy and Vision 2020 in Malaysia. This chapter gives a focus on the present situation of Malaysian Chinese education in different types of schools. The last section summarizes the achievements of Malaysian Chinese education and points out some issues in relation to Chinese teaching in Malaysia.

Introduction

The Chinese are the second largest ethnic group in Malaysia, representing 24.6% (6.39 million) of the total population according to Census 2010 (Department of Statistics, Malaysia 2010). This demographic advantage makes the Chinese community visible in national, political, economic, and social scenarios. Chinese

* This research is part of the project "The Chinese in Malaysia: Evolving Identity in a Globalizing Environment and in Nation Building" which is funded by the HIR grant from the Ministry of Education, Malaysia (UM.C/625/1/HIR-MOHE/ASH/04).

Malaysians are unique in many perspectives: (1) most of them still speak Chinese in their daily life, either Mandarin or one of the Chinese language varieties; (2) 90% of Chinese parents send their children to Chinese primary schools (Lee 2011); (3) the Chinese community has been supporting 60 Chinese Independent Schools (*Duzhong*) on their own since 1961 (Kua 1985); and (4) traditional cultural practices like the lion dance and ancestor worship are still maintained in the Chinese community (Lim 1999). As a significant minority group in a multicultural country, the development of the Chinese community has always been affected by the national sociopolitical policy. As education is a crucial issue for the community, any changes in the national education policy could cause direct and fierce reaction from the Chinese community, as did the recent Teaching Mathematics and Science in English policy. This chapter reviews briefly the development of Chinese education in Malaysia from a sociolinguistic/historical perspective. For each phase of the development, the medium of instruction, syllabus, curriculum allotment, and learning objectives are discussed against the sociopolitical background during that period. Special attention is given to the current model of Chinese education in Malaysia. The problems in the present syllabus and curriculum are addressed in the concluding chapter.

The development of Chinese education in Malaysia has always been influenced by political and economic issues in this multi-ethnic country. Since the independence from the colonial government, the political climate has moved Chinese education from private affairs into the national educational system and changed it from being a non-political independent educational entity into socioeconomic beneficial higher education. Therefore, scholars in this field tend to divide the historical phases of Chinese education according to its sociopolitical context. Wang and Xu (1985) proposed a five-phase division: (1) 1786–1920, Chinese education managed by the Chinese community when the old-style *Sishu* conducted classes in various Chinese dialects; (2) 1920–1942, Chinese education governed by the colonial government when new-style schools were established and employed Mandarin as the medium of instruction; (3) 1945–1957, pre-independence period when Chinese schools started to localize their textbooks; (4) 1958–1970, transformation of Chinese secondary schools to English-medium schools as the first step to unify the education system; and (5) 1971–1985, transformation of English schools into Malay-medium schools under the National Ideology and New Economic Policy and adoption of simplified Chinese characters and Hanyu pinyin in the new curriculum (Kurikulum Baru Sekolah Rendah, KBSR).

To contextualize the political development, two more phases are added after 1985: (6) Chinese education after the 1990s when globalization had a great impact on Malaysia and the role of science and technology was emphasized for the development of national economy; (7) current situation of Chinese education in Malaysia. In this chapter, I discuss Chinese education from the linguistic and teaching perspective, focusing on the medium of instruction, curriculum structure, teaching hours, and textbooks. While doing so, we will also take the political environment into consideration.

Chinese education in dialects and old-style *Sishu* before the 20th Century

Chinese migrants began to set up *Sishu*, the old style Chinese school, after they settled on this land. In their beliefs, education was always the priority no matter how hard life was. Malacca was reported to have three Chinese schools in 1815 and *Wufu shuyuan* in Penang was identified as the first Chinese school there in 1819 (Tan 1997). As the Chinese community at that time was segmented along the lines of dialect groups, these schools were established by various clans or dialect associations. For instance, the *Sin Kang* and *Eng Chuan* Schools in Penang were set up by the *Khoo* clan and the *Tan* clan; the *Aik Hwa School* was founded by the Hainanese; the *Han Chiang School* was started by the Teochews; the *Sum Sun School* was established by the Hock Chew group (Tan 1997). Based on the dialect of the founders of the schools, various dialects such as Hokkien, Cantonese and Hakka were used as medium of instruction in these schools. This situation remained unchanged until the introduction of *Guoyu* (Mandarin) in the beginning of the twentieth century. By 1884, there were 52 Chinese schools in Penang, 12 in Malacca, and 51 in Singapore (Tay 1998).

The early Chinese schools were left alone by the British colonial government. In general, the curriculum was imported directly from China based on a monolingual model. Classical texts were taught, such as *Qianziwen* (千字文 *The Thousand-Character Writing*), *Sanzijing* (三字经 *Three-Character Classic*), *Baijiaxing* (百家姓 *Book of Family Names*), *Sishu* (四书 *Four Books*), and *Wujing* (五经 *Five Classics*) (Tan 1997). It was believed that students could learn Chinese values and culture through these classical texts. The syllabus of *Nan Hua Free School* showed that *Xiaojing* (孝经 *Filial Classic*) and *Sishu* (四书 *Four Books*) were the main textbooks. Calligraphy and character practicing as well as memorization of the classics were the main focuses of these earlier Chinese schools (Tay 1998). *Anglo-Chinese Free School* was the only school that offered English as a subject. It was the first Chinese school to provide bilingual education (Tay 1998).

Chinese education in Mandarin and the new-style schools in early 20th Century

In late nineteenth century and early twentieth century, the old-style schools were slowly replaced by modern new-style schools in both China and Malaysia as a response to the social and cultural movements in China during that period and as a result of introduction of Western culture and civilization.

The first new-style Chinese school in Malaysia was *Chung Hwa School*, set up by *Chang Chin-Hsuh* in Penang in 1904 (Tan 2000, p. 231). In the new-style schools, the curriculum was aligned with what was taught in China. One of the salient characteristics was the teaching of *Guoyu* (国语-national language; Mandarin was established as *Guoyu*) and *Guowen* (国文-national written language). Table 7.1 shows the curriculum of *Chung Hwa School* which in 1904 (Tay 1998, p. 101).

Table 7.1 Curriculum of *Chung Hwa School*

Subjects	Content	Hours per week
Moral (*Xiushen*)	Moral textbook	2
Reading classics (*Du jing*)	*Zuozhuan* (*The Zuo Commentary*)	6
Interpreting classics (*Jiang jing*)		4
Chinese (*Guowen*)	Composition	2
	Comprehension	4
Foreign language	English	6
History	History textbook	3
Geography	Including teach map-drawing, borders	2
Mathematics	If algebra is taught, an extra class is needed.	4
Physics	Physics textbook	1
Physical Education	Mandarin Chinese (*Guoyu*)	2

It can be seen from the curriculum table that the new-style schools incorporated many new subjects, such as English, history, geography, and mathematics. Regarding teaching hours, Chinese classics (10 hours/week) and *Guowen* (6 hours/week) were allocated the most teaching hours among the various subjects. Even physical education was used to teach *Guoyu*. *Chung Hwa School* was one of the first schools in Malaysia that offered English as a subject.

According to Ser (2010), there were three types of new-style schools: (1) new schools, (2) schools transformed from old-style free schools (*Gongxue* 公学), based on a specific dialect group, (3) and schools merged from several dialectal schools. All these schools adopted Mandarin as the medium of instruction. However, dialects were still used in some schools, especially in type (2) schools. *Hou Hongjian* (1919, p. 32) recorded in his *Travel in Nanyang* (南洋旅行记) that *Yu Cai School* in Penang in 1919 used Hokkien as the medium of instruction for grades 1 and 2 and Mandarin for grades 3 and 4. This shows that both Mandarin and dialects were used at the beginning stage of the new-style schools, since the lingua franca at that time was Chinese dialects rather than Mandarin.

Localization of Chinese education in the 1950s

There were great social and political changes prior to the independence in 1957. Several political parties were founded, including the Communist Party of Malaya (CPM) and Malaysian Chinese Association (MCA). Together with the founding of the People's Republic of China in 1949, these political establishments had tremendous influence on safeguarding the welfare of the Chinese community in Malaya. During this period, the United Chinese School Teachers Association of Malaysia (UCSTAM, *Jiaozong*) and the United Chinese School Committees Association of Malaysia (UCSCAM, *Dongzong*) were established to improve Chinese education, promote Chinese culture, and strive for teachers' welfare (Tay 2001). In 1956 Nanyang University in Singapore, the first Chinese university in Southeast Asia, admitted the first batch of students. All these events had great impact on the development of Chinese education, which eventually led to the localization of Chinese education with the following characteristics:

1. Teaching Malay in grade 4 and above in Chinese schools. This policy was implemented in the second term of the 1950 academic year (Tay 2001). This means that since 1950, Chinese schools have offered three languages in their curriculum, viz. Chinese, English, and Malay. Thus, Chinese education adopted a trilingual model, which has been maintained until today.
2. Localization of textbooks. Starting in 1952, all syllabi in Chinese schools were reviewed to reflect more local life and culture. The new syllabi covered more content in relation to the Malaysian context. Since then the syllabus in Chinese schools abandoned a China-orientation and adopted a localized content.

At this stage, both English and Malay were official languages while Chinese and Tamil did not have any official status. As a result, Chinese schools received little attention. After the national election in 1955, however, the Razak Report was passed (in 1956), for the first time incorporating Chinese schools into the national education system (Kua 1985). In this report, primary schools were classified into two categories: (1) standard primary schools which used Malay as the medium of instruction, and (2) standard-type primary schools which used Chinese, Tamil, or English as the medium of instruction. From then on, Chinese primary schools were able to receive subsidies from the government. In 1957, the total number of Chinese schools increased to 1333 with a student population of 342,194 (Tay 2001). The Razak Report played a very important role in the development of Chinese education. The status of Chinese primary schools was established and has remained unchanged until today. The acknowledgement of Chinese schools and Tamil schools in the national education system consolidated the new reign at that time and retained the linguistic and cultural diversity in this country.

The evolution of Chinese schools in the 1960s and 1970s

After the independence of Malaya, an Education Review Committee was formed led by the Minister of Education, Abdul Rahman bin Haji Talib, in 1960 (Ye 2002). In the following year, the Rahman Talib Report was published and adopted by the Parliament as Education Act. This Education Act redefined two types of national primary schools: (1) national schools with Malay as the medium of instruction, and (2) national-type schools with Chinese, Tamil or English as the medium of instruction (Kua 1985).

The new Education Act also ended financial support to Chinese secondary schools. In other words, governmental subsidies were only for schools which used Malay or English, the official languages, as the medium of instruction. But in 1967, a new law, the National Language Act, was passed by the Parliament, stating that Malay was the national language and the only official language in peninsular Malaysia (Asmah 1982). English was no longer one of the official languages in West Malaysia. In Sarawak, East Malaysia, the official status of English was retained until 1985 (Asmah 1996).

During this period, racial politics became prominent. In 1969, a racial riot broke out leading the government to endorse the National Ideology. A New Economic Policy (NEP) was issued in 1970 aiming to upgrade the economic status of the Malay community (Ye 2002). Under NEP, the aim of national education was to employ Malay as the medium of instruction in all schools. As a result, all English-medium primary schools were converted to Malay-medium schools by the end of 1975 and all English secondary schools by the end of 1982 (Ye 2002). This political decision, according to Asmah (1982), was crucial for nation building because "a national ideology that aims for a just society which provides equal opportunity for everybody cannot hope to succeed in education if the national language is allowed to have competition from education in other languages" (Asmah 1982, p. 28).

Influenced by this national ideology and without government financial support, 55 secondary schools were converted from Chinese-medium to English-medium schools while 16 Chinese secondary schools remained unchanged (Tay 2003). These schools were called Chinese Independent Schools (*Duzhong*). They recruited students from Chinese primary schools and continued to use Mandarin as the medium of instruction for the various subjects. From then on, these independent schools had to regularly raise funds among Chinese communities in order to maintain school facilities and buildings. Despite radical resistance from the Chinese community, most Chinese secondary schools changed their medium of instruction from Chinese to English. In these schools, Chinese was taught as a subject but not allocated one third of total teaching hours as promised by the government. There are today 78 such national-type secondary schools (Skolah Menengah Jenis Kebangsaan SMJK) in Malaysia.

The conversion of Chinese secondary schools in the 1960s brought Chinese education into a dark period. In order to save Chinese education from further decline, UCSTAM (*Jiaozong*) started a movement from 1965 to 1967, demanding official status for the Chinese language. Although the objective of this movement was not achieved, it made the general public aware of their language rights and the importance of the Chinese language.

After the closure of the English schools, those Chinese secondary schools which converted to English schools in the 1960s had to convert again, now to Malay schools. Because of this, Chinese primary schools gained more popularity among the Chinese communities and this gave the Chinese secondary schools (*Duzhong*) a chance of revival. After the announcement of NEP, the Chinese community realized that they had to rely on themselves in all regards, whether economy or culture. Being aware of the ultimate goal of the government, a revival movement for Chinese Independent Schools was started in Perak in 1972 and in the following years spread all over the country (Kua 1985). This movement brought the number of *Duzhong* to 60 in Malaysia. The other outcome of this movement was the launch of the Unified Examination for Chinese Independent Schools by *Dongzong* in December 1975, which symbolized that a Chinese education system from primary school to secondary school had been accomplished (Tay 2003).

During the eventful 1960s and 1970s, Chinese primary schools remained in the national education system without much education regulation. A detailed description of the Chinese school syllabus in Alor Janggus, Kedah in 1965 was recorded by Maeda (1967) (see Table 7.2).

The national-type Chinese primary school used Mandarin as the medium of instruction. As shown in the table, the syllabus emphasised the teaching of Chinese which was divided into three parts: Chinese language, composition, and

Table 7.2 Syllabus of Boon Hwa National-type Chinese School in 1965 (periods* per week)

Subjects	Grade 1 & 2	Grade 3	Grade 4	Grade 5 & 6	Total
Chinese language	9	13	12	11	65
Practical composition	1	1	1	1	6
Chinese composition	–	–	2	2	6
Poetry	1	2	–	–	4
Mathematics	9	6	7	7	45
Calculation on the abacus	–	–	1	1	3
Ethics	–	2	2	2	8
History	1	–	3	3	11
Geography	–	3	4	3	13
Natural science	3	2	1	2	13
Hygiene	2	2	2	2	12
Art	7	3	–	3	23
Handicraft	–	–	3	–	3
Music	3	1	1	1	10
Physical education	4	2	2	2	16
Malay	4	5	5	7	32
English	–	6	6	7	26
Total	88	48	52	108	296

(*Note: 30 minutes per period)

poetry. The teaching allotment for Chinese varied from 11 periods (330 minutes) to 16 periods (480 minutes) per week. The teaching of Malay started from Grade 1, while English started from Grade 3 occupying longer teaching hours than Malay. Malay and English were almost equally important in this model, which reflected the sociolinguistic situation at that time. All the other subjects were taught in Mandarin. The students were also required to speak Mandarin on the school grounds although Hokkien was the dominant dialect outside of school (Maeda 1967).

KBSR and teaching simplified Chinese characters and *Hanyu pinyin* in the 1980s

After the conversion of the English schools in 1982, Malay became the medium of instruction for all national secondary schools. Along with the launch of The Forth Malaysia Plan (1981–1985), a new curriculum was designed for all types of primary schools which emphasized communication skills, literacy, arithmetic skills, and individual self-development (Lee 1988). This New Curriculum for Primary Schools (KBSR) aimed to improve the teaching of Malay language and English as a second language (Ye 2002). In National-type schools, Malay and English must be taught apart from mother tongues. Table 7.3 shows a standard timetable under the KBSR system for National-type Chinese primary schools.

Table 7.3 KBSR syllabus (1983) for National-type Chinese schools (minutes per week) (Ye 2002)

Subjects	Phase 1			Phase 2		
	Grade 1	Grade 2	Grade 3	Grade 4	Grade 5	Grade 6
Malay	270	270	270	150	150	150
Chinese	450	450	450	300	300	300
English	–	–	–	90	90	90
Mathematics	210	210	210	210	210	210
Science	–	–	–	150	150	150
Moral	150	150	150	150	150	150
Music	60	60	60	60	60	60
Physical education	90	90	90	60	60	60
Arts education	60	60	60	60	60	60
Life skills	–	–	–	60	60	60
Local studies	–	–	–	120	120	120
Class meetings	30	30	30	30	30	30
School gathering	30	30	30	–	–	–
Total	1350	1350	1350	1440	1440	1440

The medium of instruction was Mandarin in all National-type Chinese primary schools. There are great differences between the KBSR and the previous syllabus regarding the teaching of languages. To upgrade the status of Malay and integrate national ideology into education through the teaching of Malay, the allocated time for Malay increased from 32 to 42 periods while for English it decreased from 26 to 9 periods. Compared to the National (Malay) schools where the teaching of English started from Grade 1 with a total of 15 periods, the Chinese National-type schools only started English teaching in Grade 4 (Ye 2002). This caused objections from the Chinese community. Concerned about students' declining proficiency in English, the community demanded more teaching hours for English (Tay 2003). Meanwhile, suggestions for compiling textbooks and reference books in Malay and increasing Malay in music lessons were declined.

With the implementation of KBSR, a new Chinese language program was introduced to year 1 classes in 1982 with two innovations (Lee 1988): (1) the adoption of simplified Chinese characters, and (2) the teaching of *Hanyu pinyin*. The adoption of simplified Chinese characters and *Hanyu pinyin* in Malaysia was not problem-free. According to a survey conducted by Lee (1988), most teachers had difficulty in mastering neutral tone, nasal finals and retroflex.

The adoption of simplified Chinese characters and *Hanyu pinyin* in Malaysia resulted from the change of political climate in the 1970s. In 1974, China and Malaysia established diplomatic relations. Since then, there has been increasing interaction between the two countries.

At the secondary school level, all English schools completed their second conversion to become Malay-medium schools in 1982. They were the so-called national-type secondary schools. Compared to the national-type primary schools, these schools were different in that the medium of instruction was Malay for all subjects except for Chinese (*Huawen*) and English. Due to their Chinese background prior to the 1960s, these schools were different from other Malay-medium national schools. In these national-type secondary schools, the teaching of Chinese was part of the regular curriculum within school hours while the Chinese subject in national schools was allocated beyond teaching schedule (see details in section on Present Situation).

As for the Chinese Independent Schools (*Duzhong*), after the revival movement in the 1970s, they grew steadily in the 1980s. In 1989, the student population in 60 *Duzhong* had increased to 52,200 (Tay 2003). According to a survey by Tan Liok Ee, the reasons for choosing *Duzhong* include: (1) this is a very good school (20.5%), (2) the medium of instruction is Chinese (20.5%) and (3) my siblings are studying in this school (16.3%) (cited in Tay 2003). This indicates that the academic performance of *Duzhong* has been acknowledged in this country. However, the graduation certificate is not recognized by the government because Education Act 1961 stated that all graduate exams for secondary schools must be in Malay or English. This issue has been raised many times by the Chinese community leaders to the government but never resolved.

Chinese education after the 1990s

In 1990, the New Development Policy was proposed to stimulate the economy. A year later, the then Prime Minister, Dr. Mahathir announced Vision 2020 that aimed to transform Malaysia into an advanced country by 2020. To achieve this goal, the scheme of Vision School was proposed and implemented in three ways: (1) to build new schools which have two or three language streams, (2) to combine different language streams in one school, and (3) to add other language streams in the existing schools (Ye 2002, p. 44). The proposal suggested that different language streams (Malay, Chinese, and Tamil) should have their own administration systems and the common language for co-curricular activities would be Malay in Vision School. The purpose of Vision School was to unite the students from different language streams and promote the use of Malay among students from different ethnic groups. This scheme was rejected by *Dongjiaozong* as it was regarded as the first step to change the characteristics of Chinese primary school by changing the language for co-curricular activities.

During this period, the government opened the market for higher education and approved more licenses of private colleges in response to Vision 2020. These private colleges were welcomed by the Chinese community because of a quota system in the national universities that favoured ethnic Malays, leaving ethnic Chinese students few opportunities to enter national universities. Moreover, the medium of instruction in private colleges was allowed to be English according to the Private Higher Education Institutions Act 1996 (Alis 2006). The Chinese community took this opportunity setting up three colleges, The Southern College in Johor Baru in 1990, The New Era College in Kajang in 1998, and The Han Chiang International College in Penang in 1999 (Tay 2003). These colleges use Chinese as the main medium of instruction and take in graduates from Chinese Independent Schools and national-type schools. All of them established Chinese departments in their colleges. In 1997, an Education Memorandum, signed by China and Malaysia, made Chinese education more promising. Since then, exchange programs have been available to facilitate Malaysian students' tertiary education in China. This provided graduates from *Duzhong* one more country to go to for further studies in addition to Taiwan, Singapore and Western countries.

To achieve the goal of Vision 2020, the Malaysian government made another radical decision in 2002, that mathematics and science should be taught in English at all levels (Gill 2005). This is the so-called Teaching of Mathematics and Science in English (TMSE). There were two main reasons leading to this change in education policy: (1) the need to develop the national economy in the domain of science and technology, and (2) the spread of English in business and industry (Gill 2005). The Chinese, Indian, and Malay communities objected to the decision on the following grounds: the Chinese worried that Chinese schools would lose their character by changing the medium of instruction from Chinese to English; and the Malays were concerned that the students' low proficiency in English might affect their academic results. Despite the objections from different ethnic groups, the government implemented the new policy in 2003.

As a compromise and a response to the appeal of the Chinese community, the Ministry of Education allowed the Chinese primary schools to teach mathematics and science in both Chinese and English. A 2-4-3 scheme and 4-2-2 scheme were adopted for phase 1 (Grade 1, 2, 3) and phase 2 (Grade 4, 5, 6) classes respectively.

The 2-4-3 scheme means 2 periods for English, 4 periods for English mathematics, and 3 periods for English science for Grade 1, 2 and 3 as shown in Table 7.4.

Under this scheme, the teaching allotment for subjects taught in English totalled 15 periods, six periods more than the allocated time for Malay. However, without support from grass-root communities and with few teachers qualified to teach in English, as well as less satisfactory results of students' academic performance, this policy was withdrawn in 2012 after nine years of implementation (Nor Liza, Hamid & Moni 2011). In fact, many math and science teachers taught in Chinese during English periods, which ran contradictory to the objective of the policy.

Table 7.4 Change of teaching hours (minutes) in Chinese primary schools under the Teaching Mathematics and Science in English Policy

Subjects	Phase 1						Phase 2					
	Grad 1		Grade 2		Grade 3		Grade 4		Grade 5		Grade 6	
	A*	B**	A	B	A	B	A	B	A	B	A	B
Malay	270	270	270	270	270	270	180	150	180	150	180	150
Chinese	360	450	360	450	360	450	300	300	300	300	300	300
English	60	–	60	–	60	–	120	90	120	90	120	90
Mathematics		210		210		210		210		210		210
English	120		120		120		60		60		60	
Chinese	180		180		180		180		180		180	
Science.		–		–		–		150		150		150
English	90		90		90		60		60		60	
Chinese	90		90		90		90		90		90	
Moral	120	150	120	150	120	150	120	150	120	150	120	150
Music	60	60	60	60	60	60	60	60	60	60	60	60
Physical education	60	90	60	90	60	90	60	60	60	60	60	60
Arts education	60	60	60	60	60	60	60	60	60	60	60	60
Life skills	–	–	–	–	–	–	60	60	60	60	60	60
Civics	–	–	–	–	–	–	60	60	60	60	60	60
Local studies	–	–	–	–	–	–	60	60	60	60	60	60
Class meetings	30	30	30	30	30	30	30	30	30	30	30	30
Headmaster class	–	30	–	30	–	30	–	–	–	–	–	–
Total	1500	1350	1500	1350	1500	1350	1500	1440	1500	1440	1500	1440

(*A=after the policy, **B=before the policy. 30 minutes per period)
Source: *Dongjiaozong* website: ⟨www.djz.edu.my/resource/images/doc/⟩

Present situation of Chinese education in Malaysia

The 21st century saw the rise of China and the increasing importance of the Chinese language. Proficiency in Chinese language is associated with not only Chinese identity but also access to the Chinese market. Consequently, more and more Chinese and non-Chinese parents send their children to Chinese primary schools. Among the Chinese community, 90% of Chinese send their children to Chinese primary schools (Lee 2011). There were 1291 Chinese primary schools in 2010 with a student population of 604,604 (*Dongzong* website). In 2011, a new curriculum, *Kurikulum Standard Sekolah Rendah* (KSSR), was introduced in all types of schools focusing on literacy skills, creativity and innovation, information and communication technology as well as entrepreneurship (Ministry of Education 2013). The teaching hours of various languages under the KSSR are slightly different from the previous curriculum (see Table 7.5).

Table 7.5 Teaching hours of language subjects in Chinese primary schools weekly (KSSR, phase 1)*

Subjects	Periods	Minutes
Chinese language	12	360
Malay language	10	300
English language	5	150

*Source: Ministry of Education, Malaysia. ⟨http://www.moe.gov.my/bpk/kssr_docs/01_Konsep_KSSR/Konsep%20KSSR.pdf⟩

In this new curriculum, the Teaching of Mathematics and Science in English Policy has been abandoned. More periods are assigned to teach English language. Although the teaching hours for Chinese language remain unchanged, Chinese is taught as the first language and still the medium of instruction for other subjects while Malay and English are taught as a second language.

At the secondary school level, students have three choices: national schools, national-type schools, and Chinese Independent Schools. In national schools, where Malay is the medium of instruction, Chinese classes (3 periods) will be offered if more than 15 parents make a request. In national-type secondary schools (SMJK), Chinese classes are compulsory for Chinese students in most schools, as part of the school's regular curriculum. According to *Jiaozong* (*2010*), there are 124,916 students attending 78 Chinese SMJK. Among these schools, Chinese classes are offered from six or seven periods to five periods and three or four periods per week depending on the availability of Chinese teachers in the schools, even though the Ministry of Education permits SMJK to offer five periods of Chinese class per week (*Jiaozong 2010*). In SMJK, Chinese is taught as a subject and is compulsory for the Malaysian Certificate of Education exam (Sijil Pelajaran Malaysia SPM) in most national-type schools. In addition, Chinese literature is offered as an elective, covering Chinese classic and modern literature. Yet, the number of students who are willing to take this subject has been declining due to the difficulty of achieving a high grade in SPM.

In Chinese Independent Schools (*Duzhong*), all subjects except for Malay and English are taught in Chinese. If the school adopts the so-called dual-exam system (the Unified Examination by *Dongzong* and SPM by the government), the syllabus required by the governmental exam (SPM) is also taught (Tan, Ho & Tan 2005). Otherwise, the students take only the Junior/Senior Middle School Unified Examination established by *Dongzong*, which is not acknowledged by the government for entering national universities. In 2010, there were 63,675 students attending 60 *Duzhong* (*Dongjiaozong* website). The graduates from *Duzhong* have been accepted by many universities all over the world. It is popular because it emphasises discipline, learning of three languages, science and math, and the inculcation of Chinese traditional values (Tan, Ho & Tan 2005).

Table 7.6 compares the teaching hours of the three languages in *Duzhong* and SMJK.

Table 7.6 Comparison of teaching hours of three languages in *Duzhong* and SMJK

Subjects	*Duzhong** minute (period)	SMJK** minute (period)
Chinese language	280(7)	210(6)
Malay language	240(6)	210(6)
English language	240(6)	175(5)

(Source: *Form 1, *Pei Hua Duzhong*, Johor, 40 minutes per period;
**Form 2, SMJK Sacred Heart, Penang, 35 minutes per period)

Table 7.6 shows that there is not much difference between these two types of school regarding the allocated time for the three languages. However, it should be noted that the medium of instruction of *Duzhong* is Chinese while the SMJK schools use Malay as the medium of instruction for subjects other than languages. The textbooks for Chinese primary schools and national-type secondary schools are compiled by the Department of Curriculum Development in the Ministry of Education. Under the new KSSR curriculum, there are five focal points for the teaching of Chinese at the elementary level: (1) listening and speaking (90 minutes per week for phase 1 and 60 minutes for phase 2), (2) reading (150 minutes per week for phase 1 and 120 minutes for phase 2), (3) writing (60 minutes per week, write characters and sentences for phase 1 and write essays for phase 2), (4) fun Chinese (30 minutes per week), and (5) basic knowledge of Chinese (30 minutes per week) (Department of Curriculum Development 2011). After six years of education, students are expected to master 2500 Chinese characters, recite 60 classical poems, and be able to use *Hanyu pinyin*. The syllabus of Chinese emphasises language skills and its application in everyday life. In this sense, it is a language-centred syllabus (Department of Curriculum Development, 2011). At the same time, the syllabus integrates elements of Chinese culture into the teaching, such as Chinese festivals and classical poems. The contents of textbooks are more local-oriented which is aligned with the objective of KSSR.

In every perspective, Chinese education has contributed significantly to the development of the country. However, problems and challenges have never disappeared. As Tay (2003) pointed out, the lack of financial support, the shortage of well-trained teachers, and the control of the number of Chinese schools allowed are the main difficulties faced by Chinese schools. According to the statistics by *Jiaozong* (*2008*), among the 1290 Chinese primary schools, 879 schools (68%) receive only partial subsidy from the government. This also applies to the national-type secondary schools (Sinchew Daily 6/12/2012). The Chinese Independent Schools (*Duzhong*), however, are self-financed and do not receive any governmental aid. These schools also suffer from shortage of teachers (Lee 2011), which is reported in the local newspapers every year. Although the student population of the Chinese primary schools has increased since 1970, the number of schools has decreased. In contrast, more than 1500 new Malay schools were built since 1970 (*Dongzong* website). The Chinese community has to merge small schools to form bigger ones. In addition, the unstable and changing education policies have caused many obstacles to the development of Chinese schools, such as the Teaching of Mathematics and Science in English Policy.

In view of the popularity of the Chinese language, the Malaysian Ministry of Education started a new program of teaching Chinese as a second language in 1996 (Zheng 2010). This additional language class was targeted at Malay and Indian students. The allocated time was 120 minutes per week included in regular school hours (Li 2002). The textbooks for this additional language subject were compiled by the Department of Curriculum Development. Under the new KSSR curriculum, Chinese language is an elective subject in national Malay schools (Department of Curriculum Development 2010).

Concluding remarks

Chinese education in Malaysia has a long history. More than 190 years have passed since the establishment of *Wufu shuyuan* in Penang in 1819. This eventful period has seen a struggle for the survival of Chinese education (Lee 2011). There has also been a process of evolution from China-orientation to Malaysia-orientation, from old-style to new-style, from dialect-medium to Mandarin-medium, from mono-lingual education to trilingual education. This is the uniqueness of Malaysian Chinese education in primary schools, secondary schools, and tertiary institu-tions. It serves not only Chinese people but also non-Chinese Malaysians as more and more non-Chinese students enrol in Chinese primary schools, and Chinese is now offered as a second language in national primary schools.

Despite the difficulties and challenges in the past 190 years, Malaysian Chinese education has made great progress with help from devoted Chinese educationists. Over the years, Chinese primary schools have been integrated into the national education system. 20% of the Chinese primary school graduates enrol in national-type secondary schools where Chinese is taught as a subject in the regular cur-riculum. 10% enter Chinese Independent Schools which use Chinese as the main medium of instruction. The rest go to national schools where Malay is the medium of instruction and Chinese is taught if more than 15 parents request it.

Education has played an important role in the Chinese community as a way to maintain Chinese culture and identity. Through education, Chinese commu-nities protect their Chineseness in this multi-ethnic and multi-cultural society. In Malaysia, the trilingual education provides the students with the advantage of learning Chinese, English, and Malay. Pluralism has always been the pursuit of Chinese educationists in Malaysia, the opposite of monolingualism and homogenizing unitarianism held by the previous British colonial authority and the current government (Lee 2011). Chinese schools have evolved gradually to respond to the changes in the local environment and the outside world. As pointed out by Tan Liok Ee (2000, p. 249), Chinese schools "have been able to maintain a niche because they have provided alternatives that meet the changing educational needs and demands of a significant proportion of Malaysian Chinese".

Malaysia is the sole country outside of China which maintains Chinese edu-cation from primary schools to tertiary institutions. However, from secondary school onwards, Chinese is taught only as a subject except in *Duzhong*. The objec-tive of Chinese teaching should be reviewed carefully in the light of the limited teaching hours and insufficient resources.

Although problems in secondary schools have not been mentioned in published documents, several issues need to be addressed. First, the objective of teaching Chinese in national-type schools and national schools should not be the same as it is in *Duzhong*. It should be accepted that the Chinese language skills and literature knowledge of students from the national education system are not comparable to that of students in China. Their learning outcome should be assessed according to the input they have received from the various subjects. Factors such as short teaching hours, lack of well-trained teachers and inadequate teaching approaches, do affect students' performance in Chinese. Secondly, if teaching Chinese is exam-oriented, it will not stimulate students' interest in the subject. Chinese grammar and phonetics should be taught systematically in primary and secondary schools. As reported in the previous section, Chinese teachers have difficulties in the teaching of neutral tone, tone sandhi, and retroflex because these phonetic features are not found in Malaysian Mandarin (Lee 1998; Lu 2008; Wang 2006; Wong 1995). However, these contents are covered in the syllabus of primary schools and students have to memorize them for exams. Thus, the students cannot actually understand these contents which they are supposed to learn in colleges. Thirdly, Chinese literature covers modern Chinese literature, classic Chinese literature, modern Chinese literature history, and classic Chinese literature history. Given the shortage of teachers able to teach Chinese literature in secondary schools, the students have difficulties to master this subject. This further leads to the fact that the number of students opting for Chinese and Chinese Literature subjects drops sharply in national exams. Fourthly, more efforts should be put into the comprehension and appreciation of the original texts rather than memorizing standard answers to model questions.

As the Chinese language is gaining international importance, Malaysia should have a long-term macro plan for its Chinese-speaking manpower. They may have different levels of knowledge of Chinese language and culture, which will cater for different needs of the country such as linguistic experts, translators, language teachers, diplomats, businessmen, tour guides, and other people in the service sector. From the point of view of economy, the value of the Chinese language is increasing, which is definitely a positive factor for the future development of Chinese education in Malaysia.

References

Alis, P. 2006. *Language and Nation Building: A Study of the language Medium Policy in Malaysia*. Petaling Jaya: Strategic Information and Research Development Centre.

Asmah, H.O. 1982. *Language and Society in Malaysia*. Kuala Lumpur: Dewan Bahasa dan Pustaka.

Asmah, H.O. 1996. Post-imperial English in Malaysia. In *Post-Imperial English: Status Change in Former British and American Colonies, 1940–1990*, J.A. Fishman, A.W. Conrad & A. Rubal-Lopez (eds), 513–533. Berlin: Mouton de Gruyter.

Department of Curriculum Development, MOE. 2010. *Standard Document for Chinese Language for National Schools (KSSR)*.

Department of Curriculum Development, MOE. 2011. *Standard Document for Chinese Language for National-Type Schools (KSSR Phase 1)*.

Department of Statistics, Malaysia. 2010. *Population Distribution and Basic Demographic Characteristics*. Putrajaya: Department of Statistics, Malaysia.

Dongzong website:

⟨www.djz.edu.my/resource/images/doc/DataAnalysis/2010%20MICSS%20ShuJu.pdf⟩ (2 January 2013).⟨www.djz.edu.my/resource/index.php?option=com_content&view=article&id=813: 19702008&catid=75: 2009-07-31-05-27-30&Itemid=76⟩ (April 25, 2013).

Gill, S.K. 2005. Language policy in Malaysia: Reversing direction. *Language Policy* 4(3): 241–260.

Hou, H.J. 1919. *Nanyang lvxing ji* [Travel in Nanyang]. Xi Cheng Company.

Jiaozong. 2008. ⟨web.jiaozong.org.my/doc/2009/rnr/shuju/sjk_jintie.pdf⟩ (2 January 2013).

Jiaozong. 2010. ⟨web.jiaozong.org.my/doc/2010/rnr/2010smjk_survey.pdf⟩ (2 January 2013).

Kua, K.S. 1985. *The Chinese Schools of Malaysia: A Protean Saga*. Kuala Lumpur: United Chinese Committees Association of Malaysia.

Lee, K.H. 2011. The English-educated Chinese in Malaysia. In *Malaysian Chinese: An Inclusive Society*, 55–88. Kuala Lumpur: Centre for Malaysian Chinese Studies.

Lee, P.W. 1988. Perception of Chinese Language Teachers on the Implementation of the New Phonetic System in the National-type (Chinese) Primary Schools. MA thesis, University of Malaya.

Lee, T.H. 2011. *Chinese Schools in Peninsular Malaysia: The Struggle for Survival*. Singapore: Institute of Southeast Asian Studies.

Li, K.R. 2002. Maixiang Ershiyi shiji Malaixiya guanban zhongxiaoxue huawen jiaoyu de xianzhuang yu zhanwang (The present situation and future of Chinese education in governmental primary and secondary schools in Malaysia). In *Qushi yu celue* (Trends and Strategies), C.K. Lim & Y.S. Tan (eds), 254–257. Kuala Lumpur: Selangor Chinese Assembly Hall.

Lim, K.T. 1999. *Jiangou zhong de "Huaren wenhua": Zuqun shuxing, guojia yu huajiao yundong* (Construction of Chinese culture: ethnic attributes, nation and Chinese education movement). Kuala Lumpur: Centre for Malaysian Chinese Studies.

Lu, L.M. 2008. Zhengshi wo guo huawen xiaoxue Huawen kecheng yu jiaoxue wenti (Chinese curriculum and teaching in Chinese primary schools in Malaysia). *Malaysian Chinese Education* 8: 1648–1668.

Maeda, K. 1967. *Alor Janggus: A Chinese Community in Malaysia*. Kyoto: The Centre for Southeast Asian Studies, Kyoto University.

Ministry of Education, Malaysia. ⟨http://www.moe.gov.my/bpk/kssr_docs/01_Konsep_KSSR/Konsep%20KSSR.pdf⟩ (25 April 2013).

Nor Liza, A., Hamid M.O. & Moni K. 2011. English in primary education in Malaysia: Policies, outcomes and stakeholders' lived experiences. *Current Issues in Language Planning* 12(2): 147–166.

Ser, W.H. 2010. Ma Xin Huayu de lishi kaocha: Cong shijiu shiji mo dao 1919 nian [A historical investigation of Mandarin in Malaysian and Singapore: from the end of 19th century to 1919]. Paper presented at The Conference on Language Rights in a Multilingual Society, 11 December, Kuala Lumpur, Malaysia.

Sinchew Daily. Character of national-type secondary schools is threatened. 6th December 2012.

Tan, L.E. 1997. *The Politics of Chinese Education in Malaya 1945–1961*. Kuala Lumpur: OUP.

Tan, L.E. 2000. Chinese schools in Malaysia: A case of cultural resilience, in *The Chinese in Malaysia*, K.H. Lee & C.B. Tan (eds), 228–254. Shah Alam: OUP.

Tan, T.J., Ho W.F. & Tan J.L. 2005. *The Chinese Malaysian Contribution*. Kuala Lumpur: Centre for Malaysian Chinese Studies.

Tay, L.S. 1998. *Malaixiya huawen jiaoyu fazhan shi* (The history of Chinese education in Malaysia), Vol 1. Kuala Lumpur: The United Chinese School Teachers' Association of Malaysia.

Tay, L.S. 1999. *Malaixiya huawen jiaoyu fazhan shi* (The history of Chinese education in Malaysia), Vol 2. Kuala Lumpur: The United Chinese School Teachers' Association of Malaysia.

Tay, L.S. 2001. *Malaixiya huawen jiaoyu fazhan shi* (The history of Chinese education in Malaysia), Vol 3. Kuala Lumpur: The United Chinese School Teachers' Association of Malaysia.

Tay, L.S. 2003. *Malaixiya huawen jiaoyu fazhan shi* (The history of Chinese education in Malaysia), Vol 4. Kuala Lumpur: The United Chinese School Teachers' Association of Malaysia.

Wang, P.T. & Xu L.C. 1985. Malaixiya Huawen jiaoyu de huigu he qianzhan (Review and outlook of Chinese education in Malaysia). In *Wenjiao shiye lunji* (Essays on education, literature and mass media), C.K. Lim (ed.), 23–39. Kuala Lumpur: The Selangor Chinese Assembly Hall.

Wang X.M. 2006. Different medium of instruction, different destiny of language shift? A pilot study in Kuala Lumpur. *Proceedings of the 11th Conference of Pan-Pacific Association of Applied Linguistics*, 307–317.

Wong, H.C. 1995. Some Professional Problems of the New Primary School Curriculum Phase II Chinese Language Teachers in Selected National-type (Chinese) Primary Schools. MA thesis, University of Malaya.

Ye, Y.X. 2002. *Yuyan zhengce yu jiaoyu: Malaixiya yu Xinjiapo zhi bijiao* (Language policy and education: Comparison between Malaysia and Singapore). Taipei: Avanguard.

Zheng, W.L. 2010. Malaixiya guomin xiaoxue Huayu kecheng de shezhi yu yange (The Chinese class for national schools in Malaysia). *Malaixiya huawen jiaoyu* (Malaysian Chinese Education) 10: 62–76.

CHAPTER 8

Conflicting goals of language-in-education planning in Singapore

Chinese character (汉字 *hanzi*) education as a case

Zhao Shouhui & Zhang Dongbo

University of Bergen and Shanghai International Studies University / Michigan State University

This study examines the conflicting nature of official language-in-education planning goals in Singapore through analysing, firstly, the inconsistencies in curriculum reform documents at different levels of the goals and pedagogies of Chinese character (汉字 *hanzi*) teaching; and secondly, the inconsistencies between what is stated in these documents about *hanzi* and students' and teachers' perceptions as well as teaching practices related to *hanzi*. Based on student and teacher surveys, supplemented by teachers' focus group discussions and classroom observations, this chapter provides a critical evaluation of multiple dimensions of the official policies and instructional guides on *hanzi* teaching and learning in Singapore's primary schools. The study endeavors to draw attention to the humanistic dimensions of *hanzi* education such as its values in cultural heritage, artistic/aesthetic appreciation and character cultivation. It calls for a holistic evaluation of *hanzi*'s role from a broader perspective and aims to place a more proper status of *hanzi* in the next round of reform of Chinese-as-a-mother-tongue education in Singapore.

Recent development of Chinese language education: The modular curriculum

Language education in Singapore has developed against a background of diversity in both ethnic and linguistic terms. As a multiracial and multilingual city-state, Singapore has a population of 3.77 million (as of 2010), consisting of three major ethnic groups (Chinese = 74.1%, Malays = 13.4% and Indians = 9.2%) (Singapore Department of Statistics, 2011). The official language policy, as is characteristic of an overt interventionism, has been largely realised through language-in-education planning or via policy initiatives with the support from the Ministry of Education (MOE). A bilingual education model is adopted which requires all students to study two compulsory languages: English and one of the state-assigned mother tongues (MT), specific to an individual's ethnic background. These MTs are Mandarin Chinese, Malay and Tamil, all taking up an average of five class hours (30–40 minutes) per week as stipulated by MOE.

According to this model of bilingual education, the MTs of the three major ethnic groups, including Chinese language (CL), the target language of the present study, are treated primarily as repositories of cultural values, making them distinct from English whose values are assigned to economic and technological domains (Shepherd 2005). Within this paradigm, the official unwavering commitment to CL education was originally constructed to preserve ethnic and cultural traditions. However, as Wee (2003) notes, the need of Singapore to participate in a globalised economy has created a situation where the old linguistic politics related to cultural identity has been increasingly abandoned in favour of a new pragmatic position where language is valued as a commodifiable resource. Even so, the bilingual model has resulted in an intergenerational shift of the home language towards English, leading to a rapid decline of CL competence among Chinese students in Singapore (Zhao & Liu 2010). To prevent further deterioration, the Singapore Ministry of Education has initiated an innovative curriculum called the Modular Curriculum, which was formally launched in 2007 across the Island to give schools autonomy in implementing programmes to achieve optimal CL outcomes for students.

The new curriculum is to be lauded for innovations such as a greater emphasis on student-centeredness and communicative approaches. The modular approach, based on the concept of differentiated learning, intends to provide customised contents through three different modules in each unit in the new textbook series, for students from various backgrounds and with diverse abilities. The three modules are: core module, bridging module, and enrichment module. 'Core module', designed for all students, focuses on the knowledge needed for the high-stake Primary School Leaving Examination (PSLE). 'Bridging module' places emphasis on strengthening children's listening and speaking skills while introducing vocabularies useful for their learning in the core module. It caters for students who enter school with little exposure to CL, typical of children from English dominant families. Finally, the 'enrichment module', included in each lesson unit, is intended for those who have the ability and interest to learn beyond what is required by the core module.

In contrast to the new focus that emphasises an oral communication orientation, Chinese character or *hanzi* learning, particularly *hanzi* writing, has been pinpointed as an element that curtails students' CL learning interest, and teachers are advised to reduce *hanzi* writing practice and devote more time to *hanzi* recognition and reading. Given that Singapore schools operate under a highly centralised administrative system and that there is an exam-oriented educational culture in Singapore, such initiatives and guidelines are bound to have a substantial impact on schools' pedagogical priorities and practices.

Since the full implementation of the new curriculum, no projects that we know of have touched upon *hanzi* issues, despite the fact that it is one of the key focuses of the Modular Curriculum and a contested topic in the history of CL education in Singapore. Pedagogically, the issues concerning *hanzi* education can be numerous. These issues typically include prescription of the number of *hanzi* for reading/recognition and writing at different target levels, specific teaching approaches based either on cognitive or linguistic theories, assessment of students' actual *hanzi* proficiency, etc.

Drawing upon the empirical data of a large scale MOE commissioned research project carried out in Singapore primary schools, this study concerns itself with a fundamental issue from the perspective of language-in-education-planning about the interaction between CL policy and practice in Singapore. It addresses the paradoxical tension between competing policies within that interaction which underlies one important aspect of Chinese education – *hanzi* instruction. Specifically, the research questions which this chapter attempts to address are:

1. Is there a discrepancy between the instructional emphasis on *hanzi* education at the macro level and the more general objectives of CL education indicated in policy statements at the micro level?
2. Do learners themselves hold perceptions/attitudes towards *hanzi* and *hanzi* learning/teaching similar to those stipulated by policy makers and curriculum developers in CL reform documents and instructional materials?
3. How do teachers as classroom practitioners view the official *hanzi* policy, and how are their perceptions translated into classroom teaching practice?

To give a broader context for subsequent discussions, the following section is devoted to the exposition of the multidimensional facets of *hanzi* on top of its communicational functions. Then, the discrepancies between instructional guidelines for *hanzi* teaching and the general objectives stipulated for CL education at different levels of policies are discussed through inter-textual analysis. In the data analysis section, research questions are addressed one by one through examining the findings obtained from four research instruments, namely, student questionnaire survey, teacher questionnaire survey, teachers' focus group discussion, and classroom observation. In the last section, we close the chapter by expounding the broader implications of the findings about the conflicting goals between policies at different levels in Singapore.

Chinese language education: A missing link between culture transition and *hanzi* study

This section examines the paradoxicality between the instructional focuses, stipulated for *hanzi* in the policy statement report, which initiated the new round of CL educational innovation, and the general objectives of CL education as emphasised in the Modular Curriculum, the epitomisation of the educational innovation. This kind of paradox stems from an ignorance of *hanzi's* role in representing Chinese culture and its implications for linking the maintenance of Chinese culture with CL education.

Hanzi as a cultural phenomenon

In the field of teaching Chinese as a second language, *hanzi* is perhaps the most whimsical issue in terms of its place in and relevance to language acquisition. Discussions about *hanzi* almost always revolve exclusively around the pedagogical and linguistic aspects of *hanzi*, such as teaching approaches and the number of characters that should be covered in instructional materials or prescribed for proficiency tests. A commonly-held view among linguists is that script is the graphic representation of sounds and is thus detachable from the language. In teaching practice, *hanzi* has been described at worst as a Hydra, and learning Chinese without bothering to battle with *hanzi* used to be popular among speakers of western languages. For instance, John DeFrancis' Chinese language textbooks (e.g. DeFrancis & Chia-Yee 1976) were separated into a *pinyin* version and a *hanzi* version. The rationale behind such type of practices with respect to a *hanzi*-free CL curriculum seems to ignore the fact that *hanzi* is not simply a visual system to represent CL, it is also a symbol of Chinese culture.

Owing to the fact that *hanzi* is a writing system totally different from alphabetic languages such as English, which is the instructional medium in Singaporean schools, detailed quantitative learning benchmarks have been strictly adopted in Chinese curricula since the mid-1970s. Against this backdrop, issues concerning *hanzi* teaching became a serious concern in the Modular Curriculum. Because *hanzi* had been successfully computerised, the 2004 Chinese Language Curriculum and Pedagogy Review Committee decided that opportunities for writing *hanzi* be greatly reduced. Therefore, an emphasis on *hanzi* writing practice would not only increase students' learning burden and inhibit their learning motivation; it would also be in conflict with modern language pedagogies characterised by an oral communicative orientation.

However, this proposition tends to oversimplify the complex nature of the Chinese writing system. Apart from serving as a visual vehicle for written communication, *hanzi* is also characterised by its cultural and historical dimensions. The frequent set-backs of trying to reform *hanzi* in recent history are apparently a reflection of *hanzi*'s complex nature. In the literature, the pragmatic *hanzi* instrumentalism has been gradually abandoned in favour of a new postmodern narrative where the importance of *hanzi* is increasingly based on its cultural and artistic value and sentimental attachment (e.g. Wang 2008). Zhao and Baldauf (2008) noted that any optimistic treatment of *hanzi*, be it linguistically or pedagogically, tends to hit a snag if not taking into account holistically what they call the "View of Whole *Hanzi*", which suggests that beyond being a script system, *hanzi* has in Chinese life some multidimensional functions which we delineate below.

Bearer of Chinese culture

Because *hanzi* provides a multi-millennial lifeline to China's extraordinary and rich ancient works and thus ensures the vitality of the Chinese cultural heritage, it is argued that learning *hanzi* can enrich one's understanding of the spoken language as well as opening the gateway to the rich treasure of the Chinese world. Therefore, *hanzi* is regarded as the ethos of the Chinese people.

Totem of spiritual expression

The veneration of *hanzi* originated partly in its use for divinity and myth. In antiquity, *hanzi* was engraved on bones and bronze vessels, used only for divination and important official rites. As a result, *hanzi* characters "are imbued with magical, mystical quality and power, and hence are objects of reverence" (Taylor & Taylor 1995:74–76).

Genre of indigenous art (Calligraphy)

Chinese Calligraphy is a unique visual art form stemming from *hanzi*; it is one of the iconic symbols of Chinese culture. As DeFrancis (1984:78) argues, "aesthetics plays an exceedingly important role in Chinese writing, more so than any other system of writing". Aesthetic perception and artistic sense are often important considerations of Chinese learners in their decision to learn Chinese language and script.

Unifier of linguistically heterogeneous groups

Hanzi transcends chronological and geographical boundaries and enables speakers from different dialectal areas to communicate in writing. Because of great variations in other linguistic aspects (DeFrancis 1989), *hanzi* creates a common bond for peoples, which would otherwise be divided by diversified oral speeches. This is not only the case within China, but particularly more true in Chinese diasporic communities.

Cultivator of personalities

Centuries of tradition have created strict conventions governing the fluidity of strokes, dots and lines that form each character. Chinese people believe that frequently practising these writing rules results in not only profound self-expression but also a sense of aesthetics. Practicing *hanzi*-writing is often considered a desirable measure to develop children's individual personalities, such as perseverance, self-discipline and management as well as imagination and creativity (e.g. Japan, see Liu 2003, 2008). As Long (1987:2) notes, "A greater understanding of the art of Chinese calligraphy will provide a clearer insight into the character of Chinese people themselves".

Paradoxical narrative in official documents: An inter-textual analysis

In this section, we present an inter-textual analysis at both macro and micro levels of two major top-down official documents that initiated the current innovative Modular Curriculum. The two documents are the Report of the Chinese Language Curriculum and Pedagogy Review Committee released in 2004 (hereafter, the Report 2004) and the revised Chinese Language (Primary) Syllabus, known as the Syllabus 2007, developed by the Curriculum Planning and Development Division (CPDD) of MOE in 2007 and based on the recommendations made in the Report 2004. The aim of the analysis is to locate the implicit inconsistencies in the policy positions about *hanzi* education. We conduct this analysis through identifying and comparing the specific instructional guidelines and strategies recommended in the Report 2004 and the general objectives, linguistic as well as cultural, stipulated in the Syllabus 2007.

Due to the rise of China as a world economic power and the inter-generational language shift that has occurred in the past couple of decades in Singaporean Chinese families, the struggle over whether CL should be taught as a first language (L1) or a second language (L2) has intensified since the beginning of the new century (Zhao & Wang 2009; Zhao & Liu 2010). Whereas the L2 camp focuses more on language structures and communicative skills, the mother tongue or L1 camp insists that CL should be treated more as a symbolic capital of traditional Chinese heritage. Against this backdrop, the actual decline of CL among the rapid growing number of students from English dominant families motivates the government's shift towards a discourse of linguistic instrumentalism, typically manifested in constructing *hanzi* education purely through a pragmatic view of language. In the

Report 2004 (p. iii), it is recognised that "[T]here is a clear generational shift in language use at home. More of our younger students come from English-speaking homes", therefore, "[T]he way we teach MTLs in our schools must respond to and anticipate changes in the environment." Subsequently, the demotion and degrading of *hanzi* education has been repeatedly emphasised.

Not supported by strong empirical evidence, *hanzi*, particularly *hanzi* writing practice, is described as one of the major factors that stifle students' CL learning interest. Therefore, the total number of *hanzi* introduced in each learning stage is categorised into two groups, viz. characters for recognition (*rendu zi*/认读字) and characters for writing (*xixie zi*/习写字). To promote the pedagogical principle of "Recognise First, Write Later", teachers are advised to restrict curriculum time on practising *hanzi*, and instead focus more on *hanzi* recognition and reading strategies on the grounds that, with the successful computerisation of *hanzi*, the ability to write them is no longer a necessary literacy skill. This advice clearly ignores *hanzi*'s sociolinguistic functions, which we elucidated earlier in this chapter, in building up students' cultural knowledge and fostering their love for their Chinese heritage, a clearly designated objective of CL education as reflected in the Report 2004 (p. iv) – "to transmit Chinese traditional culture and values through the study of CL." According to our analysis, in the 68-page Report 2004 (excluding the annexes and the executive summary), there are at least 20 critiques or unfavourable evaluations made about approaches to teaching *hanzi* or about *hanzi* per se. In a clear contrast to that number, only three points argue positively for the necessity of introducing *hanzi* in CL learning. For instance, "an early proficiency in character recognition and reading ...... will equip students with skills to use CL more frequently and thereby sustain their interest in the language." (p. 12) The negative comments criticise the previous over-emphasis on *hanzi* (writing or stroke practice) and highlight that more time should be devoted to recognising, as opposed to writing, *hanzi*. As shown in the excerpts below, the negative evaluations appear to be centered on the assumption that students' dislike of CL learning could be attributed to the difficulty of writing *hanzi*.

- The need to memorise many Chinese words emerged as a top reason for students not liking to learn CL, across all levels (p. 7)
- Although the logographic writing system has its advantages, it poses a challenge to teaching and learning....... (p. 13)
- Students who find Chinese difficult generally attribute it to difficulty in the writing of Chinese words (p. 58)

International scholars emphasise the interaction between different language planning activities that begin at different levels. That is, they find it hard to make a consensus on to what extent macro-level policy decisions can be transmitted directly to micro-level or local contexts (e.g. Van Els 2005; Liddicoat & Baldauf 2008). In the Singapore context, studies have shown that the policies about *hanzi* instruction narrated in the reforming initiatives were realised in development of instructional materials with a high fidelity. In other words, under a centralised administration system like Singapore's, official directives and guidelines always have a significant impact on goals and priorities and on how subjects are taught in schools. For example, according to Wang (2008) and Wang (2006), students' potential to develop stronger reading and writings skills was substantially hindered by the insufficient numbers of *hanzi*. Even so, the number of *hanzi* introduced in the current textbooks for lower and mid-primary grades (grades 1–4) was further reduced in comparison with previous textbooks made under the 2002 Curriculum. In particular, the reduction of *hanzi* for writing purpose was emphasised – from 1080 *hanzi* in the 2002 textbooks for grades 1–4 to 700–750 in the textbooks compiled in alignment with the Syllabus 2007 (Wang 2010).

We now turn our attention to the conflict between the negative evaluations of *hanzi*'s role in learning CL, stated in the Report 2004, and the general objectives of CL education, stipulated in the Syllabus 2007. Aligning with the structuralist standpoint on *hanzi* instruction which regards *hanzi* as a visual-graphic system that represents speech, the Report 2004 gave little consideration to *hanzi*'s cultural dimension when it justified the reduction of time used on teaching *hanzi*. However, when it comes to articulating the objectives of language education, linguistic relativism prevails. As was true of the previous syllabi, CL education is endowed, in the Syllabus 2007, with what seems to be an inordinate function. From a theoretical perspective, it is based on the Humboldtian tradition which considers language as a repository of ancient knowledge or cultural heritage, and language acquisition is seen as essentially giving the learners a personality and a new value system or a new "worldview" (Underhill 2009). Such a Humboldtian view on the benefit of language learning has been explicitly embodied in CL syllabi in Singapore with respect to the cultural objectives of CL education.

In the Syllabus 2007, "attaching equal importance to language ability development and humanity cultivation" ("兼顾语言能力的培养与人文素养的提高"; authors' translation) is listed as the first of the six conceptual pillars of the new curriculum (p. 3). The curriculum framework illustrates an integration model where language ability development is closely connected with that of humanity enhancement and general ability (e.g. high order thinking skills, such as imagination and creation) (p. 7). Altogether, they form the three overarching objectives of CL education. Specifically pertaining to the "humanity enhancement" dimension, students should

- develop positive attitudes towards life and upright view of value;
- understand and transmit essence of Chinese traditional heritage;
- love family, care about society, and devote to the country;
- be passionate about life and develop aesthetic appreciations.

In comparing the two reform documents, our analysis shows contradictory emphases and learning objectives. The Syllabus 2007 not only underscores that language and culture are inseparable, but stipulates that learning CL entails character building as well as nurturing students' senses in aesthetics and morality. Our earlier description of the widely recognised non-instrumental functions of *hanzi* is partially germane to the additional gains curriculum developers expected of CL education in their description of learning priorities in the Syllabus 2007. In the Report 2004, cultivation of moral values and character building are also highlighted, but when it comes to pedagogical guidelines a pragmatic linguistic ideology prevails, prioritising a skill-based orientation which provides little space for the cultural and aesthetic dimensions of *hanzi* in CL teaching and learning.

Teachers' and students' perceptions of *hanzi* and *hanzi* education

Expanding on our inter-textual analysis of policy documents, this section presents an empirical study that addressed how CL teachers and students perceive *hanzi* and its place in CL education. The study drew upon data collected from a large project that aimed to evaluate the implementation of the Modular Curriculum in Singapore primary schools.

Student and teacher survey

The bilingual student questionnaire was administered to elicit students' perceptions of and attitudes towards *hanzi*'s various functions, as well as their self-assessment of their *hanzi* proficiency. In total, 364 (P2) students (207 girls and 157 boys) from 18 primary schools were sampled.[1] The questionnaire asked students to indicate the extent to which they agreed with a statement on *hanzi* on a 5-point Likert-scale (i.e. from *strongly agree* to *strongly disagree*). There were

---

1.   P2 students were selected because, according to the new curriculum, this is the first grade in which they have some experience and knowledge of *hanzi*, as P1 is devoted to *pinyin* and few *hanzi* are introduced. The schools were randomly sampled, proportional to their geographical location across the Island.

15 statements, including five for interest in *hanzi* (e.g. *I don't like to write hanzi*), three for practical functions of *hanzi* (e.g. *Writing hanzi helps me recognise them*), four for cultural-aesthetic values of *hanzi* (e.g. *Hanzi are picturesque and beautiful*), and three for self-assessment of *hanzi*-related abilities (e.g. *I am confident in writing hanzi*).

For comparative purposes, we also report below relevant findings obtained from an online teacher survey. All primary school CL teachers in Singapore were invited to participate in the survey; valid questionnaires were collected from 321 teachers (274 females and 47 males). The teacher survey included questions covering issues similar to those addressed in the student survey, but from a teacher's point-of-view.

Interest in *hanzi*

The result of the student survey suggested that the participants overall were not averse to *hanzi*. While about 25% agreed that *hanzi* were difficult to write, and about one-third reported that *hanzi* were difficult to memorise, around 60% believed that writing *hanzi* was fun, and more than 60% did not agree with "I don't like to write *hanzi*." Interestingly, the reported views of the teachers from the online teacher survey tended to show some difference from those of the students. The teachers more or less agreed that *hanzi* were difficult to learn, and believed that including *hanzi* learning as a component of the Chinese curriculum would have an unfavourable impact on students' interest in CL learning. Specifically, according to the teacher survey, around 80% of the teachers indicated that their students had voiced concerns about the difficulty of *hanzi*; more than 40% did not agree that students liked to practise writing characters; and about 60% reported that most students lacked interests in learning *hanzi*.

A difference was also found between the views of the teachers and the students on students' enthusiasm for writing *hanzi*. Most student participants (about 70%) chose that "I hope my teacher could give us more time to practise writing *hanzi* in class." The teachers' view, however, was divided on the statement "My students are enthusiastic when I ask them to practise writing *hanzi*", as 35% of the teachers agreed and 35% disagreed.

Taken together, the above findings suggest that the students' awareness of how difficult it is to write *hanzi* did not have an unfavourable impact on their interest in learning them. Some students even held a very positive attitude toward practising writing *hanzi*, hoping for more time of practice in class. In contrast, the CL teachers widely believed that their students lacked interests in *hanzi* and were not enthusiastic about learning them.

Practical functions of *hanzi*

The surveys revealed that most teachers and students agreed on the practicality of *hanzi*. Around 90% of the students agreed that more practice of writing *hanzi* would help strengthen their ability in *hanzi* recognition; and more than 80% agreed that composing in Chinese would also be beneficial. The proportions of the teachers who agreed with these views were also very high – more than 90% and 60%, respectively.

Interestingly, the result of the teacher survey also showed that for the statement "With an appropriate pedagogy, *hanzi* will never become a hurdle to the learning of the Chinese language", around 64% and 21% of the teachers chose "agree" and "strongly agree," respectively. This finding suggests that teachers in Singapore, cognisant of the importance of *hanzi*, tend to believe that effective pedagogy is a key to students' mastery of *hanzi*.

Cultural-aesthetic values of *hanzi*

Students were also largely aware of *hanzi*'s artistic, aesthetic, and cultural values. Around 65% of them agreed that *hanzi* were picturesque and beautiful. Most of them also reported that knowing *hanzi* was essential for them as ethnic Chinese. The questionnaire also asked the students about how much they knew about Chinese brushes and Chinese calligraphy. It was found that about 87% of the students knew what a Chinese brush was, which seems to suggest that they had developed some conceptual understanding of Chinese calligraphy. In addition, about 70% of the students agreed that the calligraphic works presented in the questionnaire looked beautiful, indicating that the students possessed some preliminary abilities to appreciate the cultural-aesthetic values of *hanzi* or at least displayed a potential to do so.

The teacher participants also demonstrated a strong sense of identification with the cultural values of *hanzi*. They unanimously agreed that "*hanzi* is an integral component of the Chinese language," and around 96% of them agreed that "*hanzi* should be considered a part of Chinese culture." In addition, more than 90% of them showed agreement with the values of Chinese calligraphic art in cultivating children's temperament and edifying their sentiment, including, for example, strengthening perseverance (about 80% agreement) and molding a steadfast disposition (about 74%).

The congruence of views between the teachers and the students indicates that the cultural, artistic, and aesthetic values of *hanzi* are as important attributes as their practical, communicative functions.

Students' self-assessment of *hanzi*-related abilities

Students' *hanzi* recognition and writing abilities are an important part of the Chinese curricular reform which eventually led to the implementation of the Modular Curriculum in primary schools. According to the survey, the students had fairly high assessment of their abilities related to *hanzi*. Over 80% had confidence in writing *hanzi*, reporting that they knew how to write *hanzi* before entering school. According to the teacher survey, more than half of the teachers reported that their students could actually write *hanzi*, albeit varying in number, at the beginning of Primary one, and about 95% agreed that they emphasised neat or beautiful hand-writing of *hanzi* as an important pedagogical objective. These findings suggest that students commencing primary schooling are prepared for further learning of *hanzi*, and that primary school teachers value *hanzi* writing.

The teacher survey also touched upon Chinese language teachers' perception of the attitudes of local parents toward *hanzi* learning. According to the result of the survey, over half of the teachers disagreed that "Parents often complain that their child spends too much time on practicing writing *hanzi*," and over 40% agreed that "Parents often hope that there is additional help for their child to write *hanzi*", suggesting that parents in Singapore are overall supportive of *hanzi* writing.

Finally, the student survey revealed a smaller proportion of students who had confidence in their composing abilities in Chinese. Only 62% of the students agreed that they could use Chinese to write picture compositions. Given the high proportion of students who reported confidence in writing *hanzi*, and composing entails character writing as well as sentence building, the finding could be interpreted as that the students' self-assessed abilities were lower in constructing sentences than in writing *hanzi*.

Correlations between student variables

We also examined the correlations between various student variables. As shown in Table 8.1, the correlations between the *hanzi*-related variables were largely significant. In particular, students' interest in *hanzi* ($r = .412$, $p < .001$) and their attitude toward the practical ($r = .409$, $p < .001$) and cultural-aesthetic functions ($r = .379$, $p < .001$) of *hanzi* had moderate correlations with self-assessed abilities, and all correlations were significant. In addition, students' attitude variables were also significantly correlated with their interest in *hanzi*, $r = .490$ and $r = .422$, $ps < .001$ for attitude toward practical function and cultural-aesthetic function, respectively. These significant correlations, taken together, suggest that students with a higher or more positive attitude toward the functions of *hanzi*, including the cultural-aesthetic functions, tend to have more interests in *hanzi*, and consequently, could develop better *hanzi*-related abilities.

Table 8.1 Correlations between various student variables

		1	2	3	4
1	Interest	–			
2	Attitude (practical)	.490***	–		
3	Attitude (cultural-aesthetic)	.422***	.359***	–	
4	Abilities	.412***	.409***	.379***	–

Note. Interest: interest in *hanzi*; Attitude (practical): students' attitude toward the practical functions of *hanzi*, Attitude (cultural-aesthetic): students' attitude toward the cultural-aesthetic functions of *hanzi*; Abilities: students' self-assessed abilities pertaining to *hanzi*.

The investigation and analysis above are admittedly exploratory. However, as the very first effort to examine a diverse range of variables related to *hanzi* among lower primary school students in Singapore, the present study does offer some insights into Chinese curricular reform, and Chinese language education in general. The student survey suggests a more optimistic picture of children's interests in and their awareness of the functions of *hanzi*, particularly the cultural-aesthetic functions, than what was depicted in the Report 2004. It is evident that there are some discrepancies between the views of stakeholders (such as teachers and students) and the documents of curricular policies. In Singapore, where all school curricula are mandated by the Ministry of Education and "with most teachers closely following 'curricular script'" (Towndrow et al. 2010:429), it is reasonable to expect a significant impact of the recommendations of the Report 2004, an official curricular document. It will influence both Chinese language teachers and the public in general and shape their perception of the status of *hanzi* and the teaching and learning of *hanzi*. However, given the complex nature of the educational reform, it will be advantageous that the actual impact is examined in a detailed and qualitative manner. In the following section, we further develop our analysis by focusing on teachers' views and opinions, and how they translate their perceptions into teaching practice.

Teacher interview: Focus Group Discussion (FGD)

Studying teachers' narratives of their own experiences is increasingly being seen as central to programme implementation, given that the teacher is the key, and what they think, believe and do at the level of the classroom ultimately leads to educational change and shapes the kind of knowledge that learners acquire. To conduct the FGD, 117 primary CL teachers (about 20% male and 80% female) from 17 schools were divided into 12 groups for group discussion during a one day teachers' workshop, specially organised for the FGD. Each group consisted of about 10 teachers, and each FGD session lasted 1–1.5 hours. The interview was moderated by a facilitator and a research assistant. Ten unstructured discussion questions, including two questions on *hanzi* instruction, were developed to solicit the teachers' free thoughts about or personal insights into the questions. The following analysis was based on the transcripts of the 12 FGD sessions. In the following we have selected three excerpts, with English translations, as representatives of the teachers' opinions about *hanzi* education.

> Excerpt-1:
>
> 这还用说，汉字跟文化的关系太重要了，当然了。很多中国人的概念最好用汉字解释。我一时想不起来，很多，可以说每天都碰到；现在很多老师都是拿汉语拼音来教价值观，也许可以，我不知道好不好。真的很怀疑。
>
> (Needless to day, the relationship between *hanzi* and Chinese culture is very close. Many Chinese concepts are best illustrated through *hanzi*. I can't give you a good example at the moment, but there are a lot of them; it's a daily encounter. Nowadays, many teachers teach students Chinese values in *hanyu pinyin*. It might work, but I'm not sure if it is good or not. I'm really doubtful). (G5-16-S3)[2]

This comment from a middle aged male teacher, who taught an Enrichment class at a mission school, suggests that, while many teachers had a good understanding of the "Recognise First, Write Later" pedagogical principle, others worried about the impracticality of teaching cultural knowledge as the guidance delayed the students' exposure to *hanzi* knowledge. According to a study (Shang & Zhao 2012:416), only 75 *hanzi* were taught during the first 14 weeks of study in Primary one. In this respect, this teacher's concern seems a legitimate one, because authentic understanding of Chinese culture is best achieved through *hanzi*, and illustrations of tranditional Chinese ideas and thoughts depend primarily on a good understanding of *hanzi*.

> Excerpt-2:
>
> 我认为不应该分识字跟认字，就全部都放在一起，全部教。他们应该学的就是全部要学……我看都眼花缭乱，哪里记得了这么多"识读"还是"写用"…… 你认识一个字，当然是要会用会写。所以我发觉新加坡学这个华文真的是很古怪的，很古怪啊…….
>
> (I can't see any point why there should be a division between *hanzi* for reading and writing, and for recognition. They should be combined together and learnt in one go. (Students) should learn what they're supposed to learn …… I was puzzled by the division. How can I remember which one I should teach for recognition and which one for both? Knowing a character means you should be able to write it. Therefore, I discovered that CL learning in Singapore is so bizarre, really bizarre…….). (G11-39-S1)

---

2.   A transcription code referring to the 16th paragraph/line of interview dialogue by Interlocutor 3 in FGD Group 5.

Not unexpectedly, this senior female teacher of a Core class from a neighborhood school had fairly strong concerns about the separate treatment of *hanzi* for recognition only and for both recognition and writing. The two types of approaches to *hanzi* were recommended in the Report 2004 with a hope to ease students' CL learning burden through reducing *hanzi* writing practice, so that teachers would be able to enthuse them to read within a shorter period of time. Whether or not *hanzi* writing practice should be reduced was a heated discussion in many focus groups. While some teachers appeared to contest mastery in reading as well as in writing for all pedagogical *hanzi* (i.e. supporting a necessary distinction between *rendu zi* and *xixie zi*), it remains an operational challenge for all teachers, as this excerpt shows, to figure out exactly how the recommendation should be pedagogically enacted.

> Excerpt-3:
>
> 对！二十年之后，还是需要华文老师，我相信。可是这些华文老师到前面，必须用电脑。今天我要教给大家一个字，这个字是什么，啪啪啪，打出来；如果是电脑失灵了，糟糕了，拿着笔在白板上写不出字来。
>
> (Right, in two decades, I believe that CL teachers will still be needed. But, by then, these teachers would have to use computers in front of the classes, …, (she/he) would teach like this: today I'm going to teach you this character; then, [sound of typing], the character shows up. If the computer breaks down, then how terrible, (she/he) would stand there with markers in hand but not able to write anything on the whiteboard). (G12-5-S8)

The teacher poignantly points out that modern technology with a smart *hanzi* input system by no means guarantees any *hanzi* writing ability. While the narrative was from the angle of teachers teaching *hanzi*, it is probably true for any CL-mediated communication where written form is involved. It contests the ideology in the Report 2004 that *hanzi* writing could, and should, be deemphasised with the advancement of computer technology.

To sum up, the FGD brought about mixed reactions from the teachers. Admittedly, with respect to the teachers firsthand experience of teaching the new curriculum, the overall beliefs were optimistic. On the one hand, the teachers' attitude appeared largely supportive, albeit not with overwhelming enthusiasm; on the other hand, they expressed strong opinions about some specific issues, such as *hanzi* writing. Interestingly, but not surprisingly, an apparent pattern emerged in the FGD that the more aged and experienced a teacher is, the more likely she/he is to contest the official negative interpretation of *hanzi* and *hanzi* education. A similar pattern was also found in teachers' attitudes towards the use of ICT (information and communication technology) in teaching under the same curriculum (Li et al. 2012). What worries the teachers most is the great reduction of the number of *hanzi* for writing prescribed in the Syllabus 2007. Almost all teachers agreed that such a reduction is creating an enormous challenge for composition writing, which starts from Primary three (for details, see Huang & Wang 2011). In fact, even before the current curriculum was promulgated, Singaporean students' ability in writing *hanzi* was already alarming in comparison with their counterparts in other *hanzi* dependent countries (e.g. Okita & Guo 2001). Despite their different opinions about *hanzi,* all teachers came to a consensus that practising *hanzi*/calligraphy is contributable in fostering learners' aesthetic appreciation and improving their temperament.

Classroom observation

We have thus far analysed both quantitatively and qualitatively the perspectives held by primary school students and teachers, thus shedding new light on major stakeholders' reflections on the new *hanzi* pedagogy envisioned by policymakers. As one more layer of evidence from the practitioners, it is worth an attempt to see what have actually happened in classrooms since the implementation of the curriculum under the new policy. In the aforementioned project from which the current study is derived, classroom observation was a major data collection method.

An observation system known as the Singapore Chinese Pedagogy Coding Scheme (SCPCS), modified from Luke et al.'s (2004) Singapore Pedagogy Coding Scheme, was employed to collect classroom data. The redeveloped version of SCPCS includes nine major coding categories, ranging from class organization to teaching strategy/tools and student products. The raw coding indicates the occurrence of specific teaching features. Altogether, 53 Grade 2 classes from twenty primary schools were observed, video-taped and real-time coded by the researchers using SCPCS, and the total length of coded CL lessons was 198 class hours. The data were analysed by calculating and tabulating the percentages of total time and frequency devoted to each category. The following discussion is based on the overall occurrence and non-occurrence of pedagogical features of each coded item and activity.

The findings showed that *hanzi* teaching and practicing was still a significant part in Singapore primary CL classroom. Specifically, *hanzi* focus was most evident in Students' Produced Work during classroom learning. As Table 8.2 shows, out of the eight classroom activities observed in the core module classes, the students invested nearly 18% of the total classroom time on *Hanzi* Copying, less than Short Oral Response and Oral Repetition, which accounted for 39% and 20%, respectively. The proportion, however, was far greater than all other types of Students' Produced Work, including, named in order, Written Multiple Choice/Fill in Blanks (8%), Sustained Oral Response (6%), Written Short Answer (2%), Sustained Written Text (nil) and others (4%).

Table 8.2 Students' produced work

Items	Activities	Core
	Nil	4%
	Short oral response	39%
Oral Work	Sustained oral response	6%
	Oral repetition	20%
	Character copying	18%
	Written multiple choice/fill in blanks	8%
Written Work	Written short answer	2%
	Sustained written text	0%
	Others (e.g. tests)	4%

Another learner category was Students' Modality, which aimed at recording what specific language skills students focused on in class, including Character Recognition, Listening, Reading, Speaking and Writing. The most noteworthy figures in this category were that in the Core classes, Character Recognition was the focus for 32% of the time as compared to 32% for Speaking, 16% for Writing, 13% for Reading and 6% for Listening (see Table 8.3).

Table 8.3 Students' modality

Modules	Learning Focus					
	Character recognition	Listening	Reading	Speaking	Writing	Others (e.g. drawing)
Core	32%	6%	13%	32%	16%	1%

When the comparison came to the teacher's side, in the category of Teachers' Instructional Focus, as indicated in Table 8.4, the teachers of the Core classes spent 31% of their instructional time on explaining and analysing features of *hanzi*'s physical make-up, pronunciation and writing rules, more than the 30% for Content, 24% for Vocabulary, 8% for Grammar, 4% for Content and 3% for others.

Table 8.4 Teachers' instructional focus

Modules	Teaching Focus					
	Character	Vocabulary	Grammar	Discourse	Content	Others
Core	31%	24%	8%	4%	30%	3%

The findings from the classroom observations concerning *hanzi* instruction showed that teachers did place more emphasis on *hanzi* recognition than on writing, signifying that MOE's pedagogical principle of "Recognize First, Write Later" is basically being implemented in classroom practice. However, as Louden (1991: vi) points out, "[t]eachers don't merely deliver the curriculum. They develop it, define it and reinterpret it too". Reflective teachers do in their daily teaching what they believe is practically beneficial in order to meet the immediate needs of individual learners. The above classroom observation data appear to suggest that teachers did not make special efforts to avoid *hanzi* writing practice, indicating that both teachers and students tend to agree that *hanzi* writing is still an important skill in learning CL.

Conclusion and implications

The teaching approach to and the importance of *hanzi* have long been an issue that has drawn much attention in the area of teaching Chinese as a second language. The rapid development of information technology not only offers new perspectives on *hanzi*'s merits and demerits, but also raises a number of questions that concern *hanzi*'s status in Singaporean schools.

This study critically examined the adequacy of the *hanzi* policy, adopted in the current curriculum, through a holistic view that attaches equal importance to the instrumental as well as the cultural-aesthetic and emotional aspects of *hanzi*. The study identified conflicting policies in paradoxical situations. First, the inter-textual analysis revealed the multiple competing policies emphasised in the two key reform documents, that is, the instructional approaches recommended in the Report 2004 envisioned by policy makers at the high level of educational administration and the national goals of CL education narrated in the Syllabus 2007 prepared by MOE curriculum experts to guide textbook development. Furthermore, it was found that the scenario provided in the Report 2004 was incongruent with what was reported in the student questionnaire survey (and the online teacher survey). Divergent visions between policy makers and teachers as stakeholders were also found in the teachers' FGD. The findings suggested that the negative evaluation of *hanzi*, particularly *hanzi* writing, described in the Report 2004 was not greeted with enthusiasm by classroom teachers; instead, concerns were evident among teachers that such suggestions would result in further decline of students' writing ability. The inseparability of teaching *hanzi* for recognition and for writing was also observed in classroom teaching behaviours, where once again we saw a discrepancy between the policy and the practice.

Drawing upon empirical evidence, we argue that the rationalism/instrumentalism-driven, skill-based policy on *hanzi* manifests itself in contested goals with respect to political doctrines and educational practice. On the one hand, the policy moves away from the long standing pursuance of preserving ancestral roots, of cultural heritage maintenance and nurturing all-round quality of citizenship through mother tongue acculturation; on the other hand, an overemphasis on *hanzi*'s objective and instrumental nature for a pure pragmatic purpose without empirical evidence leads to oversimplification of *hanzi*'s function in language acquisition. The implementation of such an instrumentalism-based policy confuses practitioners in pedagogic practice and creates a poor language environment for CL development. Consequently, it might diminish students' passion for and engagement in reading and improving oral skills in CL, the very goals that underlie the current round of reform programmes.

Liddicoat and Baldauf (2008: 11) emphasise that the interaction between different language planning activities begin at different levels – language decisions are typically made at macro-level institutions, but how these decisions are realised depends on decisions made at other levels. In their words, "No macro-level policy is transmitted directly and unmodified to a local context", which concurs with Bamgbose's (2004: 61) observation that "contradictory policies are adopted at different levels and what is implemented at a lower level is often different from what is prescribed at a higher level". Singapore's policy on Chinese literacy manifests a tension between the macro level at which a broad ideology is espoused by the authorities seeking to meet official goals, and the micro and meso level focusing on specific language issues.

Chinese as a state-designated mother tongue has long been promoted as a cultural protector for maintaining Chinese roots and instilling traditional values in young generations of Singaporeans. In contrast, the curricular decision to reduce the number of *hanzi* and the instructional suggestions to change *hanzi* teaching approaches were made on an instrumental basis that with the wider availability of IT devices, *hanzi* writing skills are made increasingly redundant, ignoring that *hanzi* is regarded as a culturally important symbol among school teachers and students. This approach is, in practice, unsystematic and incidental to other policy-making, and more piecemeal than rational and comprehensive. If the integrity of *hanzi* and CL/Chinese culture and the potential of extended values of *hanzi* learning/practising see continuous ignorance at the level of planning and decision making, policy and practice will inevitably be under threat of being pulled in different directions. The Singaporean experience suggests that policy makers and curriculum developers need to be cognisant of the cohesiveness of the various planning goals in formulating and implementing a language acquisition policy.

Acknowledgment

This research was supported by the Centre for Research in Pedagogy and Practice (CRPP) of the National Institute of Education (NIE) under a Singapore Ministry of Education research grant (OER 52/08 ZSH). We are thankful for the generous support from the teachers and the students in the participating schools and the hard work of many full-time and part-time research assistants. Special thanks go to Ms. Huang Meng for her contribution to data analyses reported in this chapter. Views expressed in this paper are our own.

References

Bamgbose, A. 2004. Language planning and language policies: Issues and prospects. In *Linguistics Today: Facing a Greater Challenge*, P.G.J. van Sterkenburg (ed.), 61–88. Amsterdam: John Benjamins.

DeFrancis, J. & Chia-Yee, Y.T. 1976. *Beginning Chinese: Second Revised Edition* [Yale Language Series]. New Haven CT: Yale University Press.

DeFrancis, J. 1984. *The Chinese Language. Facts and Fantasy*. Honolulu HI: University of Hawaii Press.

DeFrancis, J. 1989. *Visible Speech: The Diverse Oneness of Writing Systems*. Honolulu HI: University of Hawaii Press.

Huang, M. & Wang, C.M. 2011. Teachers' philosophies and practices towards curriculum innovation (Jiaoxue moshi chuangxin: Laizi jiaozhe de sikao yu shijian]. In *The Anthology of the 10th International Symposium on Chinese Language Teaching* (Di 10 Jie Hanyu Jiaoxue Guoji Yantaohui Lunwenji), 58–74. Beijing: Beijing Language University Press.

Li, L., Zhao, S.H. & Yeung, A.S. 2012. Teacher perceptions of curriculum reform in Singapore primary Chinese education. *International Journal of Bilingual Education and Bilingualism* 15(5): 533–548.

Liddicoat, A.J. & R.B Baldauf (eds). 2008. *Language Planning in Local Contexts*. Clevedon: Multilingual Matters.

Liu, Y.M. 2003. *Studies on Cultural Significance of Chinese Character in Japan* (*Hanzi* zai Riben de Wenhua Yiyi Yanjiu). Beijing: Beijing University Press.

Liu, Y.M. 2008. *Chinese Character in Japan* (*Hanzi* zai Riben). Beijing: Capital University Press.

Long, J. 1987. *The Art of Chinese Calligraphy*. Poole: Blandford Press.

Louden, W. 1991. *Understanding Teaching, Continuity and Change in Teachers' Knowledge*. London: Cassell.

Luke, A., Cazden, C., Lin, A. & Freebody, P. 2004. *A Coding Scheme for the Analysis of Classroom Discourse in Singapore Schools* (*Tech. Rep.*). Singapore: National Institute of Education, Centre for Research in Pedagogy and Practice.

Okita, Y. & Guo, J.H. 2001. Learning Japanese Kanji character by bilingual and monolingual Chinese speakers. In *Looking beyond Second Language Acquisition: Studies in Tri-and Multilingualism*, J. Cenoz, B. Hufeisen & U. Jessner (eds), 63–73. Tubingen: Stauffenberg.

Report 2004. *Report of the Chinese Language Curriculum and Pedagogy Review Committee*. Singapore: Singapore Ministry of Education.

Shang G.W. & Zhao S.H. 2012. Hanyu Pinyin teaching in Singapore primary schools: Current situation, problems and suggestions. In *Studies on the Conceptions and Teaching Practices of International Chinese Textbooks,* W. Xu & W. He (eds), 413–419. Hangzhou: Zhejiang University Press.

Shepherd, J. 2005. *Striking a Balance: The Management of Languages in Singapore.* Frankfurt: Peter Lang.

Singapore Department of Statistics 2011. *Census of Population 2010 Advance Census Release.* ⟨http://www.singstat.gov.sg/Publications/publications_and_papers/cop2010/census_2010_advance_census_release/c2010acr.pdf⟩ (1 April 2013).

Syllabus 2007. *Syllabus of Primary Chinese Language Curriculum.* Singapore: Curriculum Planning & Development Division, Singapore Ministry of Education.

Taylor, I. & Taylor, M. 1995. *Writing and Literacy in Chinese, Korean and Japanese* [Studies in Written Language and Literacy 3]. Amsterdam: John Benjamins.

Towndrow, P.A., Silver, R.E & Albright, J. 2010. Setting expectations for educational innovations. *Journal of Educational Change* 11: 425–455.

Van Els, T. 2005. Status planning for learning and teaching. In *Handbook of Research in Second Language Teaching and Learning,* E. Hinkel (ed.), 971–991. Mahwah NJ: Lawrence Erlbaum Associates.

Underhill, J.W. 2009. *Humboldt Worldview and Language.* Edinburgh: EUP.

Wang, H. 2010. A study on the number of *hanzi* and Chinese language teaching in Singapore (Xinjiapo Huawen yongzi liang yu jiaoxue yanjiu). *Review of Language Teaching* (Yuwen Jiaoxue Tongxun) 95: 1–7.

Wang, M.L. 2008. Script reform movement under the instrumentalism rationality at the end of Qing Dynasty (Gongju lixing xia de Qingmo wenzi gaige yundong) *Zhejiang University Journal* (*Social Science*) 38(5): 34–42.

Wang, J. 2006. Examination of *Hanzi* Teaching in "Primary Chinese Language" in Lower Primary School (Xinjiapo "Xiaoxue Huawen" Jichu Jieduan *hanzi* Jiaoxue Kaocha). MA thesis, Guangzhou, Jinan University.

Wee, L. 2003. Linguistic instrumentalism in Singapore. *Journal of Multilingual and Multicultural Development* 24(3): 211–224.

Zhao, S.H. & Baldauf, R.B. Jr. 2008. *Planning Hanzi: Evolution, Revolution or Reaction.* Dordrecht: Springer.

Zhao, S.H. & Liu, Y.B. 2010. Chinese education in Singapore: The constraints of bilingual policy from perspective of prestige planning. *Language Problems and Language Planning* 34(3): 236–258.

Zhao, S.H. & Wang, Y.M. 2009. On five critical relationships of Chinese education in Singapore. Perspective of language planning (Xijiapo Huawen jiaoyu de wu da guanxi: Yuyan guihua shjiao). *Journal of North China University* (*Social Science*) (Beihua Daxue Xuebao (Sheke Ban)) 10(3): 47–58.

CHAPTER 9

Chinese language teaching in Australia

Shen Chen & Yuzhe Zhang

University of Newcastle / University of Newcastle, Australia

Located in the Asian-Pacific region, Australia is a unique example of an English speaking country which has progressive language policies to promote Asian languages, Chinese in particular. History has witnessed three stages of development of Chinese language teaching. In the first stage, Chinese language learning was initiated and organised by local Chinese community schools featured with different curricula decided by various sub-groups. Secondly, the Australian government's multicultural and language policies have further promoted and supported Chinese language learning in community schools. Finally, the Chinese language teaching has expanded to the mainstream schools on the basis of state-based curricula. A national unified curriculum is being developed in order to meet the needs of the fast growing number of learners of Chinese in schools all over the nation. The research described in this chapter on Chinese language teaching in community schools and mainstream schools is based on a policy study of Australia and a case study through qualitative investigations at three universities in the state of New South Wales. The research has revealed some pedagogical problems of Chinese language teaching in the social and cultural context of Australia and provided some suggestions to improve the current performance of Chinese language teaching and learning.

Introduction

Australia, as a member of the Commonwealth of Nations, shares a cultural and political heritage with the United Kingdom and other Commonwealth members. Its educational system has also been strongly influenced by the United Kingdom and the United States. However, geographically it is very close to Asia. Special ties with Asian countries regarding immigration, economy, education and other socio-cultural activities have been established as a result of Australia's increasing interaction with its Asian neighbours. Phrases such as "engagement with Asia" and "Asia-literacy" have been constantly brought forward in official statements since the Hawke-Keating Government (1983–1996) and such messages are also reflected across the Australian curriculum (ACARA 2012). Chinese language education, for example, ties as well as socio-economic and cultural contacts.

In this chapter, three important issues are discussed and analysed. Firstly, features of the Chinese community are identified to situate the teaching and learning of Chinese language and culture in the socio-cultural and historical context of Australia. Secondly, a chronological investigation of Australian governments' language policies is discussed to reveal how political, economic and cultural concerns have a strong impact on the nation's language planning. Thirdly, a critical examination is made about the current Chinese language syllabi, used in mainstream schools and heritage community language schools in Australia.

Chinese migrants in Australia

Australia has been regarded as one of the most "ethnically, culturally and linguistically diverse nations on earth" for most of its history (Ingram 2002, p. 3). Apart from the indigenous population, the remainder, comprising close to 99% of Australia's population today, are immigrants or the descendants of immigrants that arrived in Australia during the past two hundred years (ACPEA 1982). Among them, Chinese-speaking people make up over 3% of the total population and is currently the largest group of speakers of languages other than English (LOTE) in Australia (Australia Bureau of Statistics 2013). The Chinese population is characterised by the following three features:

Firstly, the current Chinese community in Australia includes a number of sub-groups. There are descendants of the earliest Chinese migrants during the "Gold Rush" in the 1850s; there are economic and war immigrants from Hong Kong, Taiwan, Singapore, Malaysia, Vietnam and other Asian countries who arrived during the 1960s and 70s; there are 40,000 Mainland Chinese student-immigrants from the 1989 democracy movement; there are Hong Kong immigrants from 1997 and, lastly, investment immigrants from Mainland China in recent years. The existing large Chinese community is a combination of many sub-cultural communities providing support for the numerous Chinese community schools. These schools are operated on weekends and are an addition to the daytime mainstream schools. Chinese is taught as a subject in accordance with the curriculum guidelines issued by the state governments.

Secondly, the linguistic background of Chinese migrants is complex, depending on where they migrated to Australia. The earlier settlers speak mainly

Cantonese or other southern dialects (regional Chinese variations), whereas modern migrants from China, Taiwan and Singapore usually speak Mandarin. The two writing systems, known as simplified characters and traditional characters, add more complexity to the linguistic diversity. For example, Mandarin speakers from Singapore and P.R. China use simplified Chinese characters for written communication, whereas migrants from Taiwan use traditional Chinese characters. This complex situation has created challenges for teaching and learning Chinese language in the cultural context of Australia. Community schools are not only differentiated by the writing system the parents prefer their children to learn, but also distinguished by textbooks used, either from Singapore, Taiwan, or Mainland China. Thirdly, the Chinese population in Australia is highly concentrated in capital cities. While 66% of all people in Australia live in capital cities, the percentage is as high as 82% for the overseas-born Chinese population (ABS 2012). In the 2006 census, New South Wales and Victoria had the largest number of Chinese immigrants, with a percentage of 96.39% living in Sydney and 97.50% in Melbourne respectively. Similar high percentages of the Chinese population in urban areas are also found in the Australian Capital Territory, South Australia, Western Australia and the Northern Territory (ABS 2006). The concentration has provided more demands and opportunities for Chinese language teaching and learning, and made Chinese community schools more developed in capital cities than in regional areas.

Australia's policy on multiculturalism

The Australian governments' progressive attitude towards various languages other than English (LOTE) matches Ruíz's (1984) three categorisations of language orientation in language planning, which include *language-as-problem, language-as-right and language-as-resource* (cited in Wang 2008). *Language-as-problem* refers to the viewpoint that speaking LOTE causes problems to the society as well as hinders individuals who must learn English in order to fully assimilate into the society. *Language-as-right* indicates that speaking one's own language is part of civil and human rights, therefore LOTEs should be maintained and services in LOTEs should be provided, even in an English-speaking environment. Lastly, *language-as-resource* suggests that LOTEs and their speakers are linguistic, economic and cultural resources for a given society, thus efforts should be made to develop these languages.

The development of Chinese community schools, like that of other educational systems, has been influenced by Australia's political ideologies and language policies during different historical periods. It went from *language-as-problem* (post WWII), *language-as-right* (Galbally strategy in 1973), to *language-as-resource* (1989 policy *National Agenda for a Multicultural Australia*). Based on political ideologies and educational policies, different goals and objectives were set up aiming either at assimilation or preservation of linguistic rights or promotion of linguistic and cultural values. During the assimilation period (before the 1960s), ESL classes in schools were established, bilingual education was prohibited, and language shift was expected (Clyne 2005, 1997). From the 1970s to the 1990s, immigrant language programmes and services appeared in public domains, indicating a recognition and acknowledgment of the civil and linguistic rights of LOTE speakers. The teaching of migrant languages and cultures was established across the Australian education system, both in schools and in universities. Multicultural components were provided in teacher training programmes, and multiculturalism content was included in curricula (Clyne 2005). For the first time, the Galbally strategy identified multiculturalism as a key concept for the government immigration policy, and an inherent component of Australian society (Pietsch et al. 2010; Galbally Report 1978).

Despite 15 years articulated promotion of multiculturalism, "the proportion studying languages in senior secondary and tertiary education has been in long-term decline" and "less than 20% of school children" studied a LOTE (*National Agenda for a Multicultural Australia 1989*, pp. 39–41). The evaluation of the language situation reaffirmed the government's conviction about LOTEs as "natural resources" (p. 41). Subsequently, three successive multicultural policies have been issued by the Australian government: *A New Agenda for Multicultural Australia* (1999); *Multicultural Australia: United in Diversity* (2003); and *The People of Australia – Australia's Multicultural Policy* (2011).

"Productive diversity" (DEET 1991, p. 8) was added as one of the four principles for multiculturalism in the 1999 policy in addition to civic duty, cultural respect and social equity. Most importantly, Australia's diverse population should be able to enjoy "significant cultural, social and economic dividends" (p. 19). As an update of the 1999 policy, both policies in 2003 and 2011 readdressed the importance of the economic and social benefits of diversity by acknowledging that "Australia's multicultural character gives us a competitive edge in an increasingly globalised world" (*Australia's Multicultural Policy* 2011, p. 2).

The emphasis on the benefits for the public of learning a LOTE in the four multicultural policies reflects Australian governments' increasing focus on treating languages as natural and valuable resources. The human capital brought in by immigrants, especially their multilingual capabilities, are particularly emphasised for having placed Australia in an advantageous place in trade and business in the global age (DIMIA 2006).

Australia's policy on Asian languages

In line with the Australian governments' increasing attention to the economic benefits of its multilingual workforce, there have been great efforts to promote language education. Language diversity and multicultural imperatives, solo English language and literacy, and economically strategic Asian languages have all been at some point the priority funding area of the national language policies at some period (Ozolins 2004).

In 1987 the *National Policy on Languages* (NPL) was issued, recognising multilingualism and multiculturalism as key characters to Australia (Hatoss 2005). "A Language Other Than English for all" (NPL 1987, p. 16) was recommended to boost national consciousness, social justice, educational equity, long-term economic strategy and personal satisfaction in the country (Lo Bianco 1987, 2003). Nine languages such as Arabic, Modern Standard Chinese, French and Greek were chosen as representatives of LOTEs in schools.

In 1991 the Dawkins Report on *Australian Language and Literacy Policy* (ALLP) was published, setting English language and literacy as the primary goal for school teaching. Although LOTEs were seen as important resources, financial commitment was limited, giving the teaching and training of LOTEs approximately only 1/10 of the funding for ESL. As a result, priority was given only to "languages of broader national interest to Australia" (ALLP 1991, p. 25), which give economic benefits in trade in the Asian-Pacific region. In addition to the traditionally influential European languages such as French, German and Modern Greek, only three Asian languages – Japanese, Indonesian and Chinese – are prioritised in all States and Territories.

Three years later, the Council of Australian Governments (COAG) released a report on *Asian Languages and Australia's Economic Future,* which initiated a strategy of *National Asian Languages and Studies in Australian Schools* (NALSAS). The NALSAS Strategy was an 8-year plan (1994–2002) which gained cooperative support from the Commonwealth, State and Territory governments. It reduced the languages for the purpose of economic development down to four key Asian languages: Chinese, Japanese, Indonesian and Korean. NALSAS aimed for 60% of all Year 10 students to study one of the four Asian languages by 2004, 25% of Year 12 students to learn a LOTE and 15% of Year 12 students to study an Asian priority language.

Through the NALSAS Strategy, the government provided over $208 million to support the education and research of the four Asian languages over eight years, and an extra annual grant of $1.2 million was allotted to the Asia Education Foundation (AEF). Funding was given to support studies of Asia across all curriculum areas, especially in English, mathematics, science and history (ACARA 2013). New teaching resources, professional development and research activities related to the four languages were also given support. Subsequently, a continuation of the NALSAS was established and another four year plan was launched as the *National Asian Languages and Studies in School Program* (NALSSP 2008–2012). An additional $62 million was devoted to the promotion of the Asian languages when Rudd, a fluent Mandarin speaker, became the Prime Minister of Australia.

The realization of the importance of Asian languages in comparison with the traditional European LOTEs and increasing financial support from the Commonwealth government and State governments revealed two significant factors affecting Australia's language policy – Asian neighbours' rapid development and the changing demographics in schools.

The economic globalization and the geographical ties to Asian countries have made the Australian government realize that its economy has been increasingly relying on its Asian neighbours rather than on the traditional European trading partners. Understanding the languages and cultures of major Asian economic powers is directly linked to the national benefits of Australia. Secondly, there is an increasing need for teaching and learning Asian languages in Australian schools as a result of the demographical changes in immigrant populations. The Asian migrant intake has for the first time been overwhelming in comparison with the decreasing European migrant population. Meanwhile, there has been a very intensive internal pressure and demand from local communities to have stronger community language support, in particular for Asian language education.

The government's policy as the "top down" power and the communities' needs as the "bottom up" force have promoted the teaching and learning of Asian languages in two types of schools, namely, weekend community schools and mainstream schools. The development of teaching Mandarin, as one of the priority Asian languages, is one of the best examples to illustrate the changes under the Australian government's language policies and the local community's expectations.

Chinese Community Schools in Australia

Early Chinese community schools (1900–1990)

The first Chinese community school was established by community leaders in 1909, so Chinese language teaching has existed in Australia for more than 100 years. For most of its history in Australia, however, Chinese has been considered as a community/ethnic/minority language which was to be maintained and preserved in the light of national policies, and the teaching of Chinese language and culture has been limited to local Chinese communities (Smith et al. 1993).

In the early stage of Chinese community schools, there was no syllabus to follow and only few trained and qualified teachers. In most cases, the Chinese teachers themselves were community leaders and parents who wanted their children to learn Chinese as a cultural heritage.

Similar to the Chinese ethnic or heritage schools in other countries, Chinese community schools in Australia were usually small in scale, and it was often difficult to maintain a continuous teaching due to financial limitations and the varying availability of teachers (Smith et al. 1993). The community schools were complementary to mainstream schools, delivering Chinese language classes at night or on the weekends to students who were predominantly native Chinese speakers. The purpose of learning Chinese language was to maintain cultural identity and pass on cultural traditions and values to the coming generations in an English speaking environment.

With regard to curriculum guidelines, few Chinese community schools had clear objectives or detailed curriculum outlines, but relied largely on the teaching materials available at that time. Lack of teaching materials and teaching facilities were characteristics of the community schools, not to mention the lack of professional training for the teachers (Sun 2007). Therefore the teaching content and teaching methods varied to a great extent.

Because of the heterogeneity of the early Chinese migrants who came from different regions and countries, teaching "Chinese language" might refer to different varieties of Chinese language as these migrants formed their own sub-communities and community schools, and determined their own teaching contents regarding language and culture. For instance, in Melbourne, a cluster of Chinese language schools were organized and sponsored by the Taiwanese "Committee of Overseas Chinese" before Australia established diplomatic relations with P.R. China. The Chinese Association of Victoria, consisting of migrants from Singapore and Malaysia followed the syllabus issued by the Singapore government. Obviously, in addition to the linguistic variations of the "Chinese language", the cultural content differed within various sub-groups.

Recent development in Chinese community schools – the case of Xinjinshan School

Over the past 20 years, new migrants from P.R. China have brought new ideas and new resources to the local Chinese community schools.

Xinjinshan School in Melbourne, the largest community school in Australia, is a typical example of innovative community schools run by a group of qualified teachers, educational administrators and community leaders. Xinjinshan School is located in the Eastern suburbs of the greater metropolitan area of Melbourne and has a total number of 4200 students and 300 teachers, scattered over various campuses. In Xinjinshan School, the Chinese syllabi include "General Chinese Learning" (GCL) and Chinese for "Victorian Certification of Education" (VCE). The former is open to all children and adults who wish to learn Chinese for various purposes. The courses are organized in accordance with proficiency levels (beginning, intermediate and advanced) and divided in two strains, Chinese as a first language and Chinese as a second language. There are no official and detailed curriculum guidelines for the GCL programme, but the teachers follow a textbook series, entitled "Zhongwen" issued by Overseas Council of Chinese Government.

The VCE programme, however, is designed exclusively for Year 11 and Year 12 students who also learn Chinese as a LOTE subject in the mainstream school system. Xinjinshan School and other similar community schools function as a supplement to provide these students with additional tutorials after school or during weekends.

Among the entire student population of 4200, approximately 780 students are enrolled in the VCE Chinese programme. The teaching of VCE strictly follows the Chinese syllabus, developed by the educational authority of the Victorian State Government. This cohort of learners is taught by professional trained and certified teachers of Chinese language. Most of them are actually full-time or part-time Chinese teachers in mainstream State schools (personal communication).

The school is supported by the Victorian government, from which it receives $190 per student enrolled. Apart from the certified teachers for the VCE programme, the teachers receive 10 weeks teacher training, organised by local universities and sponsored by the state government. Xinjinshan School also sends teachers to private schools to help establish their Chinese programmes. Work relations with after-school care centres have enabled Xinjinshan School to establish partnerships with 16 primary schools, where Chinese language learning programmes start as early as at lower primary level.

Chinese community schools began flourishing after the establishment of the Commonwealth Sponsored Community Schools Programme in 1981. During 1980's, Chinese community schools were established in all major population centres in Australia (Smith et al. 1993), and student enrolment reached 11, 274 by 2005 (Orton 2010).

Chinese programs in mainstream schools

Getting started

The community schools continued to grow although the funding for these schools had been transferred to and was administered by state governments under the Ethnic School Program (ESP). Recognising the important roles played by ethnic communities in providing language maintenance classes, the ESP determined to "work closely with the relevant community groups" and to "improve the quality of provision", especially in terms of addressing the common issues of accessing the "best teaching materials" and using the "most effective teaching methods" (ALLP 1991, p. 16). The government was committed to linking and aligning the teaching of community languages with mainstream language programmes in the official educational system. Chinese teaching began to be widely incorporated into mainstream schools after the ALLP was issued in 1991.

With the states of Victoria and New South Wales taking the lead, Mandarin began to be taught in Australia nationwide as part of the curriculum in primary and secondary education systems, including State, Catholic and independent schools. By 2010, 319 schools in Australia offered Chinese language programmes, with an enrolment of 77,453 students in primary and secondary schools and 4,534 students (5.85%) in Year 12 for the HSC examination (Orton 2010).

But not every school provides Mandarin programmes. If students from a mainstream school, regardless of their background, want to learn Chinese but the classes are not offered in their school, they are encouraged by the state government to study in one of the local Chinese community schools after school hours. Classes can be conducted face to face, but distance education is also offered. Credit points gained in the assessments can be converted and used in the mainstream school system.

Chinese language teaching materials and syllabi in mainstream schools

The lack of appropriate teaching materials was a major problem for community schools in the past. With the commitment to developing a successful LOTE programme, funding was given to design appropriate textbooks for mainstream school students. Peter Chang et al. (1985, 1986, 1990) from Griffiths University developed the first set of three textbooks for Chinese teaching for beginner, intermediate and advanced levels in the mid-1980s. In subsequent years, these textbooks were adopted widely by both community schools and the mainstream schools. The contents were gradually treated by the states as a brief syllabus guideline for Chinese teaching used nationally for primary and secondary schools. However, the contents were designed for all learners across the country at two levels, namely the K-10 years and the 11–12 years, regardless of their background. The government also decided that Modern Standard Chinese (Mandarin) should be the speaking form, and simplified Chinese characters the writing form, although the study of traditional Chinese characters was not excluded.

Taking the Chinese syllabus in New South Wales as an example, the Board of Studies (BOS) issued two sets of syllabi for Chinese teaching in 2003: one for K-10 years and one for 11–12 years. The syllabi classified six stages of learning

Chinese. From Stage 1 to 3, in years K to 6, students were expected to "develop an awareness" of Chinese language (BOS 2003, p. 22). From year 7–10, 100 hours per 12 months were allocated to the study of Chinese, just as for any other LOTE (see also Figure 9.1). Compared with the previous syllabus, the 2003 syllabus in NSW extended and broadened the standards of learning outcome (NSW BOS 2003).

Differentiated learners in mainstream schools

The newly developed Chinese language syllabus did not, however, resolve all the problems regarding learning outcomes. In the first place, the curriculum framework, used for the Chinese syllabus, was similar to those used for other LOTEs. In other words, the learning objectives, learning hours and expected learning outcome were the same as for other European languages, such as French and German. Research shows that English-speaking learners need much more time to learn Chinese than a European language if they wish to reach an equivalent level of proficiency (Smith et al. 1993). Allocating the same number of teaching hours was not realistic although necessary if the goals set up in the language policies were to be achieved.

In addition, the backgrounds of learners were becoming extremely complicated (Lo Bianco & Liu 2007). Different learner background and proficiency level in the same class caused problems in teaching and learning. Using the same type of syllabus for both ethnic Chinese students and for students without a Chinese background was unjustified and unfair. As a matter of fact, when the former became the majority of learners in a Chinese class, the latter often felt intimidated and threatened, leading to a high dropout rate at the senior level (Orton 2010). On top of that, the Chinese community schools often provide ethnic Chinese students with additional enforcement of the Chinese syllabus used in the mainstream schools. This extra resource may not necessarily be available to non-Chinese students.

To overcome these problems streamed syllabi of Chinese were written for Year 12 students. As a result, when students have reached Stage 6, i.e. the Higher School Certificate (HSC) level, they have four choices based on their linguistic background and needs: Stage 6 Syllabus – Chinese Beginners; Chinese Continuers; Chinese Extension; and Chinese Background Speakers. Among the four syllabi, the first three were designed for students with little linguistic background in Chinese. The last one was designed specifically for students who speak Mandarin or a Chinese dialect at home, and who have received formal school education in Chinese before migrating to Australia. The streamed syllabus is illustrated by the continuum of the Chinese curriculum for K-12 in NSW, as demonstrated in the following figure:

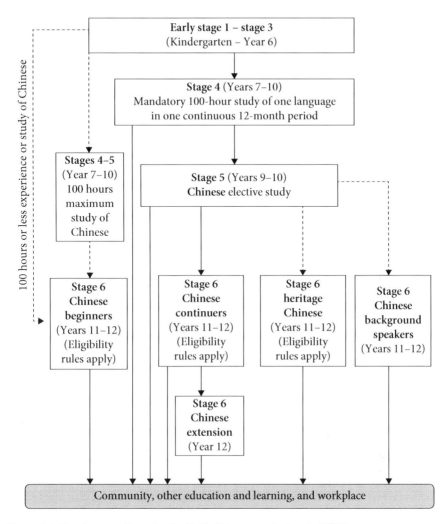

Figure 9.1 Continuum of learning for K-12 Chinese curriculum in NSW

(Source: Board of Studies, NSW, Heritage Chinese State 6 syllabus)

The division between non-background learners and background speakers in the syllabus design was linguistically justified, so it seemed that learners of Chinese, regardless of gender, race and ethnicity, were equally treated. However, the definition of background and non-background learners could be problematic due to parents' intercultural marriage and speakers' birth place. Therefore, the four types of syllabus were unable to accommodate all of the various needs of the learners.

In 2010, New South Wales initiated a new national project for developing heritage language programmes for the four key Asian languages (Lo Bianco & Slaughter 2009). The target group was background students who were born in

Australia, but not eligible to take background speakers examination for HSC. These Australian-born background students usually have higher proficiency in speaking and listening skills but have limited reading and writing skills. Unlike the overseas born background speakers, they do not have access to sustained period of immersion education in Chinese. These students may have received most of their formal education in either English or other non-Chinese languages, but have also studied some Chinese in Australia, or in schools using Chinese as medium of teaching up to age 10 (NSW BOS 2010).

The new heritage language programme led to further changes in the Chinese language syllabus for various background speakers as shown in Figure 9.1, where heritage learner was included as an independent category of Chinese language learner.

With regard to culture integrated in the Chinese language, the NSW HSC syllabus made an explicit statement: "The ability to communicate in Chinese contributes significantly to the sociocultural and economic understanding between Australia and Chinese-speaking countries and enables students to gain insights into the contributions that have been made by Chinese-speaking communities to Australian, and indeed to global, society" (BOS 2012, p. 7). According to this view, Chinese should be learned for intercultural communication. However, the syllabi seem to put more attention on learning the culture of Chinese speaking countries and communities than on how to get Chinese speaking people to understand Australian culture. In particular, how to link Chinese language learning with real life in Australia remains a common problem.

A critique of Chinese syllabus in NSW

Jointly with the Australian Commonwealth Government and all other states and territories of Australia, NSW has made an effort to develop a nationally unified Chinese language curriculum. There are, however, still several issues that need to be addressed. In order to understand how efficient and functional the NSW Chinese syllabus is, we conducted a qualitative research to seek evaluative views from various teaching professionals, including five teacher educators, five student teachers and four graduates of the Chinese teacher education programmes in three universities in NSW. Using in-depth interview as a tool for data collection, the 14 participants provided their perspectives on the new syllabus. The background information of the participants is described in Table 9.1.

In spite of the state governments' effort to provide a streamed syllabus for students with different backgrounds, our analysis shows that the teaching professionals have three major concerns.

Table 9.1 Participants' background

	Participant code	1st Language	Experience with Chinese language teaching	Work place
Teacher Educators	TE1	Chinese	Over 20 years with Chinese teaching and teacher training in Australia	Regional area
	TE2	Chinese	Over 20 years with Chinese teaching and teacher training in Australia	Urban area
	TE3	English	Over 20 years with LOTE teaching and teacher training in Australia	Urban area
	TE4	English	Over 10 years with LOTE teaching and teacher training in Australia	Urban area
	TE5	English	Over 20 years with LOTE teaching and teacher training in Australia	Rural area
Student teachers	ST1	Chinese	50 days' practice teaching in Chinese	Regional area
	ST2	English (Chinese background)	25 days' practice teaching in Chinese	Urban area
	ST3	English (Chinese background)	1 year school teaching in Chinese, over 10 years teaching in English	Urban area
	ST4	English	1 year school teaching in Chinese, over 10 years teaching LOTE	Regional area
	ST5	English	1 year Chinese teaching, over 20 years LOTE teaching	Regional area
Graduates	G1	Chinese	Almost 20 years teaching Chinese in Australia	Urban area
	G2	English	Almost 20 years teaching Chinese and other LOTE in Australia	Regional area
	G3	English	Almost 20 years teaching Chinese and other LOTE in Australia	Regional area
	G4	English	Almost 20 years ESL teaching in Australia	Regional area

Syllabus content

Firstly, the requirements for language study in the syllabus are considered too demanding. This challenge is reflected mainly in the number of Chinese characters required by the syllabus. Being aware of the linguistic differences between alphabet and logographic languages, TE3 is concerned that vocabulary size is hard to increase for most of the English-speaking students because Chinese characters do not "have links to English". However, the number of characters to be mastered in the NSW Chinese syllabus is overwhelming for the English-speaking students in high schools. For example, in the syllabus for Chinese beginners, the students are required to master 167 characters, and the number increases to 350 for continuers. Comparatively, in Japanese the requirement for Kanji is 79 for beginners and 150 for continuers (NSW, BOS 2009). With the same 100 hour curriculum time, the learning of characters in Chinese is much less "digestible" (ST2) than in Japanese.

The large amount of characters to be mastered in the limited study hours is considered a big challenge for both background Chinese students and, to a much greater extent, students from a non-Chinese background.

TE3 and G1 point out that background students need to spend as much time on practicing writing as non-background students although they are usually advanced in listening and speaking skills. Unless they are encouraged, or sometimes forced, by their parents to commit substantial hours to practicing Chinese characters, these students would learn no more characters than non-background students, as Chinese is "such a vocab based language" (ST2). Insufficient vocabulary size might easily lead to difficulties in reading and writing (ST2), which account for a significant proportion in the HSC examination.

As an experienced Chinese language teacher, G1 observed that many background students have been encouraged by their parents to study basic Chinese at a young age, either at mainstream or community schools, for both educational and cultural reasons. But parents and students are realistic when it comes to "serious study", namely preparing for entering a selective high school or for HSC examination. If the background students realised that they do not have much advantage in HSC Chinese, they drop Chinese and focus on other more promising subjects. ST2 acknowledges that most background students find the contents "hard and irrelevant". Amongst all the school subjects, ST4 thinks Chinese is the most difficult subject for Year 7 or 8 students.

Compared to other LOTE students, Chinese language learners progress at a slower pace. The characteristics of Chinese as a logographic language, which has little indication of pronunciation of characters, tend to slow down the learning process of English-speaking students. ST2 comments that "this could be extremely frustrating". Therefore, once learning Chinese is no longer compulsory, many students drop the study, which causes the overall low retention rate (6%) of Chinese language program in Australia beyond compulsory years (Orton 2010).

The views from the teachers and teacher educators suggest that there is a gap between the government's expectation of Chinese teaching and the students' interest in and need for Chinese learning. TE2 considers such an expectation from the government to be "unrealistic" within the short period of a few years' study. Consequently, to achieve a satisfactory proficiency and contribute to economic exchanges with China is unlikely to be attainable. If the goal for promoting Chinese in the education system is based on the economic rationale, TE2 continues, then "students will get disappointed and drop the classes when they obviously cannot even reach the minimum level".

TE2 suggests that the syllabus should set realistic goals for Chinese teaching in Australia by lowering the goal from professional and vocational use of Chinese learning to basic social purposes. TE2, ST2, and ST3 recommend as more fruitful, especially at beginners' level, to focus on developing basic conversational skills through immersion practice in speaking and listening, instead of emphasizing mastery of Chinese characters through repetitive drills. If the students had some basic conversation in Chinese with native speakers, they would experience a sense of success and thus be motivated to learn more. The current requirement for learning Chinese characters has brought the standard to a "very high level" (TE2) so that the unrealistic goals have become "empty talk" (TE2).

Teaching resources and support

Secondly, the prescribed syllabus does not come with adequate and suitable teaching resources, mainly because of the short history of Chinese teaching in NSW schools.

Admitting that there are "tons of" Chinese textbooks in the market at present, ST3 remarks "a few of them are considered good textbooks and have been widely used in Australian schools". However, when introducing a Chinese language programme in his school, ST3 had a frustrating experience locating a good textbook. Many available ones are identified by ST3 as either "not interesting", "very dry" or "not challenging enough", and overall not "relevant" to his teaching. Eventually in order to develop a set of suitable teaching materials for the primary students who are predominantly non-background students, ST3 has had to spend a lot of time on-line searching for resources that are "unique", engaging and appealing to the students.

The lack of teaching resources is also evident despite the generous supportive resources from China. G1 teaches in an urban public school where there is a large Chinese community and the students are exclusively background Chinese. According to G1, because of the increasing enrolment in this program, the school is eligible for sufficient teaching aids and resources from the state government through the sponsoring organisation Hanban in P. R. China. These abundant resources demonstrate the commitment to Chinese teaching in Australia, from both the Australian and the Chinese governments. However, G1 comments that many of the textbooks are developed by scholars in China, and do not always cater for the teaching and learning in an Australian classroom. Thus many of these resources are not used in his teaching, including visual and audio materials.

When Chinese teachers have to devote a large amount of time in an often futile effort to develop new resources, it is very easy to "feel isolated and lonely", and "get a bit deflated…(think) it's not fair…very down" (G2). The situation is exacerbated by the fact that many Chinese teachers are the only teacher of Chinese (such as G1, G3), the only Asian language teacher (such as G2), and even the only LOTE teacher (ST3, ST5) in the school. Especially for teachers of Chinese who work in regional and rural areas in Australia, "it's quite a lonely journey" (TE3), because the proportion of Chinese population outside urban areas is very low. In this situation, it is vital that the Chinese teachers "grab the lifeline" (TE3), reach out to their peers through online forums and attend regular meetings, seminars or conferences.

Although the interviewed teachers of Chinese deeply appreciate and welcome such organised support, they suggest that the efficiency of the communication could be improved. As G1 comments, during the conferences, "the consultants… they talked about many theories, and envisioned the developments of Chinese teachings. That is good. But when it comes down to instructing my classroom teaching, facing my 20 students today, how can these consultants solve my direct problem in my class?" ST3 suggests local Chinese teacher associations organise small scale meetings based on frequent and flexible schedules, where only "the best resources" and "most effective things" that have been proved to "work really well" in the teaching should be shared. It is also considered to directly benefit the teachers' classroom teaching if the Chinese teachers could have the opportunity to observe each other's class (G1).

The comments and suggestions indicate that teachers are passionate and enthusiastic about teaching Chinese language. Developing teaching resources requires collaboration between teachers, text writers and academics who take into consideration the students' learning environments and interests. Compared with teachers of well-established languages in Australian schools, according to G2, teachers of Chinese are "pioneers" who often need to "take a lot more" to develop a Chinese program from scratch. They cannot "only teach classroom and go away, instead, they need to "think of the ideas, create it, invite people along…plan the events…plan (the) classes".

Teaching method

The third concern is regarding efficient teaching methods. Although professional training programmes are available for teachers in NSW universities, specialised Chinese language methodology courses have not been effectively developed due to funding and resource limitations.

While the Australian government has undoubtedly taken the lead when offering teacher training programmes for Chinese language teachers at universities, two issues related to Chinese syllabi may have had great influence on the training outcome.

First of all, a majority of the Chinese language teachers in both community schools and mainstream schools are predominantly native speakers of Chinese who have received teaching degrees in China and taken in-service training in Australia. When attending training programmes offered at universities, they found that specific Chinese method courses for student-teachers to learn about the state syllabus and effective ways to teach the syllabus were insufficiently provided. Two of the three investigated universities used to offer Chinese method courses. However, due to cuts in funding and lack of educational resources, and the declining enrolment over the last two decades, it became "very uneconomic" (TE1, TE2) and thus only generic LOTE method courses are now available. As a result, these qualified Chinese language teachers learned all the basic knowledge, namely Chinese content knowledge, general education theories and theories in LOTE teaching. Upon graduation and after 25–50 days practicum in schools, they had little understanding of the syllabus, hardly enough to enable them to implement the syllabus effectively (ST1).

Secondly, student-teachers and graduates from different language and cultural backgrounds may have different teaching styles that affect their interpretations and implementations of the syllabus. According to TE1, in general, these teachers can be divided into two groups – Chinese background teachers and Australian teachers from non-Chinese background. The former tends to have good Chinese language proficiencies but are less informed in educational concepts, learner needs and the workplace environment in Australia, while the latter shows the opposite characteristics. It is hoped that through a common training programme, student-teachers from different backgrounds will reach a competent level (TE3, TE4). However, the influence of language and cultural background on teaching styles cannot be easily changed, even by 3–5 years' university training.

Interestingly, the same group division occurred at schools based on student population. Native Chinese-speakers tend to be given classes where students are mainly native or background learners, whereas English speakers teach non-background learners. For example, G4, as an English-speaker, was constantly rejected to teach in schools where the students were predominantly Chinese, even though she achieved a high level of Chinese language competence. Similarly, in most regional areas and in some urban schools where the majority students are non-background learners, school managements prefer to have Chinese language teachers who are from the same background as the students, so their experiences as Chinese learners can help them understand the challenges their students might encounter (TE1, TE3).

The voices from the participating teachers and teacher educators clearly show that there is a gap between curriculum design and curriculum implementation. To fill the gap, curriculum evaluation and innovation are urgently needed. Currently, a new version of the Chinese syllabus has been drafted and consultations are sought by the Australian Curriculum Assessment and Reporting Authority (ACARA). Needless to say, this is a new milestone for teaching and learning Chinese in both mainstream and community schools across Australia.

Conclusion

In conclusion, three important points seem to be noteworthy and should be considered in the further development of Chinese language teaching and learning in Australia:

Firstly, the development of Chinese language teaching and learning in Australia needs to be closely linked to the changing composition of Chinese migrants and the evolution of multiculturalism, promoted in the Australian socio-cultural context.

Secondly, Australia was one of earliest English-speaking countries that issued a series of government policies on multiculturalism and made Chinese language teaching available, not only in community schools but also in the mainstream educational system.

Finally, the entire national syllabi of Chinese language teaching and learning have been constantly undergoing change on the basis of social changes and Australia's changing relations with Asian countries, in particular the P.R. China. A national curriculum of Chinese is now in preparation to meet the political and economic needs of Australia with respect to economic ties, business, tourism and cultural exchange.

References

ABS (Australian Bureau of Statistics) (2012, 12 December 2012). *Cultural Diversity in Australia.* ⟨http://www.abs.gov.au/ausstats/abs@.nsf/Lookup/2071.0main+features902012-2013⟩ (29 January 2013)

ABS (Australian Bureau of Statistics) 2006. *Language Spoken at Home by Sex-1996, 2001, 2006 by State and Statistical Division.*

ACARA (Australian Curriculum, Assessment and Reporting Authority) 2013. *Asia and Australia's engagement with Asia.* ⟨http://www.australiancurriculum.edu.au/CrossCurriculumPriorities/Asia-and-Australias-engagement-with-Asia⟩ (29 January 2013)

ACPEA (Australian Council on Population and Ethnic Affairs) 1982. *Multiculturalism for all Australians: Our Developing Nationhood.* Canberra: Australian Government Public Service.

BOS (Board of Studies), NSW 2012. HSC (Chinese) syllabi.

BOS (Board of Studies), NSW 2003. Chinese K-10 syllabus guide.

Chang, P., Mackerras, A. & Yu, H. 1985. *Hanyu 1: Chinese for Beginners.* Melbourne: Griffith University Press.

Chang, P., Mackerras, A.& Yu, H. 1986. *Hanyu 2: Chinese for Beginners.* Melbourne: Griffith University Press.

Chang, P., Mackerras, A. & Yu, H. 1990. *Hanyu 3: Chinese for Beginners.* Melbourne: Longman Cheshire.

Clyne, M. 2005. *Australia's Language Potential.* Sydney: University of New South Wales Press.

Clyne, M. & Kipp S. 1997. Trends and changes in home language use and shift in Australia, 1986–1996. *Journal of Multilingual and Multicultural Development* 18(6): 451–473.

COAG 1994. *Asian Languages and Australia's Economic Future: A Report Prepared for the Council of Australian Government on a Proposed National Asian Languages/Studies Strategy for Australian Schools (Rudd Report).* Brisbane: Queensland Government Printer.

Department of the Prime Minister and Cabinet and Office of Multicultural Affairs, July 1989. *National Agenda for a Multicultural Australia: Sharing Our Future.* Canberra: Australian Government Publishing Services.

DEET 1991. *Australia's Language: The Australian Language and Literacy Policy.* Canberra: Australian Government Publishing Services.

DIMIA (Department of Immigration and Multicultural and Indigenous Affairs). 2006. *Multicultural Australia: United in Diversity.* Canberra: Australian Government Publishing Services.

Galbally, F. 1978. *Migrant Services and Programs: Report of the Review of Post-arrival Programs and Services for Migrants.* Canberra: Australian Government Publishing Service.

Hatoss, A. 2005. *Sustainable Multilingualism as an Essential Characteristic of Multicultural Societies: The Case of Australia.* Paper presented at Language, Attitudes and Education in Multilingual Cities, 27–29 May 2004, Brussels, Belgium.

Ingram, D.E. 2002. *Language and Culture Policy in Multicultural Australia.* Brisbane: Centre for Applied Linguistics and Languages, Griffith University.

Lo Bianco, J. 1987. *National Policy on Languages.* Canberra: Australian Government Publishing Service.

Lo Bianco, J. 2003. *A Site for Debate, Negotiation and Contest of National Identity: Language Policy in Australia,* Strasbourg: Council of Europe.

Lo Bianco, J. & Liu G. 2007. Australias language policy and ecology of Chinese language education. *Chinese Teaching in the World (Shi jie Hanyu jiao xue)* 3: 120–131.

Lo Bianco, J. & Slaughter, Y. 2009. *Second Languages and Australian Schooling.* Victoria: Australian Council for Educational Research.

Orton, J. 2010. *The Current State of Chinese Language Education in Australian Schools.* Melbourne: The University of Melbourne.

Ozolins, U. 2004. Language policy and its rationales. *Current Issues in Language Planning* 5(4): 361–375.

Pietsch, J, Graetz, B & McAllister, I. 2010. *Dimensions of Australian Society.* Melbourne: Palgrave Macmillan.

Ruíz, R. 1984. Orientations in language planning. *NABE: The Journal for the National Association for Bilingual Education, 8*(2), 15–34.

Smith, D., Chin, N.B., Louie, K. & Makeras, C. 1993. *Unlocking Australia's Language Potential, Profiles of 9 Key Languages in Australia,* Vol.2: *Chinese.* Canberra: National Languages and Literacy Institute of Australia.

Sun, H. 2007. 海外华人教育 *The Education of Chinese Language from Abroad.* Shanghai: Shanghai People's Publishing House.

Wang, S.C. 2008. The ecology of the Chinese language in the United States. In *Encyclopaedia of Language and Education,* Vol. 9: *Ecology of Language,* A. Creese, P. Martin & N.H. Hornberger (eds), 169–181. Dordrecht: Springer.

PART IV

Chinese language, culture and identity

CHAPTER 10

Speaking of identity?

British-Chinese young people's perspectives on language and ethnic identity

Becky Francis, Ada Mau & Louise Archer
King's College, London

Young people's constructions of the relationship between language and ethnic identity is discussed, drawing on data from 60 British-Chinese complementary school attendees, and 38 young people of Chinese/mixed heritage that constructed themselves as not being able to speak Chinese. Those young people attending Chinese complementary school strongly foregrounded fluency in heritage language as essential to Chinese identity. Indeed some of these young people drew on moral and nationalistic discourses to challenge the possibility of identification as 'Chinese' without fluency in 'mother tongue'. However, it was also found that, for those young people not able to speak the language, this did not preclude their identification as Chinese: these young people drew on a range of signifiers of Chinese culture, connection, and engagement to position themselves as wholly or partly 'Chinese'. The impact of the different diasporic family histories for the two sample groups is discussed in relation to the young people's different constructions, and theoretical implications of the findings considered. It is argued that, despite discourses that produce idealised notions of 'essential' features of Chinese culture, in practice young people demonstrate agency in their diverse productions and understandings of 'Chineseness'.

Introduction

In her powerful work *On (not) speaking Chinese*, Ang (1994) ruminates on the consequences of speaking (or not speaking) the 'Mother tongue' for inclusion/ exclusion from particular identifications and claims of belonging. In this chapter we seek to reflect on findings from our research with British-Chinese young people, concerning their perceptions of the import or otherwise of Chinese language competence for their lives in Britain.

We draw on findings from two studies. The first is an ESRC-funded project[1] that sought to explore British-Chinese complementary school pupils' experiences and constructions of this schooling. This project built on earlier ESRC-funded research[2] instigated by our interest in the identities and attitudes to education among a high-achieving minority-ethnic group within the British education system – the British-Chinese (see Francis & Archer 2005a, 2005b; Archer & Francis 2006a, 2007). We found that complementary Chinese schools were positioned by the participating pupils and their parents as providing a pivotal role in the transmission of the Chinese language and culture, and in their provision of an additional source of learning (Francis & Archer 2005a). In this sense, these parents and pupils portrayed complementary schools as contributing both to the educational achievement of British-Chinese pupils, and (relatedly) to their ethnic identity (see also Martin et al. 2003; Archer et al. 2009).

The second study which will be briefly drawn on in this chapter was in turn precipitated by the complementary school study – as findings that we shall discuss below concerning the importance (or otherwise) of speaking Chinese provoked Ada Mau to explore ethnic identifications among those British Chinese that *cannot* speak Chinese. We hope that our work contributes to understandings of the moral and ideological discourses underpinning the impetus (or otherwise) to learn 'mother-tongue', and the ways in which these are interpolated in constructions of ethnic identity. Our work also provides insights as to how (a) 'mother-tongue' competence can be constructed as fundamental to Chinese identity, but also, (b) how some young people may reject 'mother-tongue' competence as a vital component to Chinese identity, drawing instead on other narratives and practices to populate 'Chineseness'.

Conceptual background

Our studies are foregrounded in the literature on identity work, educational attainment, and on Chinese complementary schooling. We very briefly here situate our work within research findings on complementary schooling, before explaining the theoretical perspective we adopt with regard to the concepts of 'identity' and 'culture'.

---

1. ESRC project 'British-Chinese Pupils' Identities, Achievement and Complementary Schooling' (RES000231513).

2. ESRC project 'British-Chinese Pupils' Constructions of Education, Gender & Post-16 Pathways' (R000239585).

Numerous studies had elucidated the diverse benefits of complementary schooling for minority ethnic children (see e.g. Archer et al. 2009; Creese et al. 2006; Dove 1993; Hall et al. 2002; Martin et al. 2003; Reay & Mirza 1997; Strand 2002). However, at the point of our study's inception relatively little attention had been paid to the constructions of complementary schooling among the user populations – particularly the pupils. Our research sought to make a distinctive contribution by focusing on how minority ethnic pupils and parents construct complementary schooling in terms of purposes, benefits and functions.

With regard to our understanding of identity, we draw on postcolonial and sociological work that has developed nuanced understandings of identity, culture and ethnicity, and attended to the ways in which these are played out within diasporic spaces and collectivities. The identities generated within diasporic communities blend and synthesise a host of different cultural elements, challenging and transcending 'old' boundaries (Bhabha 1994). Concepts such as 'hybridity' have been offered as productive ways for grappling with the complex cultural and identity formations that characterise diasporic identities. As Hall (1992, p. 235) explains, "identity lives with and through, not despite, difference: by hybridity". Our interest lies especially in understanding the complex workings of power that are involved in negotiations between parents, teachers and pupils over the symbols and markers of 'culture' and 'ethnic identity' (notably struggles around 'hybridised' or 'authentic' cultural identities; see Archer et al. 2010). We apply a conceptual framework that understands culture and identities as processes of 'becoming' – unstable moments that are subject to the continuous flows of history, culture, context and power (Hall 1992) and which are inter-cut by structural axes of 'race', gender, social class and so on.

Such analyses that see identities as 'in process' have been increasingly applied in the field of language learning (Norton & Toohey 2011; see also Cummins & Early 2011; Kinginger 2004; Norton 2010). He (2006, p. 1) argues that Chinese heritage-language development "takes place in a three-dimensional framework with intersecting planes of time, space, and identity", and a learner's language development "depends on the ability to find continuity and coherence in multiple communicative and social worlds in time and space and to develop hybrid, situated identities and stances". Proficiency in heritage language is seen as an important signifier relating to ethnic identity among diasporic communities (Ang 2001); however, as Oriyama's (2010) study shows, level of heritage language proficiency does not always correlate to the degree of identification with the heritage culture or group.

We approach ethnicity, culture and identity as discursive constructs. In contrast to dominant, popular views of 'culture' as something fixed, static and definable, we adopt a poststructural view of 'culture' as fluid, performative, and produced by discourses which delineate 'truth', fixity and status and that are infused with desire and morality (see e.g. Foucault 1972). This approach recognises that the construction of boundaries around 'culture' (what 'counts' and should be taught/preserved, and so on) is a social and political process (Chun 1996). As we observe elsewhere (Francis et al. 2009), it is imperative to recognise the highly politicised and stratified nature of language, and its power as a system of reification and/or marginalisation; and the related impact of such discursive practices on identities. This extends to 'mother tongue' and languages often seen as marginalised in British contexts (for brief discussion of hierarchies of 'Chinese' languages and dialects, see Francis et al. 2009).

The concept of the 'imagined community' (Anderson 1991) has been used by a number of scholars (e.g. Kanno & Norton 2003; Norton 2001; Pavlenko & Norton 2007) to examine the discourses characterising construction of different 'communities' and the implications for associated identities and language learning. Norton and Toohey (2011) suggest that such imagined communities can have a strong impact on how learners engage in language learning and imagined identities. When a language is linked to a national identity, the symbolic status of a language can "create identity and discontinuity, and can both unite and divide, as it can become a battleground, an object of oppression and a means of discrimination" (Blommaert & Verschueren 1998, in Blackledge 2004, p. 71). Language, in a similar manner to cultural practices, can be used to draw boundaries and mark differences in 'culture' and 'values' in other ethnic/linguistic communities. This important recognition and emphasis on the operation of power via discourses pertaining to culture and identification also reminds us of the role of social structure and material embodiment within these constructions, and in relations of power. For example, the way that the physical, 'raced' body often remains the vehicle around which discourses on ethnicity and culture can be targeted and re/produced.

Methodology

The ESRC-funded study of British-Chinese complementary school pupils was a qualitative study based on interviews with parents, teachers and pupils, and classroom observations in six different Chinese complementary schools (for further details see e.g. Francis et al. 2009). The data discussed here are drawn from individual interviews with 60 British-Chinese secondary school-age pupils. Mau's doctoral study is based on individual interviews with 38 British-Chinese young people who constructed themselves as not being able to speak Chinese.

Table 10.1 Outline of the two projects

	Chinese complementary schools (Francis, Archer & Mau 2009) ESRC-funded study of British-Chinese complementary school pupils	On not speaking 'much' Chinese (Mau 2013) Doctoral study of British Chinese pupils with limited Chinese language skills
Purpose	To explore the experiences and identities of young people attending Chinese complementary school, and the practices of Chinese school	To explore the identities of young people of Chinese heritage with limited Chinese language skills
Respondents	60 11–16 year old pupils from six Chinese complementary schools	38 11–18 year old young people of Chinese heritage who do not have fluent Chinese
Respondents' country of birth	UK 53 (88%) Mainland China 4 (7%) Hong Kong 2 (3%) Macau 1 (2%)	UK 33 (87%) Malaysia 2 (5%) Australia 1 (3%) Hong Kong 1 (3%) USA 1 (3%)
Mixed heritage pupils within the samples	1 Chinese & White British	6 Chinese & White British 1 Chinese & Greek Cypriot 2 Chinese & Italian 1 Chinese and Pakistani
Questions to respondents	About their reasons for attending complementary school, their perceptions of the purposes of Chinese complementary schooling and their experiences of it, their views on the importance or otherwise of 'mother-tongue', and their views on the comparison between their complementary and mainstream schooling	About their experiences of growing up with no/limited Chinese language abilities, the impact on their constructions of learner and social identities, and their perspectives on 'Chineseness' and Chinese and British 'culture' relating to the role of languages within the Chinese 'community' and greater British society
Methods	Individual interviews with 60 young people, across six Chinese complementary schools, and observation of classroom interaction and practices at each school across England.	Individual interviews with 38 young people and some observations across a range of sites in Southern England.

Constructions of the import of speaking Chinese

For the 60 pupils interviewed in our Chinese complementary school study, overwhelmingly the primary reason for attending Chinese school was to learn, or improve competency in, the Chinese language. Additional explanations – to learn about Chinese culture, to be 'more Chinese', to facilitate future work in Hong Kong – also tended to evoke the intentions of replication of 'culture' and continued links with 'Motherland' which infused the responses of many pupils. Perhaps not surprisingly, given their construction of learning/improvement of the Chinese language as the main purpose of attending Chinese school, 87% (52 pupils) said that it is important to learn the language. Only 3 pupils (5%) said that it is not important, with a further 5 pupils (8%) providing ambivalent or qualified responses. Table 10.2 depicts the *reasons* provided by those pupils declaring it important to learn Chinese:

Table 10.2 Reasons provided as to why they consider it important to learn the Chinese language

EXPLANATION	BOYS	GIRLS	TOTAL
For communication with relatives	6	11	17
For future work	5	4	9
To facilitate communication if travelling/living in HK/China	4	5	9
To help relatives	0	1	1
Identity/'good face'	7	7	14
To broaden vocabulary in English and Chinese	0	2	2
To know an extra language	2	0	2
It is important to my parents	0	1	1
To pass on to the next generation	1	0	1
Not sure	0	1	1

As Table 10.2 illustrates, identity emerged as a key motivation for learning Chinese. Indeed, some of our respondents took this as self evident, puzzled at our question as to why they wished to learn the language, simply responding 'because I'm Chinese'. We turn now to explore those themes that emerged in response to our questions regarding the purposes and benefits of Chinese schooling, as they relate to language and identity. It is important to explain that our study reveals various other constructed benefits – for example, of Chinese schools as an ethnic enclave, and a sanctuary from 'minoritisation' and exoticisation (see Archer et al. 2010); and as positively impacting broader learner identities (Archer et al. 2009). Indeed, in our original project on the respondents' perceptions of the benefits of Chinese language acquisition, we focused on constructions of Chinese language as providing social and cultural capital, as well as an aspect of identity (see Francis et al. 2009). However, here we intend to focus exclusively on respondents' constructions of language in relation to social identity.

This being said, it is important to acknowledge that such 'separating' out of investments in language in relation to identity – as opposed to, say, practical, or instrumental investments – is problematic, given that many of these motivations and desires are intermeshed. For example, it became strikingly evident in our fieldwork how many of these children retain strong links and affiliations with Hong Kong. That they identified with Hong Kong was hardly surprising given that very many of them described having extended family still living there, whom they continued to visit regularly (annual trips back to Hong Kong were common among our sample). This contact with Hong Kong facilitated direct, ongoing access to aspects of Hong Kong popular culture, such as films and pop music ('Cantopop'). Many of the pupils had access to Chinese language television channels at home. This familiarity and affiliation with Hong Kong appeared in turn to impact on many pupils' perceptions of the future, opening up possibilities of future work and residence in Hong Kong later in life. Hence the practical application of the Chinese they learned in complementary schools in Britain during travel to Hong Kong emerged as a strong incentive for learning. Here practical application and identification with Hong Kong were often firmly interwoven. This was also the case with instrumental constructions where proficiency in Chinese was presented as cultural capital for respondents in a cosmopolitan global marketplace, facilitating their saleability in the international jobs market (Francis et al. 2009).

Nevertheless, speaking Chinese was for many complementary school pupil respondents intimately related to their ethnic identities, and it is this that we wish to attend to in this chapter.

Language and identity

As we have seen, the overwhelming majority of pupils saw learning the Chinese language as important, and when asked why, issues around identity emerged as a strong theme. Time and again, pupils responded that they needed to learn the Chinese language *because* they are Chinese: Wai Yan Lee (M, age 12) explains it is important he learn Chinese "because Chinese people learn Chinese"; and Lihuan Yang (M, age 14) agrees, "Because it's what I am, is like Chinese". For these pupils, it seemed to be unquestioned that as Chinese people they ought to be able to speak Chinese: many seemed puzzled at our question, reflecting the 'taken-for-granted' position they appeared to adopt in relation to the answer. It appeared that dominant discursive practices on 'Chineseness' impose necessity of 'mother-tongue' fluency as a qualification for ethnic identification rarely questioned (or perhaps unquestionable) by respondents.[3] Indeed, the perceived necessity for young people of Chinese origin to be proficient in the Chinese language emerged as grounded in powerful moral discourses of duty, identity and inclusion/exclusion, which appeared to retain a profound hold on the experiences and understanding of identity among pupils across social class groups. This is illustrated in the following responses:

I: Ok. How come you wanted to come here then? Why are you interested?
R: Well it's because I'm Chinese so I should actually learn Chinese.
I: So do you think it matters if *you* couldn't speak Chinese then?
R: Yeah. It would be a disgrace if I couldn't speak Chinese, yeah!
I: You think it would be a disgrace for you or your parents or both or...?
R: Like all my relatives speak Cantonese so if I can't speak Cantonese I'm like some outsider...and it's not good so I have to learn Chinese.

(Pui Ming Cheung [F, age 13])

I: So why is it important for you to learn the Chinese language?
R: Because I'm Chinese. A Chinese person doesn't know Chinese is an extreme disgrace.

(Yong Jie Zhang [M, age 13])

Similarly, Joe Yui (age 14) maintains that one would "just feel ashamed" if one did not "know about your own language"; Katie Wang (age 13) asserts that "my parents are Chinese and stuff and it might be, like a bit more embarrassing if you can't [speak Chinese]"; Benjamin Yuen (age 14) says that if you are Chinese but cannot speak the language "you might get teased or something"; and Vivienne Lau (age 14) explains that "sometimes when you see some people that are obviously Chinese but they don't know how to speak it, it's very embarrassing." It is important to note the highly-charged language pupils used – words such as 'disgrace', 'ashamed', 'embarrassing' – emotive words evoking powerful tropes of shame/pride, exclusion/inclusion. This illustrates the discursive power of those narratives and practices that present Chinese language proficiency as both central to Chinese identification and recognition: nationalist discourses present proficiency as an issue of morality and loyalty, while essentialist discourses on 'race' position the production of language fluency in 'racially-appropriate' bodies as natural, and of dissonance in this regard as unnatural. Such discourses are perpetuated both by

---

3. These discourses may be perpetuated by those of Chinese heritage (as recorded in our study), and/or by non-Chinese who expect Chinese heritage young people to be able to perform 'Chineseness' via Chinese language proficiency; see Archer & Francis (2006b).

many Chinese in Britain (Francis et al. 2010) and by wider British society (Leung et al. 1997; Archer & Francis 2006b).

Indeed, many of the pupils who used such language initially seemed to struggle to articulate their responses when prompted about them. Often after providing such an originally emotional reaction, their justification for their position would be a practical one rather than a moral one. We see this in the transcript extract from Pui Ming, above, where she claims it would be "a disgrace" if she could not speak Chinese, but then explains her position as premised on how she would not be able to communicate with her relatives (rather than elaborating on the shame/rejection evoked by the word 'disgrace'). Likewise, Cedric Tse (age 12) explains his statement that he needs to learn Chinese "because I'm Chinese" by elaborating, "you need to learn it in case you go to China some day and you need to look for a job and stuff." Hence the pupils' (practical) explanations seemed to qualify and rationalise the original emotional response: it seemed that they were unable, or unwilling, to articulate the moral premises underpinning their language.

However, not all the pupils were so reluctant. Oreina Yip (age 13) was prepared to state quite openly what she saw to be the issues at stake:[4]

I: And do you think it's important for you to learn the Chinese language?

R: Yeah as a Chinese person I think it is really important

I: Why do you say that?

R: Because like I said before, if you're Chinese and you only speak something like English it's still a little embarrassing. If a Chinese person comes up to you and starts speaking Chinese and you don't understand it's really embarrassing. Like they say in Chinese, the BBCs who don't speak Chinese are like bananas because they're Chinese on the outside and inside they're completely English.

The application here of the concept of the 'banana' is particularly interesting in theoretical terms due to the apparent slight distinction from the more widely-known concept of the 'coconut' ('Black on the outside, White on the inside') which it echoes. Both metaphors suggest that racial embodiment is insufficient in itself to constitute one as authentically 'Black' or 'Yellow': one's identity, as well as one's body, must delineate the appropriate ethnicity in order for one to be considered authentic. Yet there appears to be a subtle difference between the two cases in what may be considered as *constituting* identity. For these Chinese pupils the Chinese language appears to be a key – or perhaps *the key*– delineator of Chinese identity, whereas aspects of identity other than language (for example, political iden-

---

4. This openness is not, as might be surmised, related to shared ethnicity with the interviewer: Oreina was interviewed by a White researcher.

tity, attire, behaviour and institutional affiliation) may be as salient as proficiency in heritage languages in the case of 'Black' identities. In the Chinese case as it is presented by our respondents, language appears to subsume and express identity, rather than the other way around.

This notion of proficiency in the Chinese language as constituting 'Chineseness' was also evident in the concept of 'full Chinese' (or 'not full Chinese') emerging in some pupils' interviews, also in relation to Chinese language proficiency.

This construction of language as the signifier of ethnic authenticity is illustrated by Jessica Lee's (age 15) reflection that "if I couldn't speak Chinese at all I'd probably not feel very Chinese." And the signifying power of Chinese language appeared to be interwoven with threads of nationalism in connection to China/Hong Kong. The following interview extract with Wai Yiu (M, age 12) is illustrative:

R: Because if you're Chinese and you can't speak Chinese, bit embarrassing for your parents.
I: It would be embarrassing for you as well then?
R: Yeah.
I: How come it's embarrassing then?
R: Because you're supposed to learn the language from the country you come from.
I: Uh-huh, but you were born here though?
R: Yeah.
I: So even though you were born here you still feel that you should…?
R: Yes.

Wai Yu is 'caught out' because, according to his argument, having been born in England he should be learning English (as of course he has). But the point is that he clearly sees himself more profoundly as 'coming from' China. Fredrick Tam (age 16) constructs a similar discursive position when he explains that he wants to learn Chinese to enable him to pass the language on to his future children, "so they won't grow up knowing English which is *not normal* for them" [our italics]. Some of the young people of Chinese heritage in Mau's (2013) study, who could *not* speak Chinese fluently, commented on such perceptions. For example, Louise (aged 17), who grew up in an English speaking household, articulated the disapproval she had received in the past due to her limited Chinese abilities:

> Sometimes if you meet um, like some old aunties and things, they'll sort of look at you and shake their heads, and the older people tend to, quite, they think it's sort of, there's something quite wrong with me for not being able to, and a lot of people think it's very strange.

Clearly issues of embodied 'race', nationality and identity are extremely difficult to disentangle in these productions. The 'raced' body, marked as 'Chinese', is expected to perform 'Chineseness' as constructed within the imagined community, including re/production of Chinese language. Furthermore heritage language is a signifier of (and experienced by the young people as a fundamental aspect of) 'correct' ethnic identity. The complexity is heightened by the issues of inclusion and exclusion, appropriation and rejection, that the notion of *not* learning Chinese evokes.

On not learning Chinese

So far, we have highlighted young people's articulations of the *importance* of learning Chinese. But what of those who do not agree, and/or do not learn it? As we have seen, of the 60 complementary school pupils interviewed, only three said they believe it is not important to learn the Chinese language; with a further five pupils providing ambivalent responses. However, given that pupils overwhelmingly considered the learning of the Chinese language to be the primary purpose of Chinese schooling, and that we only interviewed young people *engaged* in this Mother-tongue schooling, it could be argued that these 'refusers' are especially significant. Explanations for the lack of importance of learning Chinese (and hence of complementary schooling) fell into three categories. The first was articulated by a small handful of pupils who spoke Cantonese at home, but did not use – nor see the use for – the written language.

Other pupils felt Cantonese was irrelevant to their lives altogether. Michelle Tong (age 11) says that she does not consider it important that she learn Chinese, explaining, "there aren't very many Chinese people that I speak with in my English school. So I just normally speak English." Prompted, she argues that 'lots of people know more English than Chinese', and includes her family in this. Here we see an argument emerging that Chinese becomes less relevant to younger (second and third) generations of people of Chinese heritage in Britain. For some of these younger generations it then became difficult to see the point in maintaining the language, especially when they did not enjoy Chinese school. Lai Ki Li (F, age 12) finds the learning tedious, and maintains that she sees no benefit in attending as, "no point doing it if I'm not going to do anything [with it] in my future".

The third argument for the irrelevance of their complementary education was that Putonghua ('Mandarin') will supersede Cantonese. This is a counter-perspective to the perception of some pupils that the Chinese they were learning at school would become *more* relevant due to China's meteoric rise as a global economic power. Sienna Sze (age 11) reflects that, "sooner or later, I think you might have to learn Mandarin, because in Hong Kong like Cantonese might die out, you know what I mean. Then you have to start learning Mandarin." Likewise Hannah Yue (age 14) considers the Chinese she learns in complementary school unlikely to be useful later in life, explaining, "some English people want to talk Chinese but then that's Mandarin, so then Cantonese would be just like wiped out basically in the future".

These arguments discursively position Cantonese as archaic and 'under threat'; the property of an older generation, irrelevant to younger generations in both social and economic terms. Such discourse stands in opposition to the idea of Chinese language as fundamentally relevant to the constitution of Chinese identity, as well as discourses of Chinese language as capital. It is not difficult to see how these discourses may be mobilised relationally in debates within the diasporic community. It was precisely this point that generated Mau's interest in those British-Chinese young people that are not proficient in Chinese.

Minority ethnic pupils are often assumed to inherit, or are born into, language traditions that 'transcend questions of the actual language use of individuals and collectives' at mainstream schools, and they are commonly thought to possess expertise in their home or community language (Leung et al. 1997). This expectation or automatic assumption of knowing one's heritage language is shared by many within the British Chinese community. It appears assumed that being racially embodied as 'Chinese' somehow should give one 'natural' abilities and an obligation to learn or speak Chinese no matter where the said individual were born or raised, and failing to do so could be seen as unnatural and even disgraceful (see above).

However, many young people in Mau's study challenged such beliefs of what constituted being Chinese (or British). Alongside language fluency, a number of other both traditional and contemporary cultural practices, of which many were influenced by home culture, also appeared to make up a 'package' of being 'Chinese' in the UK. Such traditional practices included, for example, the celebration of Chinese festivals and maintenance of customs; and contemporary cultural engagements included the consumption of Chinese/Asian drama series and popular culture. However, as illustrated by the range of responses from these young people, these practices are not a check-list of 'necessary' alternative signifiers of 'Chinese culture', rather they often inter-linked with each other and the young people's environments, and individuals relate to them differently.

Many of the young people who had limited or no Chinese language knowledge were comfortable with hybrid identities, with identification with 'Chineseness' remaining a strong aspect within this. Several went further to express ethnic pride and close connection to their Chinese heritage. For example, although Emma (age 17) acknowledged that both herself and her UK university-educated parents were 'very Westernised', she felt Chinese and was proud of her heritage. She believed that certain cultural practices, such as eating rice and respect for elders, were 'ingrained' in her and would 'always make me Chinese'. Likewise, Louise (age 17) asserted the authenticity of her identification as Chinese by explaining that her inability to speak Chinese was 'only one part of something a lot bigger' in being Chinese, as she felt that 'everything else about my [English speaking] family is Chinese, apart from language'. She described feeling 'very Chinese' because her family celebrated all the festivals, ate Chinese food regularly, and met and ate with their extended family every Sunday like many other Chinese families. Postcolonial theorists, such as Hall (1992, 1997) and Bhabha (1994), have shown how understandings of identity and culture that are based on fixed, inherent, and measurable characteristics fail to understand complex, hybridised identities and cultural practices in the context of increased societal changes and globalisation. Mau's study illustrates the diversity and complexity at stake, highlighting young people's agency to challenge and resist static and simplistic interpretations of 'Chineseness'. These young people are able to draw on different narratives and signifiers around 'culture', globalisation, and nation to assert their identities as Chinese. Her findings demonstrate how these non-Chinese-speaking young people of Chinese heritage are comfortable with negotiating their Chinese and British (and other) identities in situated, fluid terms.

Additionally, the prominence of China on the global stage within the last decade has provided new ways of connecting to a celebratory, China-based Chinese identity and representation within the mainstream society. Mandarin (the official language of China) has been promoted at British schools and is seen as a key to access the growing Chinese market. Some of the participants discussed learning Mandarin at mainstream/complementary school or their desire to learn Mandarin in the future; or their parents' desire and encouragement for them to learn Mandarin as a way to increase their cultural capital given the rise of China. For example, although Emma's parents used Cantonese between themselves in their predominantly English speaking household, she felt that her parents sent her and her brother to Chinese school to learn Mandarin because "they think Mandarin is more important in today's worlds and because Cantonese is a dialect, erm, so yeah Mandarin is like the main Chinese language." Mau's study reiterates the point that some Cantonese-heritage young people (and parents) feel that Cantonese, the former lingua franca of the British Chinese community, is being usurped, and potentially gradually replaced, by Mandarin in British Chinese circles. When learning the family Chinese language, such as Cantonese, becomes less relevant or holds less instrumental value among partially or fully English speaking households, learning Mandarin can serve as a symbolic tie to their Chinese heritage, regardless of their original family dialects, as well as a possible asset in the job market in the future.

Discussion

We have shown that for the majority of Chinese complementary school pupils, the purpose of complementary school is to teach the 'mother-tongue'; and the primary benefit of this replication of heritage language proficiency relates to ethnic identity, with a more diverse range of potential additional benefits. We have argued that this understanding reflects the demographics of those attending Cantonese complementary schools (Francis et al. 2009); and this hypothesis is supported by Mau's (2013) findings. The vast majority of pupils in the complementary school sample were second generation, with at least one parent born overseas (97%), and often speaking Chinese (at least to some extent) at home (88%). We suggested that such experiences may be decreasingly representative of the British-Chinese community as a whole. Professional families constituted a small minority among attendees (12%), while the many third generation British-Chinese and/or mixed-heritage young people were largely not represented in the study of complementary school pupils, as they did not attend.

We have also analysed how complementary school pupils often saw proficiency in Chinese as the key signifier of Chinese identity. This view of language *as* culture/identity raised important questions around the conception of ethnic identity. As we discuss elsewhere, the complementary school pupils' discussion of the importance of knowing Chinese language, and what they saw as the implications of failure (disgrace, embarrassment, exclusion and so on) also raises some uncomfortable questions about the effects of practices around cultural reproduction within and without the "imagined community" (Francis et al. 2009).

However, the findings from Mau's (2013) study of young people of Chinese heritage with limited Mother-tongue abilities demonstrates that for those 'not speaking Chinese', this did not preclude their identification as Chinese (or Chineseness remaining an important aspect of their identity). The profundity and diversity of these respondents' variously hybrid identities was striking, and notably hard to capture in existing conceptual terminology (Mau 2013). More than this though, as the earlier study argued, representations of 'Chineseness' are themselves diverse and heteroglossic at both macro and micro levels (see also Ang 1994, 1998, 2001; Chun 1996). These young people were drawing on a range of signifiers of Chinese culture, connection, and engagement to position themselves as wholly or partly 'Chinese' (albeit of course these signifiers may be rejected as inauthentic by others). These productions are heteroglossic in terms of cultural expression, language practice, individual experience, and extent of hegemony. Arguably, although as we have seen, there are monoglossic efforts at reproduction of idealised notions of 'essential' features of Chinese culture, in practice young people demonstrate agency in their heteroglossic understandings and productions of 'Chineseness'.

References

Anderson, B. 1991. *Imagined Communities*. London: Verso.

Ang, I. 1994. On not speaking Chinese: Postmodern ethnicity and the politics of diaspora. *New Formations* 24: 1–18.

Ang, I. 1998. Can one say no to Chineseness? Pushing the limits of the diasporic paradigm. *boundary* 2 25(3): 223–242.

Ang, I. 2001. *On not Speaking Chinese: Living between Asia and the West*. London: Routledge.

Archer, L. & Francis, B. 2006a. Challenging classes? Exploring the role of social class within the identities and achievement of British Chinese pupils, *Sociology* 40(1): 29–49.

Archer, L. & Francis, B. 2006b. Constructions of racism by British-Chinese pupils and parents. *Race, Ethnicity and Education* 8(4): 387–407.

Archer, L. & Francis, B. 2007. *Understanding Minority Ethnic Achievement: Race, Gender, Class and 'Success'*. London: Routledge.

Archer, L., Francis, B. & Mau, A. 2009. 'Boring and stressful' or 'ideal' learning spaces? Pupils' constructions of teaching and learning in Chinese supplementary schools. *Research Papers in Education* 24(4): 477–497.

Archer, L., Francis, B. & Mau, A. 2010. The culture project: Diasporic negotiations of ethnicity, identity and culture among teachers, pupils and parents in Chinese language schools. *Oxford Review of Education* 36(4): 407–426.

Bhabha, H.K. 1994. *The Location of Culture*. London: Routledge.

Blackledge, A. 2004. Identity in multilingual Britain. In *Negotiation of Identities in Multilingual Contexts*, A. Pavlenko & A. Blackledge (eds), 68–92. Clevedon: Multilingual Matters.

Blommaert, J. & Verschueren, J. 1998. The role of language in European nationalist identities. In *Language Ideologies, Practice and Theory*, B.B. Schiefflin, K.A. Woolard & P.V. Kroskrity (eds), 189–210. Oxford: OUP.

Chun, A. 1996. Fuck Chineseness: On the ambiguities of ethnicity as culture as identity, *boundary* 2 23(2): 111–138.

Creese, A., Bhatt, A., Bhojana, N. & Martin, P. 2006. Multicultural, heritage and learner identities in complementary schools, *Language and Education* 20 (1): 23–43.

Cummins, J. & Early, M. (eds) 2011. *Identity Texts: The Collaborative Creation of Power in Multilingual Schools*. Stoke-on-Trent: Trentham Books.

Dove, N. 1993. The emergence of black supplementary schools. *Urban Education* 27(4): 430–437.

Foucault, M. 1972. *The History of Sexuality*, 1. London: Penguin Books.

Francis, B. & Archer, L. 2005a. British-Chinese pupils' and parents' constructions of the value of education. *British Educational Research Journal* 31(1): 89–107.

Francis, B. & Archer, L. 2005b. British-Chinese pupils' constructions of gender and learning. *Oxford Review of Education* 31(4): 497–515.

Francis, B., Archer, L. & Mau, A. 2009. Language as capital, or language as identity? Chinese complementary school pupils' perspectives on the purposes and benefits of complementary schools. *British Educational Research Journal* 35(4): 519–538.

Francis, B., Archer, L. & Mau, A. 2010. Parents' and teachers' constructions of the purposes of Chinese complementary schooling: 'Culture', identity and power. *Race, Ethnicity and Education* 13(1): 101–117.

Hall, S. 1992. New ethnicities. In *'Race', Culture and Difference*, J. Donald & A. Rattansi (eds), 252–259. London: Sage.

Hall, S. 1997. *Representation: Cultural Representations and Signifying Practices.* London: Sage.

He, A. 2006. Toward an identity theory of the development of Chinese as a heritage language. *Heritage Language Journal* 4(1): 1–28.

Hall, K., Ozerk, K. Zulliqar, M. & Tan, J. 2002. 'This is our school': Provision, purpose and pedagogy of supplementary schooling in Leeds and Oslo, *British Educational Research Journal* 28(3): 399–418.

Kanno, Y. & Norton, B. (eds) 2003. Imagined communities and educational possibilities. *Journal of Language, Identity, and Education* 2(4): 241–249 (special issue).

Kinginger, C. 2004. Alice doesn't live here anymore: Foreign language learning and identity construction. In *Negotiation of Identities in Multilingual Contexts,* A. Pavlenko & A. Blackledge (eds), 219–242. Clevedon: Multilingual Matters.

Leung, C., Harrs, R. & Rampton, B. 1997. The idealised native speaker, reified ethnicities, and classroom realities. *TESOL Quarterly* 31(3): 543–560.

Martin, P., Creese, A. & Bhatt, A. 2003. *Complementary Schools and their Communities in Leicester: Final Report to the ESRC.* Leicester: University of Leicester.

Mau, A. 2013. On not Speaking 'Much' Chinese: Identities, Cultures and Languages of British Chinese pupils. Ph.D. dissertation, University of Roehampton.

Norton, B. 2001. Non-participation, imagined communities, and the language classroom. In *Learner Contributions to Language Learning: New Directions in Research,* M. Breen (ed.), 159–171. London: Pearson Education.

Norton, B. 2010. Language and identity. In *Sociolinguistics and Language Education,* N. Hornberger & S. McKay (eds), 349–369. Bristol: Multilingual Matters.

Norton, B. & Toohey, K. 2011. Identity, language learning, and social change. *Language Teaching* 44(4): 412–446.

Oriyama, K. 2010. Heritage language maintenance and Japanese identity formation: What role can schooling and ethnic community contact play? *Heritage Language Journal* 7(2).

Pavlenko, A. & Norton, B. 2007. Imagined communities, identity, and English language teaching. In *International Handbook of English Language Teaching,* J. Cummins & C. Davison (eds), 669–680. Berlin: Springer.

Reay, D. & Mirza, H. 1997. Uncovering Geneaologies of the Margins: Black supplementary schooling. *British Journal of Sociology of Education* 18(4): 477–99.

Strand, S. 2002. *Surveying the Views of Pupils Attending Supplementary Schools in England 2001.* Slough: NfERNelson.

CHAPTER 11

Chinese language learning by adolescents and young adults in the Chinese diaspora

Motivation, ethnicity, and identity*

Duanduan Li & Patricia Duff
University of British Columbia

Issues connected with motivation, ethnicity, and identity among adolescent and young adult heritage language learners are the subject of a growing amount of research in diaspora communities. However, until recently, this research has tended to be quantitative, and the constructs were theorized and operationalized in a categorical or essentialist manner. This chapter aims to (1) describe some of the changes in theory that are relevant to Chinese heritage language (CHL) learning, seeing it as a much more dynamic, multilingual, nonlinear, and contingent process; (2) review recent research examining these socio-affective factors among CHL learners; (3) present a study on the longitudinal trajectories, motivations, and identities of four individuals learning CHL in a Western Canadian university program; and (4) consider implications of this work for improving curriculum, pedagogy, learning materials, and policies.

Introduction

There is now a rich and growing body of case study research on young children's learning of heritage languages (HLs), including Chinese, often in conjunction with early bilingualism/biliteracy and multilingualism, in both home and school contexts (e.g. G. Li 2006a, 2006b, 2007; Maguire & Curdt-Christiansen 2007).

* The authors acknowledge, with thanks, funding from the Social Sciences and Humanities Research Council of Canada, which supported the preparation of this chapter for our project "Languages, Literacies and Identities of Chinese Heritage-Language Learners" (D. Li, Principal Investigator). An earlier version of this paper was presented at the World Congress of Applied Linguistics in Essen, Germany in 2008.

However, issues of motivation, ethnicity, and identity, often characterized as social-psychological or affective variables, are not central to all such studies of young children, given their still-developing cognition, self-awareness, and identity formation. Rather, the focus is often on the children's emerging oral and literate practices, repertoires, and the texts and cultural themes they engage with (e.g. Chiu 2011; Curdt-Christiansen 2003, 2008).

With older learners, research traditionally of a more quantitative and social-psychological nature (reviewed below) has examined how motivation, ethnicity, and identity are connected with Chinese heritage language (CHL) learning and use in a variety of geographical and cross-linguistic settings (e.g. Australia, Canada, Japan, UK, U.S.). These studies generally involve survey questionnaires that ask students to reflect on socio-affective dimensions of their cultural heritage or "Chineseness" and their CHL learning in the past or present. For example, their attitudes and motivations toward CHL, as well as their CHL linguistic and literate practices, are explored. In comparison with the work on young children, less *qualitative* research in the form of in-depth ethnographic case studies has documented older children's and young adults' experiences, and especially their reasons for learning Chinese and how those relate to perceptions of their ethnicities and identities, or to the decisions they make regarding their HL development at different points in time. Fortunately, that trend is beginning to change though, generating understandings based on individual, contextualized cases of learners' educational and emotional connections with Chinese from various educational and social experiences.

In this chapter, some foundational and recent studies examining CHL in adolescence and young adulthood are briefly reviewed. We then describe how key constructs such as motivation, identity, and agency are being reconceptualized in current research and present data from a study conducted in western Canada with CHL learners that drew on these. Finally, the chapter concludes with recommendations for future research and pedagogy.

Examining linguistic and cultural "inheritance" and trajectories in CHL

Examining CHL among adolescents and young adults cannot be done without considering the seminal earlier formative experiences, including family language policies (see chapters by Curdt-Christiansen and Duff, this volume), that inevitably affect subsequent ones, in potentially positive, negative, or more ostensibly neutral ways. The term *HL learners*, unless otherwise noted, generally refers to students who have had at least some prior exposure to a Chinese language (or "dialect") in the home, possibly with grandparents or other relatives, if not their own parents (following e.g. Valdés 2000). Given the growing Chinese diaspora internationally, which in many contexts has existed for several generations or even centuries, CHL learners in classes often include Generation 1.5, 2, or 3 students, not all of whom have had previous home-language exposure to any variety of Chinese (Li & Duff 2008). What is more, the profiles of HL students are very diverse even for those coming from the *same* generation of immigration, linked to differences in their proficiency levels across skills, dialects they speak, political, social, and cultural backgrounds stemming from the places they come from or identify with, their aspirations, and the means by which they learn and use Chinese. Therefore, the label *CHL learner* includes a very wide range of experiences and profiles and is far from monolithic (Li & Duff 2008; Wong & Xiao 2010).

It can therefore be helpful to look at the HL learner in terms of the three dimensions proposed by Leung et al. (1997): *inheritance* (i.e. in this case, learners' Chinese heritage and thus their likely disposition to the language); *expertise* (how proficient they may already be in the language); and *affiliation* (how strongly they identify with the language and culture). Just *being Chinese*, although providing some sense of ethnolinguistic inheritance, by no means ensures expertise in or affiliation with the language or its speakers. Bourdieu's (1991) concept of *habitus* (linguistic, social, and cultural contexts and dispositions) is highly compatible with such a view of inheritance (Dai & Zhang 2008; see also Duff this volume). However, an even more dynamic, agentive, constructivist view of habitus and identity as always being under negotiation, construction, and in the process of transformation or "becoming" is found in Maguire and Curdt-Christiansen (2007). This view is consistent, moreover, with the principle that any discussion of HL linguistic/cultural *maintenance* should carefully examine the appropriation, (co)construction, adaptation, hybridization, syncretism, or shedding of aspects of habitus rather than simply assume that habitus is "inherited" wholesale through biological and cultural transmission or socialization. Indeed, an interesting aspect of Dai and Zhang's (2008) discussion of habitus is the notion of *intimacy* – and not just future *desires* – that emerges among CHL learners when remembering their early experiences with and attachments to CHL. As a typical CHL participant in He's (2010) study remarks,

> My home language is Chinese. My parents are from China. They praised me, scolded me, all in Chinese.... My Chinese is really bad. I can't read and I can only write my name. But when I think of Chinese, I think of my mom, dad, and home. It is the language of my home, and my heart.... (p. 66)

This emotional or affective connection to the language of one's childhood is powerful. For people who did *not* speak or hear the HL during their childhood, there may instead be an idealization or romanticization of the distant past mediated by that language and especially if those were considered good times within family lore. On the other hand, youth may also perceive their heritage as traditional, "old world," and incompatible with the cultural habitus surrounding them in dominant contemporary society, or may be positively disposed to it but later disillusioned by their negative experiences as HL students in high school or university courses, as in Wiley's (2008) and Kelleher's (2008, 2010) case studies.

Blackledge and Creese (2008), in a view consistent with ours, tease apart language and heritage as well, noting that the two cannot automatically be equated or conflated. Just because a CHL student decides to study Chinese does not mean that the learner is heavily invested in his or her cultural "heritage" (or traditional cultures). By the same token, learners of Chinese deeply invested in the language may not be strongly affiliated with Chinese culture or communities (Duff et al. 2013).

Thus, in research on CHL it is important to ascertain learners' identification with the heritage (home or other) culture and language to understand their ongoing emotional and intellectual investments in language learning and acculturation or socialization. Furthermore, how they are positioned by others in relation to the HL language and culture may constrain or enable them to take up particular subject positions that may impact their learning opportunities. From an online survey of university HL students conducted by Kagan (2012), for example, one respondent asked to self-identify by ethnic category replied cryptically: "[I'm] Asian-American.. kuz in america ur asian.. and in asia ur american.. the question is pointless.. it's how others identify you" [sic] (Kagan 2012:73). This statement reflects others' identifications or positionings that may then be taken up or contested by individuals, which Taylor (1994) calls the "politics of recognition" in multicultural society and is in turn related to people's self-esteem and identity. Yet even being positioned (either positively or negatively) as "Asian" or "Asian-American" or "Chinese" does not mean that one will be more inclined to take up Asian languages and cultural practices. On the contrary, it may compel people to want to be seen as less Asian and in greater conformity to local non-Asian-background "American" students, as in Kagan's context.

Motivation, identity, agency, and autonomy: New directions in CHL research

Motivation is an important construct with a relatively long and distinguished history in applied linguistics and (social) psychology. In comparison with earlier accounts, it has recently come to be seen as much more fluid, complex, and socially contingent phenomenon – and not simply a stable, deterministic trait. Norton

(2000) proposed a complementary notion, *investment*, that is more sociological than psychological. Ushioda and Dörnyei (2012) chart the progression in second language acquisition (SLA) studies of motivation from 1959 as follows: the *social-psychological period* (to 1990); *cognitive-situated period* (1990s); *process-oriented period* (2000s); and what they currently call the *socio-dynamic* period, stressing "dynamic systems and contextualized interactions" in "the modern globalized world" (p. 397–398). Current treatments of motivation such as these, influenced by complexity and dynamic-systems science, examine interactions between the individual learner (including motivation, cognition, and emotion) and the social learning environment, both of which are constantly changing and co-adapting together (Tasker 2012). The approach examines the "possible selves" of learners, their *vision* of their *ideal self* and what it might take to achieve that ideal (Dörnyei 2010; Dörnyei & Ushioda 2009; Ushioda & Dörnyei 2009, 2012; see Xie 2011, for a CHL- and non-HL college-level study applying Dörnyei's work).

Thus, whereas earlier motivation research defined students' language learning orientations in terms of a stark integrative-instrumental dichotomy that was fairly static and categorical regardless of changing circumstances, recent conceptions have placed greater emphasis on the situated, organic individual, and the dynamic nature of motivation and its relationship to one's sense of "self." The learner's "ought-to" versus "ideal L2 self" is differentiated (Dörnyei 2010; Ushioda & Dörnyei 2012). This construct of *ideal self* is similar to Norton's (e.g. McKinney & Norton 2008; Norton & Toohey 2011) notion of "imagined identity" – that is, the kind of person (self) the CHL learner desires to be in terms of the HL and not just his or her sense of obligation to be a particular type of person.

Identity (e.g. in terms of gender, language, ethnicity, and sense-of-self) has therefore also been at the center of many of these motivation studies (e.g. Block 2007a, 2007b; Menard-Warwick 2005; Norton 2000), although it has only recently entered into CHL research as a major poststructuralist or social-constructivist theoretical construct (e.g. He 2006, 2008, 2010, 2011; Hornberger & Wang 2008). Naturally, there are differences in how sociologists (e.g. Chow 2001), (social) psychologists, and applied linguists approach notions of (ethnic) identity theoretically and methodologically. Sociologists, for example, might be more interested in externally observable or reportable aspects of identity performance, such as the social networks and institutions that HL learners participate in (e.g. Chinese churches, language schools, and community or home celebrations). Social psychologists, in contrast, traditionally have designed surveys and interviews to uncover less visible, internal psychological or emotional attachments to language and culture (e.g. Ushioda & Dörnyei 2010).

Applied linguistics and CHL are also being influenced, increasingly, by Bakhtin's (e.g. 1981) concepts of *voice, ideological becomings, heteroglossia,* and *identity enactments* (e.g. Lei 2012; Lo-Philip 2010; Maguire & Curdt-Christiansen 2007). This work represents a sharp contrast with erstwhile group-based quantitative approaches to identity, ethnicity, and motivation, and incorporates more interpretive epistemologies, as well as narrative and discourse analysis. (Swain & Deters 2007 and Zuengler & Miller 2006 provide overviews reflecting some of these recent epistemological shifts in applied linguistics.)

Furthermore, this new understanding of desire, voice, and identity in language learning takes into account learner *agency* to a greater extent (Duff 2012). Unlike the learning of Chinese by young children of Chinese descent, whose parents usually make the "choice" for them (meaning the children have little choice in the matter, at least initially), or non-Chinese learners of Chinese, who typically have chosen to learn that language from among a variety of possible languages (Duff et al. 2013), Chinese-background adolescents and young adults typically have more agency and autonomy with respect to their language learning decisions, behaviors, and identities.

The roles of socially-mediated agency, identity, and autonomy in language learning and their intersections with motivation have garnered considerable recent attention, particularly with the poststructural, social/sociocultural, and narrative "turns" in the field of SLA (see Block 2007a, 2007b; Duff 2012; Duff et al. 2013; Kramsch 2009; Lantolf 2000; Norton & Toohey 2011; Swain & Deters 2007; Ushioda & Dörnyei 2009, 2012; Zuengler & Miller 2006). With the growing complexity of language learning in transnational, globalized, and lingua franca contexts, for example, these approaches are now being applied to research with HL learners as well. In what follows, we examine how these constructs can shed light on the lives, choices, motivations and identity positions of CHL learners and their trajectories of CHL learning and socialization.

The study

To study CHL students' ethnolinguistic identities, motivations, and CHL trajectories, we recruited CHL students in the Chinese language program at a large Canadian university who had participated in our earlier questionnaire-based survey of Chinese learners regarding their attitudes and motivations toward various aspects of Chinese (see Li & Duff 2008). The survey generated a sense of their histories, affiliations, expertise, identities, and investments in CHL. From those who volunteered to take part in follow-up, semi-structured interviews of about an hour in length, 20 participants were selected. We were also able to conduct follow up interviews or correspondence with many in the larger group three years later. The interviews were conducted by the first author in English primarily. The participants were chosen based on maximum variation, according to their countries of origin, histories, CHL proficiency level, and home-language dialects. From that larger sample, we report on four students below to illustrate some of the issues described earlier in relation to CHL learning and Chineseness.

Our original research questions were as follows:

1. What are the major factors that motivate students to enroll in HL classes at university?
2. What features characterize their language learning trajectories? More specifically, what has their history of HL learning and use been within family, local community, and other settings? What global, societal, and local factors promoted or inhibited intergenerational HL transfer, maintenance, and development? How did – or might – opportunities for travel enhance their access to and integration within Chinese-speaking communities?
3. How do social, political, economic, and cultural values affect the attitudes of HL learners from different regions and subcultures of Chinese (e.g. from Taiwan, Mainland China, Hong Kong) toward different varieties of spoken and written Chinese?
4. What is the role of Chinese HL learning in students' ongoing negotiation of their multiple or hybrid identities at home, at university, and in the wider, global community?

Findings

Short profiles of the four participants – Amy, Flora, Katie and Tony – are shown in Table 11.1. All four were in their early twenties at the outset of the study. They grew up in Canada, Hong Kong, China (Beijing), and Indonesia, respectively. Participants in the larger study also came from Malaysia, Taiwan, and other regions where Chinese is spoken, but space does not permit their inclusion here. In addition to their different countries of origin, the four focal participants represented a range of L1s (Mandarin – Beijing and Taiwan varieties, Cantonese and English, Indonesian), different ages at which they had first come to Canada (from birth to age 18), diverse academic majors at university, and levels of Chinese attained prior to the first year of the study. They also had enjoyed different levels and types of societal support for their retention and development of Chinese when they grew up. All three female participants, for example, had been well supported in their Chinese language maintenance at home and in their local communities, whereas not all of their siblings had fared as well in that regard, given the stigma of being "ESL" learners and the peer pressure to assimilate into the local Anglophone culture. However, as we shall see, the male participant in our study, from Indonesia, had attempted to learn Chinese under much more challenging conditions in his home country.

Table 11.1 Profiles of four CHL learners

Name (pseudonym)	Birthplace	L1(s)	Other languages	Age of arrival in Canada	Mandarin proficiency course level at university in 2005	Occupation/residence in 2008
Amy	Canada	Cantonese & English	French Mandarin	N/A	Began 1st yr level elementary HL courses to intermediate	Dental hygienist in Canada
Flora	Mainland China	Mandarin	English French Cantonese	5 yrs old	Started in an elementary level 1st yr HL course at university; in 2nd yr in 2005	University administrator in Canada (co-op program)
Katie	Hong Kong	Cantonese & English	English German, Danish, Mandarin	18 yrs old (age 12 to 18 in Denmark)	Started in intermediate-level HL course; in advanced in 2005	Graduate student in Canada doing research in Shanghai
Tony	Indonesia	Indonesian	English Mandarin	18	Started in 2nd yr HL course	(unknown, possibly China?)

The participants are discussed below based on the age at which they arrived in Canada. Amy and Flora are paired together, as Generation 2.0 immigrant students in many respects (although Flora came to Canada as a young child), having received all or most of their (K-12) education in Canada and still living with their parents. Katie and Tony are paired together because both first arrived as international (visa) students in Canada at age 18, albeit from completely different linguistic backgrounds and exhibiting distinct trajectories. Yet all four were enrolled in sections designated for CHL learners in the Mandarin program when the study began, the first two in elementary HL courses and the latter two in intermediate-level ones.

Amy and Flora: "Traditional" HL learners in Canada

Amy represents a fairly typical "overseas Chinese" HL learner in Canada in the mid-to-late late 20th century – one who was born in Canada, or had immigrated to Canada at a very young age and spoke (some) Cantonese at home, but learned (some) Mandarin in community HL programs and at university as well. Amy's parents were from Hong Kong and Macao. She spoke both Cantonese and English as home, accompanied her grandmother to a Chinese church, and lived in an area of the city with many Cantonese and Mandarin speakers.

When she was young, Amy and her family returned to Hong Kong for some time and then settled back in Canada permanently. When she began school in Canada, Amy said she was weak in English and "had a lot of trouble" communicating with teachers, which precipitated her linguistic shift to English, following in her older sisters' footsteps. As she reported,

> I cannot verbalize it [problems in class in English]. So then ... I always follow my sister, Sandra, cause they spoke all English. So, I am "Okay, I should speak all English too." And so for most of when I was younger, like from kindergarten and after, I spoke English. But then I thought I got older, and started realizing that I need also to perfect my Chinese as well and then I began to speak more Chinese. And I speak with my parents usually Chinese whereas my sisters usually speak English.

Therefore, among the three sisters in her family, she was the only one who persisted with both Cantonese and Mandarin, making a conscious decision from about Grade 8 to speak more Chinese, while her sisters became virtually monolingual in English through language shift.

Like many other young second-generation immigrants, Amy had attended weekend Chinese HL schools for many years – Cantonese in elementary school and later Mandarin, the latter for three years during high school but in a community program. However, to her chagrin, Amy lamented that she "didn't learn much" in those programs. Because the family often moved, both transnationally and within Canada, her placement in Chinese community classes (regardless of the dialect) was often with younger children, which she found demotivating. Amy also studied French for 12 years in total (K-11), yet felt her French was worse than her Mandarin. When she entered university she considered taking French to improve it but chose Mandarin instead, in part at her mother's urging (because neither the mother nor father spoke Mandarin well, but an uncle, in real estate, spoke it fairly well and felt it was important). Therefore, she took Mandarin for mostly pragmatic reasons – to earn easy credits and perhaps have more work opportunities later – rather than because of any personal identification with that variety. She also conceded that her choice represented a form of "respect" for her parents and their Chinese heritage and a way of "fitting in" with a local Chinese peer group that she affiliated with in high school, stating:

> When I was in a group like people who all speak Chinese and sort of you are the one who does not know how to converse ... like joking and fun.... when you cannot do that you are sort of like lost out. So I mean that's another reason why I like to just to fit in... [... refers to ellipsis of fillers or repeated phrases]

As an ESL tutor to new immigrant children, moreover, Amy expected that Mandarin would help her communicate with the children and their families.

Three years later in our follow-up interview, Amy had graduated and was working at a dental clinic as a hygienist, speaking colloquial Mandarin with some patients whose English was limited. But she noted that she lacked technical dental terms in Mandarin. She viewed herself more as Canadian than Chinese (but still said "I may go *back* to Hong Kong") and now felt "proud of being able to speak" relatively unaccented Mandarin as a Cantonese L1 speaker and that her Mandarin was "better than my sisters' and better than the rest of my family". Her relatives in turn were very impressed by her, such as when she accompanied them to China and served as their language broker.

Unlike Amy, our second participant, Flora, was not born in Canada and represented a newer wave of young Mainland Chinese or Taiwanese immigrants who already had a good foundation in colloquial Mandarin before studying Chinese in Canada. Flora had immigrated with her parents from Beijing when she was five. Like Amy, she spoke some Chinese L1 at home and was a longtime student of French in Canadian schools. Flora loved French so much that enrolled in late French immersion from Grade 6. Both she and Amy used French as their language requirement for university, not Mandarin. Interestingly, although Flora's home language was Mandarin, she later pursued Cantonese as well – thus adding both languages to her repertoire but in a reverse order to Amy's experience. After immigrating, Flora's parents had tried to teach her Mandarin and by her estimate she had acquired 200–300 (written) characters but was reportedly not very interested in Chinese literacy when younger and, as in Amy's situation, Chinese was not offered at her public schools in Canada. Nevertheless, at high school Flora met some Chinese speakers from Taiwan and Hong Kong and started speaking Mandarin with them. That was her first time using Mandarin outside the home with peers, she stated, and was quite comparable to Amy's situation of embracing Mandarin at that age. Flora subsequently began her formal Mandarin study at university and then went to Hong Kong to study Cantonese. She then returned to Canada to resume her university studies, including Mandarin, which she described as being "a very difficult, uphill battle," primarily due to the difficulty of Chinese literacy. At the time the study began, she was an international relations major who still considered herself more more proficient in French than Chinese. But she insisted that both languages were very important to her as a Chinese Canadian:

> Personally, I think I could not have done without either [French or Chinese]. French being a part of Canada, I think French is really important to know, just because it is our second national language or official language, but also having a Chinese heritage, Chinese is also extremely important for me.

Whereas French was symbolic of her Canadian identity, responsibility, and national affiliation, she had a much stronger, more intimate identification with Chinese based on her ethnic heritage. She also viewed it as a form of cultural capital that might prove valuable careerwise. She put it thus:

> I study Chinese because it is part of my heritage. I love learning languages, so why not study my own language? Also for the future, I'd like to do business with Asia, which is kind of a big thing. So I find it very important to know some Chinese.

Like Amy, therefore, investing in her identity and home language constituted an investment in her career as well, given the growing business ties between Canada and China, in particular, but also the growing number of Mandarin speakers in Canada. Cultural dimensions of the language and her heritage appeared to be foregrounded to linguistic aspects.

As with many CHL learners, Flora's main focus in university Chinese courses was her reading and writing skills and developing more sophisticated oral registers. Even in 2008, three years after the study began and when she was working as a university administrator in Canada involved in co-op programs, she still expressed the acute need to develop her proficiency further but now framed it in terms of an attachment to her "roots in China":

> because you know I have Chinese heritage and my parents read, speak and write Chinese and that's- that really is the first language I grew up with before English, so even though I am more familiar with English I am still quite attached to my roots in China.

That sentiment about her Chinese roots, her investment in the literacy practices of her parents, and in her own identity and not just her "roots" but also Chinese cultural "traditions" and "heritage" was conveyed perhaps most explicitly by Flora of the four participants in 2008:

> I'm definitely more Chinese now than I feel I was before [three years earlier], the thing is to BE Chinese…. I am in an environment where I am comfortable with … the traditions and the things that I am involved with …Chinese heritage.

Moreover, having a friend who was born in Canada and also "very strongly connected to her Chinese heritage" had also helped retain and build up her Chinese identity. That person had apparently "been a great supporter of me and bringing out you know the more comfortable side of accepting the Chinese culture and Chinese heritage." Such peer influences in late adolescence and early adulthood, which Amy also noted, can be very compelling, either pushing people to retain their ethnolinguistic ties (Amy and Flora), or pulling them away from them, as was the case with Amy's sisters. In effect, having a trusted peer group that embraces, invests in, and shares a co-ethnic HL identity and engages in contemporary multilingual and cultural practices can be among the most motivating factors of all for youth, offering new possibilities of "ideal selves" or imagined/enacted identities that were previously not imagined or sought. Indeed, peer language socialization can be a dynamic site of both innovation and contestation of HL practices and deserves more attention.

Katie and Tony: "Nontraditional" HL learners in Canada

Katie and Tony both had come to Canada at age 18 from their respective source countries, Hong Kong and Indonesia, not as immigrants but as international university students. Their linguistic and geographical journeys and multilingual profiles, while by no means unusual in the world of CHL learning, were quite distinct from many of the others in our larger study. For one thing, Katie did not *look* Chinese. Her father was European (Danish) and her mother Chinese (Cantonese). She spent her first twelve years growing up in Hong Kong where, in addition to her exposure to Cantonese and English, she learned Mandarin at an intenational school. Her father, who had done business in or with Hong Kong and China and had lived in Hong Kong for more than 26 years, was fluent in Danish, German, and English but spoke no Chinese, according to Katie. In contrast, her mother spoke Shanghainese, Mandarin, Sichuanese, German and Danish, in addition to Cantonese and English. The family relocated from Hong Kong to Denmark when Katie was 12 and she soon became proficient in Danish and later German (through German-speaking friends, another outcome of peer socialization). In short, Katie came from a linguistically and culturally "superdiverse" transnational background and her own travels were far from over. Hoping to get into foreign relations or foreign service, she came to Canada to study political science, but also majored in Chinese. When the study began she was enrolled in intermediate to advanced Mandarin courses and was also taking intermediate German. Given her formative adolescent years in Denmark, she was more proficient in Danish than Mandarin. What is more, despite being a native speaker of Cantonese (and English), she said she liked the sound of Mandarin better than Cantonese, that it was "softer and more sophisticated."

Like her mother, Katie had a very rich and complex multilingual repertoire to both draw upon and cultivate. Three years into the study, she was doing graduate studies in sociology at another Canadian university and was happily based in China, collecting ethnographic data among rural-urban migrant families in Shanghai. She was using her Mandarin, and likely Shanghainese as well, to full advantage with her research participants, giving not only her but also her own research participants a kind of "voice" by which to convey issues related to their housing needs, her research focus. She reported that Chinese enabled her to talk to them "about their predicaments and aspirations."

In our first extended interview with Katie in 2005, she spoke about her connection with Chinese and her Sinophone identity (both linguistic and cultural) in the following way, underscoring the sense of cultural affiliation and "duty" that came with learning Chinese:

> I find it very important in terms of my cultural background, that for me it is basically to fulfill my interest towards the Chinese culture and tradition and language. So that's why I am learning Chinese right now… and I feel almost like it's a duty for me to carry on my pursuit in learning the Chinese language.

She also reported that learning Chinese earlier in her life and now at university "really … helps me to understand what kind of person I am and that I know I am Chinese. It also gives me more confidence." Given her non-Chinese appearance and her history in Europe, learning Chinese provided strong affirmation of her roots, and likely evoked her early years in Hong Kong. It was interesting that for such an accomplished and well-travelled, multilingual young woman, proficiency in Chinese conferred upon her a degree of "confidence" in herself as well. However, like Amy, she was studying Mandarin (her L3) and not her mother tongue, Cantonese. That she would later, through her thesis research, be able to use her Chinese to mediate her sociological research was an unintended major benefit of that sustained commitment to the Chinese dimension of her multifaceted identity.

Tony's story, the last of the four, was fraught with apparent tension, regret, shame, sociopolitical contestation, and very deep-seated desire. Unlike Amy, Flora, and Katie, Tony tried to avail himself of opportunities to connect with his ethnolinguistic heritage in ways that his own parents, as Chinese Indonesians, had been denied during their lifetime. He recounted growing up in a "Chinese family" in Indonesia, except for a year in which they had fled to Malaysia because of anti-Chinese race riots in Indonesia. His grandparents were Chinese speakers (Mandarin and Cantonese) but his parents spoke Indonesian and English, not Chinese, which they had been politically forbidden from learning. Tony said he had studied Chinese off and on, "but we were just singing… having fun" in small, illegal, underground language courses. Deeply disappointed not to be able to speak Chinese with his grandparents, he had learned Indonesian, English, and basic French instead.

In 2005, Tony was a young international business major in Canada, heading to Singapore the following semester for an exchange program. His goal was to later work in Shanghai. Unfortunately, of the four participants, given his mobility and lack of Canadian family or institutional ties – particularly after graduating – we were unable to locate Tony to track where his career had taken him three years later and what role Chinese might have played in that process. He was, however, very candid in his first interview about what learning Chinese meant to him, declaring "I'm a Chinese, so I should speak Chinese." He then provided a narrative of what had been a disquieting encounter with someone in Canada that underscored what was for him a deep and inextricable link: *speaking Chinese, being Chinese,* and *being recognized or validated as Chinese* by others:

> I'm a Chinese. I remember a person asked me where was I from. I said "Indonesia." But he said "You don't look like a person from Indonesia, you look like a Chinese." I said "Yeah, I'm a Chinese born in Indonesia." And he said "Then you could speak Chinese?" I said "I can't" and I'm very embarrassed. So I want to speak Chinese then I can be recognized as a Chinese.

Tony also felt that not just being Chinese but being able to speak Chinese would mark him as "a clever person" and, since "China was developing beautifully," it would give him a means of enhancing his international business career possibilities as well. So for him CHL was saturated with deep intergenerational connections and regrets, a sense of personal cultural integrity, and a form of both symbolic and cultural capital and habitus that would likely pay significant dividends in his planned international business pursuits. Whereas Katie sought to build up her confidence with a deeper knowledge of Chinese, Tony sought to mitigate the deep shame he felt due to his lack of proficiency.

Discussion

The four participants' very complicated transnational and linguistic histories, investments, and desires in relation to Chinese were quite evident. Collectively, they had had prior experience with different dialects of Chinese, ultimately including Mandarin, which they studied at the Canadian university where the study took place after some earlier sanctioned or unsanctioned (clandestine) attempts to learn Chinese through HL programs, either by their own or their parents' choice. All had also learned English (with some reported early ESL difficulties for the Chinese-Canadian children entering English-medium schools in Canada) and had expertise in other non-Chinese languages too: principally, French, Indonesian, Danish, and German. Furthermore, even during the three-year span of our study (2005–08), they moved from Canada to other countries to pursue work or further education – to Hong Kong (Flora), Denmark, Canada, and China, in turn (Katie), and Singapore (Tony) and possibly China as well in his case. This mobility illustrates the transnationalism and different forms of cultural, symbolic, linguistic, and economic capital at the disposal of these students and quite likely many other Chinese youths in North America seeking to retain Chinese. Their geographical location and movement affected not only their personal agency regarding the choice and use of different languages, but also their dialect and script preferences – which changed over time in some cases (e.g. from Cantonese to Mandarin, or traditional to simplified characters). They also seized upon additional languages, such as German (Katie) and French (Amy, Flora, and Tony), in the interim, either because of peer influences (Katie), their emerging Canadian identities (Amy and Flora), or because it was novel yet politically neutral (which we infer from Tony's learning of French). These cases demonstrate anew that motivation to learn, use, and retain HLs, therefore, is highly mediated, by one's social networks (family and peers), by geographical circumstance and opportunity, by experiences with the languages themselves through formal and informal education or exposure, and by the ideologies surrounding those languages in learners' worlds. Language learning motivation is also temporal and situated, and thus subject to change as new visions of oneself and one's future possibilities in the world unfold across time and space. In a word, it is very *dynamic* – echoing Ushioda and Dörnyei's (2012) characterization of current motivation research as "socio-dynamic" – and is inextricably linked with learners' identities (past, present, and future).

Indeed, longitudinal research such as this with CHL adolescents and young adults who now more than ever may have future opportunities to use their Chinese knowledge in other settings is therefore very worthwhile and important, particularly if participants agree to take part in research that spans different geopolitical regions, time, space, and languages and have enduring forms of contact, such as a longterm email address, rather than a temporary university address.

These four participants' experiences represent those of our larger set to some extent and those in studies cited earlier in this chapter (e.g. He 2010), although being on the west coast of Canada (as they all were at some point) likely offered them more subsequent transnational opportunities to learn and use Chinese and more like-minded peers from similar HL backgrounds than might exist in other parts of the continent. However, some of the issues the participants encountered are shared by non-ethnic-Chinese learners of Chinese as well. The adult *non*-CHL (Anglo-Canadian) learners of Chinese featured in Duff et al. (2013) exhibited similarly diverse trajectories, transnational migration, goals, achievements, and even misgivings vis-à-vis learning and using Chinese at certain points, especially given the demands of both literacy and oral language knowledge and struggles with attrition in this during periods of disuse (which Flora also mentioned in relation to Chinese literacy). For both groups, of non-Chinese and Chinese ethnicity, we also documented the oft-cited challenges in learning spoken and written Chinese, dilemmas and choices regarding which oral dialects and orthographic systems to acquire (or not acquire), and in what sequence, and the need to negotiate access to communities of (Mandarin) Chinese speakers and to identities as legitimate, (multi)literate, cosmopolitan, transnational speakers of Chinese and other languages. For the CHL learners described above, access to Sinophone communities with whom to cultivate meaningful and enduring relationships was more or less a given, since their parents (except in Tony's case), grandparents, and other older relatives typically spoke at least one variety of Chinese.

Conclusion and implications

In this chapter, we have reviewed existing socio-affective research on the learning of Chinese as a HL in North American diaspora contexts primarily. Just ten years ago, there was relatively little discussion of identity and motivation in terms of poststructural or sociocultural theory or employing qualitative (ethnographic, phenomenological, discourse analytic, and other interpretive) methods in research in Chinese language education. Applied linguistics and CHL have made great strides toward more socially situated, dynamic, and contingent understandings of how and why children, adolescents, and adults engage with Chinese languages, literacies, cultures, and semiotics over time. It is possible to track their nonlinear trajectories as a result. The result is a greater convergence of traditionally positivist and interpretive perspectives. The "heart of [Chinese] heritage" (He 2010) is also beginning to take center stage in emerging research, and not just the (psycho) linguistic developmental milestones or mechanics of learning. This trend underscores the very profound personal significance of cultural and linguistic connectedness to one's background and relations for many individuals, families, and communities, particularly in the Chinese diaspora. Conversely, it also points to the often devastating impact of language loss (see e.g. Kouritzen 1999; Pavlenko & Lantolf 2000), of the sort that Tony had begun to experience before he began more formal Mandarin studies.

Case studies of learners across and along the lifespan in home, school, extra-curricular, and community settings demonstrate the ambivalence, desires, pressures, positionings, and struggles associated with CHL for many learners. Yet they also illustrate the intense source of pride, confidence, intellectual and social stimulation and challenge, social connectedness, and opportunity that proficiency in Chinese affords. Future research, we hope, will continue in this vein, particularly with a wider range of Chinese-background learners, including those from mixed ancestry, and in other transnational contexts (e.g. G. Lee 2010).

There are some very practical implications of this research. It is our hope that educational programs for learners of Chinese descent wishing to affiliate with their history and seeking to attain a multilingual identity and repertoire (forms of expertise) that includes Chinese will respond by creating more intrinsically motivating materials, media, instruction, participation frameworks, and opportunities for students to harness their existing knowledge as well as their passion and dreams (see also Duff, this volume). The constructs of (positive) self-determination, self-concept and self-esteem, identity, agency, and autonomy, as we have seen, are strongly associated with not just resilience but deep and enduring satisfaction with sustained involvement in high quality HL programs and Chinese learning. Unfortunately, these positive sentiments regarding HL learning do not appear to be commonplace in many CHL contexts for youth, judging from our earlier study (D. Li & Duff 2008) and related research.

Yet there are promising signs that meaningful curricular, pedagogical, and policy reform is taking place. Wu and Chang (2010) document ways in which they attempted to motivate adolescent CHL learners in the U.S. through a summer camp that included such topics as:

> the Chinese Exclusion Act and Chinese immigration, history and personal memories of Chinatown, intergenerational relationships, personal border-crossing experiences, and pop music in Mandarin speaking regions. A class blog was used to further enhance HLLs' motivation and language production (p. 23).

They reported that the curriculum enabled the students to take "active ownership of their learning, dispelling the image of adolescent heritage language learners as lacking motivation to learn about their cultural roots and heritage languages, as portrayed in the literature" (p. 23). Instruction of this type goes a long way to creating the kinds of intrinsically motivating learning situations that Comanaru and Noels (2009) characterize as promoting "imagination and creativity, curiosity and enthusiasm" (p. 134) and not just rote memorization of grammar structures, vocabulary, and Chinese characters, ubiquitous elements of CHL instruction at many weekend schools. The more appealing topics and activities contribute to students' sense of agency as lifelong language learners and users. Similarly, Lu and G. Li (2008) found that "in addition to promoting students' integrative motivation, Chinese language teaching at college level should also include curriculum and teacher professional development that addresses students' mixed abilities and needs, and fosters individual students' sustained interest in the language" (p. 89). Much more work remains to be done at all curricular levels in both credit- and non-credit contexts (Duff 2008; D. Li 2008). Curriculum and materials need to be updated and revitalized by tapping into the exciting affordances of new media, pop culture, and digital technologies and other engaging tools. Chinese language learning experiences need to become more rewarding for *all* learners regardless of their backgrounds, to enhance students' longer-term learning Sinophone trajectories, identities, and experiences. In this way, students stand a better chance of reaching higher levels of Chinese proficiency and becoming lifelong learners – and users – of Chinese.

References

Bakhtin, M. 1981. *The Dialogic Imagination*. Austin TX: University of Texas Press.

Blackledge, A. & Creese, A. 2008. Contesting 'language' as 'heritage': Negotiation of identities in late modernity. *Applied Linguistics* 29(4): 533–554.

Block, D. 2007a. *Second Language Identities*. London: Continuum.

Block, D. 2007b. The rise of identity in SLA research, post Firth and Wagner (1997). *Modern Language Journal* 91(5): 863–876.

Bourdieu, P. 1991[1982]. *Language and Symbolic Power* (J.B. Thompson, Ed., G. Raymond & M. Adamson, Trans.). Cambridge: Polity Press.

Chiu, L. 2011. The Construction of the 'Ideal Chinese Child': A Critical Analysis of Textbooks for Chinese Heritage Language Learners. MA thesis, University of British Columbia, Canada.

Chow, H. 2001.The challenge of diversity: Ethnic identity maintenance and heritage language retention in the Canadian Mosaic. Commissioned by the Department of Canadian Heritage for the Ethnocultural, Racial, Religious, and Linguistic Diversity and Identity Seminar Halifax, Nova Scotia. ⟨www.metropolis.net⟩

Comanaru, R. & Noels, K. 2009. Self-determination, motivation, and the learning of Chinese as a heritage language. *The Canadian Modern Language Review* 66(1): 131–158.

Curdt-Christiansen, X.L. 2003. Growing up in Three Languages: Triliteracy Practices of Immigrant Chinese Children in Quebec. Ph.D. dissertation, McGill University.

Curdt-Christiansen, X.L. 2008. Reading the world through words: Cultural themes in heritage Chinese language textbooks. *Language and Education* 22(2): 95–113.

Dai, J.E. & Zhang, L. 2008. What are the CHL learners inheriting? Habitus of the CHL learners. In *Chinese as a Heritage Language: Fostering Rooted World Citizenry*, A.W. He, & Y. Xiao (eds), 37–51. Honolulu HI: University of Hawai'i National Foreign Language Resource Center.

Dörnyei, Z. 2010. Researching motivation: From integrativeness to the ideal L2 self. In *Introducing Applied Linguistics: Concepts and Skills*, S. Hunston & D. Oakey (eds), 74–83. London: Routledge.

Dörnyei, Z. & Ushioda, E. (eds). 2009. *Motivation, Language Identity and the L2 Self*. Bristol: Multilingual Matters.

Duff, P. 2008. Issues in Chinese language teaching and teacher development. In *Issues in Chinese Language Education and Teacher Development*, P. Duff & P. Lester (eds), 5–48. Vancouver: University of British Columbia Centre for Research in Chinese Language and Literacy Education.

Duff, P. 2012. Identity, agency, and SLA. In *Handbook of Second Language Acquisition*, A. Mackey & S. Gass (eds), 410–426. London: Routledge.

Duff, P. & Li, D. 2008. Negotiating language, literacy and identity: Chinese heritage learners' language socialization. World Congress of Applied Linguistics, Essen, Germany, August.

Duff, P., Anderson, T., Ilnyckyj, R., VanGaya, E., Wang, R., & Yates, E. 2013. *Learning Chinese: Linguistic, Sociocultural, and Narrative Perspectives*. Berlin: Mouton De Gruyter.

He, A.W. 2006. Toward an identity theory of the development of Chinese as a heritage language. *Heritage Language Journal* 4(1): 1–28.

He, A.W. 2008. An identity-based model for the development of Chinese as a heritage language. In *Chinese as a Heritage Language: Fostering Rooted World Citizenry*, A.W. He, & Y. Xiao (eds), 109–124. Honolulu HI: National Foreign Language Resource Center, University of Hawaii.

He, A.W. 2010. The heart of heritage: Sociocultural dimensions of heritage language acquisition. *Annual Review of Applied Linguistics* 30: 66–82.

He, A.W. 2011. Heritage language socialization. In *The Handbook of Language Socialization,* A. Duranti, E. Ochs, & B. Schieffelin (eds), 587–609. Malden MA: Wiley-Blackwell.

He, A.W. & Xiao, Y. (eds). 2008. *Chinese as a Heritage Language: Fostering Rooted World Citizenry.* Honolulu HI: National Foreign Language Resource Center.

Hornberger, N.H. & Wang, S. 2008. Who are our heritage language learners? Identity and biliteracy in heritage language education in the United States. In *Heritage Language Education: A New Field Emerging,* D. Brinton, O. Kagan, & S. Bauckus (eds), 3–35. New York NY: Routledge.

Kagan, O. 2012. Intercultural competence of heritage language learners: Motivation, identity, language attitudes, and the curriculum. *Proceedings of Intercultural Competence Conference* 2: 72–84.

Kelleher, A. 2008. Placements and re-positionings: Tensions around CHL learning in a university Mandarin program. In *Chinese as a Heritage Language: Fostering Rooted World Citizenry,* A.W. He, & Y. Xiao (eds), 239–258. Honolulu HI: National Foreign Language Resource Center, University of Hawai'i at Manoa.

Kelleher, A. 2010. Policies and Identities in Mandarin Education: The Situated Multilingualism of University-Level "Heritage" Language Learners. Ph.D. dissertation, University of California, Davis.

Kouritzen, S.G. 1999. *Face[t]s of First Language Loss.* Mahwah NJ: Lawrence Erlbaum Associates.

Kramsch, C. 2009. *The Multilingual Subject: What Language Learners Say about Their Experience and Why It Matters.* Oxford: OUP.

Lantolf, J. 2000. *Sociocultural Theory and Second Language Learning.* Oxford: OUP.

Lee, G. S–C. 2010. A study of an Overseas Chinese College Student Learning Mandarin in Taiwan. MA dissertation, Ming Chuan University.

Lei, J. 2012. Socio-psychological factors affecting heritage language education: A case study of Chinese American adolescents. *New Waves. Educational Research & Development* 15(1): 62–88. ⟨http://www.caerda.org/journal/index.php/newwaves/article/view/56⟩

Leung, C., Harris, R., & Rampton, B. 1997. The idealised native speaker, reified ethnicities, and classroom realities. *TESOL Quarterly* 31(3): 543–560.

Li, D. 2008. Issues in Chinese language curriculum and materials development. In *Issues in Chinese Language Education and Teacher Development,* P. Duff & P. Lester (eds), 49–69. Vancouver: University of British Columbia Centre for Research in Chinese Language and Literacy Education.

Li, D. & Duff, P. 2008. Issues in Chinese heritage language education and research at the post-secondary level. In *Chinese as a Heritage Language: Fostering Rooted World Citizenry,* A.W. He, & Y. Xiao (eds), 13–33. Honolulu HI: National Foreign Language Resource Center, University of Hawai'i at Manoa.

Li, G. 2006a. Biliteracy and trilingual practices in the home context: Case studies of Chinese Canadian children. *Journal of Early Childhood Literacy* 6(3): 359–385.

Li, G. 2006b. What do parents think? Middle-class Chinese immigrant parents' perspectives on literacy learning, homework, and school-home communication. *The School Community Journal* 16(2): 25–44.

Li, G. 2007. Second language and literacy learning in school and at home: An ethnographic study of Chinese-Canadian first graders' experiences. *Journal of Language Teaching and Learning* 11(1): 1–40.

Lo-Philip, S.W. 2010. Towards a theoretical framework of heritage language literacy and identity processes. *Linguistics and Education* 21: 282–297.

Lu, X. & Li, G. 2008. Motivation and achievement in Chinese language learning: A comparative analysis. In *Chinese as a Heritage Language: Fostering Rooted World Citizenry,* A.W. He, & Y. Xiao (eds), 89–108. Honolulu HI: University of Hawai'i Press.

Maguire, M. & Curdt-Christiansen, X.L. 2007. Multiple schools, languages, experiences and affiliations: Ideological becomings and positionings. *Heritage Language Journal* 5(1): 50–78.

McKinney, C. & Norton, B. 2008. Identity in language and literacy education. In *The Handbook of Educational Linguistics,* B. Spolsky & F. Hult (eds), 192–205. Malden: Blackwell.

Menard-Warwick, J. 2005. Both a fiction and an existential fact: Theorizing identity in second language acquisition and literacy studies. *Linguistics and Education* 16(3): 253–274.

Norton, B. 2000. *Identity and Language Learning: Gender, Ethnicity and Educational Change.* London: Longman.

Norton, B. & Toohey, K. 2011. Identity, language learning, and social change. *Language Teaching* 44(4): 412–446.

Pavlenko, A. & Lantolf, J.P. 2000. Second language learning as participation and the (re)construction of selves. In *Sociocultural Theory and Second Language Learning,* J.P. Lantolf (ed.), 155–177. Oxford: OUP.

Swain, M. & Deters, P. 2007. "New" mainstream SLA theory: Expanded and enriched. *The Modern Language Journal* 91(5): 820–836.

Tasker, I. 2012. The Dynamics of Chinese Learning Journeys: A Longitudinal Study Of Adult Learners of Mandarin in Australia. Ph.D. dissertation, University of New England, Australia.

Taylor, C. 1994. The politics of recognition. In *Multiculturalism: Examining the Politics of Recognition,* A. Gutmann (ed.), 25–73. Princeton NJ: Princeton University Press.

Ushioda, E. & Dörnyei, Z. 2009. Motivation, language identities and the L2 self: A theoretical overview. In *Motivation, Language Identity and the L2 Self,* Z. Dörnyei & E. Ushioda (eds), 1–8. Bristol: Multilingual Matters.

Ushioda, E. & Dörnyei, Z. 2012. Motivation. In *The Routledge Handbook of Second Language Acquisition,* S. Gass & A. Mackey (eds), 396–409. New York NY: Routledge.

Valdés, G. 2000a. Introduction. In *Spanish for Native Speakers: AATSP Professional Development Series Handbook For Teachers K-16,* Vol. 1, N. Anderson (ed.), 1–20. New York NY: Harcourt College.

Wiley, T. 2008. Chinese "dialect" speakers as heritage language learners: A case study. In *Heritage Language Education: A New Field Emerging,* D. Brinton, O. Kagan, & S. Bauckus (eds), 91–105. New York NY: Routledge.

Wong, K.F. & Xiao, Y. 2010. Diversity and difference: Identity issues of Chinese heritage language learners from dialect backgrounds. *Heritage Language Journal* 7(2): 153–187.

Wu, M.-H. & Chang, T.-M. 2010. Heritage language teaching and learning through a macro-approach. *Working Papers in Educational Linguistics* 25(2): 23–33.

Xie, Y. 2011. Representations of L2 Motivational Self System with Beginning Chinese Language Learners at College Level in the United States: Heritage and Nonheritage Language Learners. Ph.D. dissertation, Liberty University, online.

Zuengler, J. & Miller, E.R. 2006. Cognitive and sociocultural perspectives: Two parallel SLA worlds? *TESOL Quarterly* 40(1): 35–58.

Index